the
ZEN
WORKS
of
STONEHOUSE

the ZEN WORKS of STONEHOUSE

*Poems and Talks of a
Fourteenth-Century
Chinese Hermit,
Translated by Red Pine*

MERCURY HOUSE
SAN FRANCISCO

Published in the United States of America by Mercury House, San
Francisco, California, a nonprofit publishing company devoted to the
free exchange of ideas and guided by a dedication to literary values.

United States Constitution, First Amendment: Congress shall make no
law respecting an establishment of religion, or prohibiting the free ex-
ercise thereof; or abridging the freedom of speech, or of the press; or
the right of the people peaceably to assemble, and to petition the
Government for a redress of grievances.

Mercury House and colophon are registered trademarks of
Mercury House, Incorporated.

Printed on recycled, acid-free paper. Manufactured by
Hignell Book Printing, Winnipeg, Manitoba, Canada.

Design and typesetting by Thomas Christensen and Kirsten
Janene-Nelson. Chinese typesetting and proofreading by
Katherine Loh Graphic Design.

Cover: Detail from the Fu-ch'un River Scroll painted in 1350 by
Huang Kung-wang (1269–1354), inspired by the scenery of
Chekiang province and used with the kind permission of the
National Palace Museum, Taipei, Taiwan, Republic of China.

This book has been made possible by generous support from
The Witter Bynner Foundation for Poetry and
the National Endowment for the Arts.

Library of Congress Cataloguing-in-Publication Data:
Ch'ing-hung, 1272-1352.
[Works. English. 1999]
The Zen works of Stonehouse : poems and talks of a fourteenth-
century Chinese hermit / Translated by Red Pine.
p. cm.
Chinese and English.
ISBN 1-56279-101-X (pbk. : alk. paper)
1. Ch'ing-hung, 1272-1352.—Translations into English.
I. Pine, Red. II. Title.
PL2694.C57P56 1999
895.'144—DC21 97-25577
CIP

9 8 7 6 5 4 3 2 1
FIRST EDITION

for Stefan Hyner & Mimi Steele

Contents

PREFACE

More than a decade ago, while I was working on a translation of the poems of Cold Mountain, I carried around an edition published by Taipei's Hsin-wenfeng Publishing House that included the poems of several other Chinese Buddhist poets. When I finished Cold Mountain's last poem, I turned the page and found the *Mountain Poems* of Stonehouse. I liked them so much I translated them as well, and in 1986 I published a limited edition of hand-bound copies with my friends at Empty Bowl. While I was preparing an introduction for that edition, I came across a second volume of Stonehouse's poems entitled *Gathas,* as well as a record of his *Zen Talks* in the archives of Taiwan's Central Library. With the help of a grant from the National Endowment for the Arts, I was able to devote most of 1987 to translating the *Gathas* but have delayed their separate publication, hoping to publish all three of Stonehouse's surviving works in one volume. Having finally found the opportunity to do so, I have revised my earlier work, added additional notes, and have also revised the introduction that follows. I have included the Chinese text of the poems as well so that others might make use of this book in their study of classical Chinese or Yuan-dynasty vernacular.

Red Pine
Port Townsend, Washington
Thanksgiving, Year of the Rat

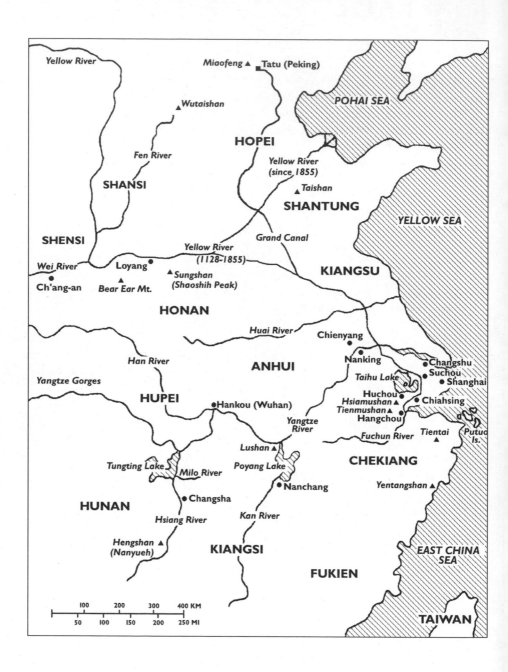

INTRODUCTION

Stonehouse 石屋 was born in 1272 in the town of Changshu, not far from where the Yangtze empties into the East China Sea. He took his name from a cave at the edge of town. The cave was on Yushan, which was named for Yu Chung-wei, whose nephew founded the Chou dynasty in North China around 1100 BC. This is where the uncle was buried. Yushan is also known for its pine trees, its rock formations, and its springs, in particular a spring that flows out of a cave as big as a house. Locals call the cave *Shihwutung*, or "Stonehouse Cave." This part of the mountain was also frequented by the painter Huang Kung-wang, whose work appears on the cover. Huang was born in Changshu three years before Stonehouse, and by the time he died, four years after Stonehouse, he was regarded as one of the greatest painters of the Yuan dynasty. Among Huang's favorite subjects were the scenes of Yushan, and he was buried just beyond the cave that also impressed a young Buddhist novice, if not with its beauty then perhaps with its serenity.

The cave was located at the western end of Yushan. At the eastern end was Hsingfu Temple. First built at the end of the fifth century, Hsingfu was one of the great monastic centers south of the Yangtze. Buddhist historians liken it to Hangchou's Lingyen Temple, Chenchiang's Chinshan Temple, and Changchou's Tienning Temple. In 1292, Stonehouse became a novice there under Master Yung-wei, and three years later, he was formally ordained and given the Buddhist name Ch'ing-hung 清琪.

One day not long after his ordination, Stonehouse saw a monk walk past his door wearing a straw hat and carrying a hiking staff. Stonehouse asked the monk where he was going. The monk said he was going to the Tienmu Mountains to see Master Kao-feng, who was one of the great Zen masters of the age, and he asked Stonehouse to join him. Stonehouse agreed, and the two monks journeyed by boat along the Grand Canal past Suchou to the provincial capital of Hangchou. From Hangchou, the two monks continued overland to Kao-feng's hermitage on Tienmu's West Peak.

Following their arrival, Kao-feng asked Stonehouse his reason for coming. Stonehouse said, "I've come for the Dharma." Kao-feng answered, "The Dharma isn't so easy to find. You've got to burn your fingers for incense." To this Stonehouse replied, "But I see the Master before me with my own eyes. How could the Dharma be hidden?" Kao-feng nodded his approval and suggested he study the koan "All things return to one."*

Stonehouse stayed with Kao-feng for three years serving him with diligence

---

*During the preceding Sung dynasty, the koans, or recorded conversations, of previous Zen masters were compiled into books and used as subjects for meditation and aids to enlightenment.

but without deepening his understanding of the Dharma. When Stonehouse finally said he was leaving, Kao-feng told him, "You're still a blind mule. In the Huai region north of the Yangtze, there's a master named Chi-an. Why don't you go see him?" So Stonehouse crossed the Yangtze at Nanking and found Chi-an at West Peak Temple near Chienyang.

Chi-an asked Stonehouse where he had come from, and Stonehouse told him, "From Tienmu." Chi-an asked, "What instruction did you receive?" Stonehouse said, "All things return to one." Chi-an asked, "And what does that mean?" Stonehouse didn't answer. Chi-an said, "Those words are dead. Where did you pick up such rot?" Stonehouse bowed and asked to be instructed. Chi-an said, "Tell me what this means: 'Where buddhas dwell, don't stop. Where buddhas don't dwell, hurry past.'" Stonehouse answered, "I don't understand." Chi-an replied, "More dead words." Stonehouse still didn't understand, but he decided to stay with Chi-an.

One day Chi-an asked him again what the koan meant, and Stonehouse answered, "When you mount the horse, you see the road." Chi-an said, "You've been here now for six years. Is this all it amounts to?" Exasperated, Stonehouse turned and left. But on his way down the mountain, he looked up and saw a pavilion.* Suddenly he understood. He hurried back and told Chi-an, "'Where buddhas dwell, don't stop.' Those are dead words. 'Where buddhas don't dwell, hurry past.' Those are dead words too. Now I understand living words." Chi-an asked, "And what do you understand?" Stonehouse answered, "When the rain finally stops in late spring, the oriole appears on a branch."** Chi-an nodded his approval. Later, when Stonehouse decided to leave, Chi-an told him, "In the future, we will both share the same niche."

Not long afterward, Chi-an was asked to take over as abbot of Huchou's Taochang Temple, and Stonehouse joined him there. Chi-an told the assembly, "Here is a rare fish that slipped through the net and entered the Dharma Sea."

The Buddhists of his day viewed Stonehouse with great respect. And after several years with Chi-an, Stonehouse was invited to become the meditation master of Hangchou's famous Lingyin Temple. But after a short stay, he decided he preferred the mountains. And in 1312, at the age of forty, he moved to Hsiamushan, twenty-five kilometers southwest of Huchou, and he built a hut just below its 450-

---

*West Peak Temple was located on Langyashan, three kilometers southwest of the county seat of Chienyang, which is now called Chuchou. Halfway up Langyashan stands Tsuiweng Pavilion, which still bears the name given to it by Ou-yang Hsiu during his tenure as magistrate of Chienyang in 1046. It remains the area's most famous sight and was, I presume, the pavilion that prompted Stonehouse's insight into Zen. Its name means "Pavilion of the Old Drunkard" and is taken from Ou-yang Hsiu's inscription of the same name, which Stonehouse would have known by heart. It ends, "Birds know the joys of the mountains and forests, but they don't know the joys of people. And people know the joys of accompanying the Magistrate on his hikes, but they don't know the joy that their joy gives the Magistrate. He who can share their joy while drunk and can describe it while sober, this is the Magistrate. And who is the Magistrate? Ou-yang Hsiu of Luling."

** Confucius says, "When the oriole rests, it knows where to rest. Is it possible man isn't equal to this bird?" (*Tahsueh*: 3.2)

meter summit. A contemporary wrote that Stonehouse lived a hard life, refusing to beg for food in nearby villages as was the custom among other monks. When he ran out of food, he survived on water. He was hard on himself but kind and generous to others.

Stonehouse enjoyed the seclusion of the mountains for nearly twenty years. Then, in 1330, Emperor Wen ordered Fuyuan Temple in neighboring Chiahsing Prefecture rebuilt. The temple was originally built by Emperor Wen's father in 1312, and because of his reputation Stonehouse was asked to take over as the temple's second abbot. Stonehouse at first declined but was admonished, "If monks are supposed to work for the benefit of the Dharma, how can they succeed while living in idleness and isolation." In the spring of the following year, Stonehouse left Hsiamushan and took up his post as abbot of Fuyuan Temple, one hundred kilometers to the east.

However, temple life did not suit Stonehouse. After eight years as abbot, he pleaded old age and in 1339 returned to his former mountain home. He was sixty-seven. During this second stay on Hsiamushan, he compiled his *Mountain Poems,* completing them shortly before his death.

In the spring of 1352, in recognition of his reputation as one of the age's great Dharma masters, the empress presented Stonehouse with a golden robe. His disciples were in awe, but Stonehouse remained unmoved. In autumn of the same year, on the twenty-first day of the seventh moon, he told his disciples he was feeling ill. And on the night of the twenty-second, his disciples gathered around to say good-bye. One of them asked him if he had any parting words. Stonehouse picked up his writing brush and wrote:

> corpses don't stink in the mountains
> there's no need to bury them deep
> I might not have the fire of samadhi
> but enough wood to end this family line

He threw the brush down and died. He was eighty-one. Mindful of Chi-an's premonition that someday he and Stonehouse would share the same niche, Stonehouse's disciples put his cremated remains next to those of Chi-an, which had already been interred on Hsiamushan. A portion of Stonehouse's relics was also sent to the Korean monk, Taego, who in turn presented them to his ruler, King Kongmin. Taego first visited China in 1347 and impressed Stonehouse enough to be called his true Dharma heir. Taego is still revered in Korea as the founding patriarch of the Chogye Order, which united the various schools of Zen in his country.

Three hundred years after Stonehouse's cremation, a seventeenth-century official is reported to have opened Stonehouse's relic pagoda. The relics emitted such an intense golden light the official was unable to move. Only after others had re-interred the relics and repaired the pagoda did the light stop and the official recover. Thus ends Stonehouse's grave inscription.

In the fall of 1991, I had the opportunity to visit the places where Stonehouse once lived while I was gathering material for a series of radio programs on the region south of the Yangtze. I was joined by my friends Steve Johnson and Finn Wilcox, and we began with Stonehouse's hometown of Changshu and Hsingfu Temple at the foot of Yushan. On the road leading to the temple's front gate, we passed a cemetery containing the graves of its most famous monks. I didn't recognize any of their names, but their nicknames were colorful enough: Yen-jan, Subduer of Tigers; Ch'ang-ta, Conqueror of Dragons; Huai-shu, Patched Robe Monk Who Sits in the Sun; and Wu-en, Reader of Sutras in the Moonlight. The temple had undergone a certain amount of renovation and was flourishing once again, though more as a center of local tourism than Buddhist practice. I talked with several monks, including the abbot. But no one at the temple had heard of Stonehouse. We left Changshu and headed south for the town of Huchou and Hsiamushan.

In Taiwan I had located Hsiamushan on a declassified military map, but I had neglected to bring the adjoining map sections with me and had no idea how to reach the mountain from Huchou. I looked at the route map on the bus station wall and picked Teching, a town about thirty kilometers to the south. The Sha River flowed past Teching, and I remembered that Stonehouse's *Mountain Poems* began with the line: "Built my hut west of the Sha." I figured if we hiked into the mountains west of Teching, sooner or later we would stumble onto Hsiamushan. I went to the ticket window and asked for three tickets on the next bus to Teching. Not many foreigners pass through Huchou, and when the ticket seller saw us, she left and returned a few minutes later with the station master. I told him we wanted three tickets to Teching. He nodded and sold us tickets on a bus due to leave in another thirty minutes.

Meanwhile, a crowd of onlookers had gathered, and he suggested we would be more comfortable waiting in his office. We gladly accepted. After exchanging introductions, I asked the station master if he had ever heard of Hsiamushan. But neither he nor anyone else at the station recognized the name. Perhaps the name had changed. While our host left to get us some tea, I gazed around his office. On the wall behind me was a detailed topographic map of the entire county. It took me about thirty seconds to find Hsiamushan. It actually existed, and after six hundred years the name was still the same. When the station master returned, we told him to forget Teching, we wanted to go to Hsiamushan, and I pointed to it on the map. He not only refunded our tickets, he went to hire a car to take us there. While we were waiting, I continued to pore over the map and found Taochangshan. Mount Taochang was where Stonehouse lived with Chi-an before moving to Hsiamushan.

A few minutes later, we were headed for Taochangshan. Two kilometers south of town, we turned off the main road and drove as far as we could up a rutted side road. A trail led us the rest of the way to Wanshou Temple, which was located about halfway up the mountain. A thousand years ago, Taochangshan's Wanshou Temple was considered one of the ten greatest Zen centers in all of China. It had since fallen on hard times.

Inside the main hall, we met Abbot Hsiang-sheng. He said the Red Guards destroyed just about everything except the main hall's T'ang-dynasty pillars, a T'ang-dynasty well, and the Sung-dynasty pagoda on the ridge behind the temple. Then he invited us to join him for tea and a dessert of fried rice pudding. I showed him some of Stonehouse's poems and asked him if he had heard of Stonehouse or his teacher, Chi-an. But he just shook his head. We chatted for a while, and as soon as we finished our dessert, we said good-bye. The day was half over, and we were anxious to find Hsiamushan and the scene of Stonehouse's *Mountain Poems*.

We returned to the main road and headed south again. I should have borrowed the station master's map, or at least traced the major roads and landmarks. We spent the next hour stopping every few kilometers to ask villagers if we were headed in the right direction. Everyone shrugged, and we continued on in ignorance. Finally, we crossed a set of railroad tracks and headed off on a dirt road just wide enough for a single car. The road led several kilometers to a small village at the base of a mountain. As luck would have it, the villagers called their mountain Hsiamushan.

Just beyond the village, we turned off on an even narrower track that led up the west side of the mountain. It was slow going, but our driver managed to keep his battered blue Polish sedan going far beyond where sense would have suggested he stop. A few hundred meters below the summit, a chain barred our way, and we had no choice but to park next to a set of blockhouse buildings. Before anyone inside had time to come out, we jumped over the chain and started up a trail that led the rest of the way to the top of the mountain.

A few minutes later we arrived at the summit, but there wasn't much to see. First of all, the bamboo was so high it was impossible to see the surrounding countryside. Second of all, there was something other than bamboo at the summit. There was a big metal dish for relaying electronic signals. There was also a bunker from which several soldiers came running with rifles pointed in our direction.

But once again the gods smiled. Just then, the base commander came puffing up the trail. I explained that we were looking for traces of a monk who had lived on the mountain six hundred years ago. I showed him a copy of Stonehouse's poems that I had published several years earlier with the Chinese text and my English translations. His eyes opened wide, and he smiled. He waved the soldiers away and then led us straight into the bamboo. It was a variety known as arrow bamboo, which produces the tenderest shoots but which grows incredibly thick.

The commander and his machete disappeared. We tried to follow. But even following his path as best we could, the bamboo was so dense, we sometimes found ourselves stuck, unable to move either arms or legs. Somehow we always got loose and managed to find the path again, such as it was. After twenty minutes and maybe two hundred meters, we finally emerged at a small farmstead and open vistas.

The commander said that before the telecommunications base was built, the farmhouse was the only structure on the mountain. A farmer appeared in the doorway and waved for us to come inside. He said the place had been a small Buddhist temple, but the monks had been forced to leave during the Cultural Revolution.

According to his contemporaries, Stonehouse attracted so many disciples toward the end of his life, his hut had expanded into a small temple. In the intervening six hundred years, the place hadn't changed much. His thatched roof was now tiled and the walls were made of rock, but it still had a dirt floor, and the

Current incarnation of Stonehouse's hut on Hsiamushan. Photo © Bill Porter.

spring he called Sky Lake still flowed from the rocks in back, and the slopes were still covered with valley-mist tea and arrow bamboo, and a couple of pines were still holding on.

The farmer invited us inside for a cup of tea. Like Stonehouse, he lived there alone. His children had grown up, and his wife lived in the village at the foot of the mountain. He had been living at the summit by himself for twenty years. Like Stonehouse, he didn't have much to say:

> I built my hut on Hsiamushan
> ploughing and hoeing make up my day
> half a dozen terraced fields
> two or three men of the Way
> I made a pool for the moon
> I sell wood to buy grain
> an old man with few schemes
> I've told you all about me.

the ZEN WORKS of STONEHOUSE

福源石屋琪禪師山居詩

元參學門人至柔編

清海天精舍學人校梓

余山林多暇瞌睡之餘偶成偈語自娛

紙墨少便不欲紀之雲衲禪人請書蓋

欲知我山中趣向於是靜思隨意走筆

不覺盈帙故掩而歸之復囑慎勿以此

為歌詠之助當須參意則有激焉

Stonehouse's preface to the Mountain Poems: Here in the woods I have lots of free time. When I don't spend it sleeping, I enjoy composing gathas. But with paper and ink so scarce, I haven't thought about writing them down. Now some Zen monks have asked me to record what I find of interest on this mountain. I've sat here quietly and let my brush fly. Suddenly this volume is full. I close it and send it back down with the admonition not to try singing these poems. Only if you sit on them will they do you any good.

吾家住在霅溪西　水滿天湖月滿溪
未到盡驚山險峻　曾來方識路高低
蝸涎素壁粘枯殼　虎過新蹄印雨泥
閒閉柴門春晝永　青桐花發畫胡啼

柴門雖設未嘗關　閒看幽禽自往還
尺璧易求千丈石　黃金難買一生閒
雪消曉嶂聞寒瀑　葉落秋林見遠山
古柏煙消清晝永　是非不到白雲閒

荒冢纍纍沒野蒿　昔人未葬盡金腰
有求莫若無求好　進步何如退步高
貪餌金鱗終落釜　出籠靈翮便沖霄
山翁不管紅塵事　自種青麻織布袍

紙窗竹屋槿籬笆　客到蒿湯便當茶
多見清貧長快樂　少聞濁富不驕奢
看經移案就明月　供佛簪瓶折野花
盡說上方兜率好　如何及得老僧家

1. Stonehouse's hut was west of the East Fork of the Sha River. §*Sky Lake* was the name Stonehouse gave to the small spring next to his hut. During the Yuan dynasty, it was also the name of a temple near the summit of Mokanshan, the next highest mountain to the south. §Hermits in China still report seeing the South China tiger, which, fortunately for them, is much smaller than its Siberian and Bengali cousins. §The paulownia is the only tree on which the phoenix will alight. Here the bird that is China's emblem of virtue is replaced by the insect that symbolizes rebirth and immortality and whose distinctive rhythmic drone announces the end of spring and the beginning of summer.

2. The second line suggests there was so little going on in Stonehouse's hut that birds that normally avoided humans were building nests under his eaves. §The fourth-century Buddhist monk Chih Tun became the butt of jokes when he tried to buy a mountain from the hermit who lived on it (*Shihshuo Hsinyu:* 25.28). §The *peaks* were those of the Tienmu Mountains to the south.

3. Gold seals were the perogative of royalty and high-ranking officials. §The graves of the elite of the preceding Southern Sung dynasty were east of Hangchou along the Chientang Waterway and beyond the city of Shaohsing. They were not only abandoned to weeds but desecrated in 1278 by the Central Asian monk-official Yang-lien Chen-chia, who reportedly dug up more than a hundred royal graves and pillaged the surrounding area in the years immediately after the founding of the Yuan dynasty.

4. The paper used for window panes was treated with oil to make it waterproof. §The hibiscus is often used to form hedges in the warmer regions of South China. §Wormwood, or *Artemisia annua,* is used as an antipyretic and in chronic dysentary. §Sutras are the sermons of the Buddha. §The bookstand was used to hold texts that were being studied or chanted. I am indebted to Burton Watson for his correction of my earlier reading of this line. §*Tushita* is the name of the highest heaven in the realm of desire. It is also where bodhisattvas are reborn before their final rebirth.

BOOK ONE:
MOUNTAIN POEMS

1. I made my home west of the Sha
   where water fills Sky Lake and the moon fills the river
   people are frightened when they see the heights
   but once they arrive they know the trail
   dried snail shells on rock walls
   fresh tiger tracks in the mud
   my door stays open when spring days grow long
   when paulownias bloom and cicadas call

2. Outside the door I made but don't close
   I glimpse the movements of unfamiliar birds
   a handful of jade is worth a whole mountain
   but gold can't buy a lifetime of freedom
   the sound of icy falls on a dawnlit snowy ridge
   the sight of distant peaks through leafless autumn woods
   mist lifts from ancient cedars and days last forever
   right and wrong don't get past the clouds

3. Grave upon grave buried beneath weeds
   before their funerals they carried gold seals
   but desire is no match for detachment
   ambition can't compete with restraint
   lured by bait fish end up in kettles
   uncaged a bird flies high
   worldly affairs don't concern a hermit
   I weave my robe from homegrown hemp

4. Paper windows bamboo walls hedge of hibiscus
   when guests arrive wormwood soup serves as tea
   the poor people I meet are mostly content
   rare is the rich man who isn't vain or wasteful
   I move my bookstand to read sutras by moonlight
   I honor the buddhas with a vase of wild flowers
   everyone says Tushita Heaven is fine
   but how can it match this old hut of mine

道在人宏孰可憑　發言須與行相應

貪心似海何時足　妄念如苗逐日增

幾樹梅花清處士　一園芋子樂閒僧

而今隨例菴居者　見道忘山似不曾

動則乖真靜則差　非思量處更淆訛

無心未合祖師意　有念盡為煩惱魔

白雲曳曳方拖練　又被風吹過綠蘿

矮屋朝陽寒氣少　疏籬種菊晚香多

松下雙扉冷不扃　一龕金像照青燈

眠雲野鹿驚回夢　落澗獼猴墜折藤

得意看山山轉好　無心合道道相應

多時不向門前去　蘚葉苔花積幾層

二十餘年住嶺西　钁頭邊事不吾欺

一園春色熟茶筍　數樹秋風老栗梨

山頂月明長嘯夜　水邊雲煖獨行時

舊交多在名場裡　竹戶長開待阿誰

5. Confucius said, "A man can glorify the Way, but the Way does not glorify a man" (*Lunyu:* 15.28). When Tzu-chang asked how he should act, Confucius replied, "To your words be true, in your conduct be sincere" (15.5). §The plum blossom's association with purity and seclusion was immortalized in the poems of Lin Ho-ching, a Sung-dynasty recluse who lived outside Hangchou. §Zen masters often summarize the Buddhist path with the saying, "When I first entered the Way, I saw mountains. After a while, I saw that mountains were not mountains. Now I see that mountains are just mountains."

6. Movement is the practice of mortals, and stillness is the practice of monks. §Bodhidharma says, "While ordinary people keep giving birth to the mind, claiming it exists, disciples of the Hinayana keep wiping out the mind, claiming it doesn't exist. But bodhisattvas and buddhas neither create nor annihilate the mind" (*The Zen Teaching of Bodhidharma:* 53). §The Patriarch of Zen is often pictured meditating while facing a wall. Meanwhile, T'ao Ch'ien, the poet of recluses, entered samadhi while picking chrysanthemums along his fence (see his *Drinking Poems:* 5). §Clouds are often used as metaphors for thoughts, while vines represent the convoluted logic of the mind.

7. The *blue light* suggests the dying flame of an oil lamp. The scene that comes to mind is that of a small forest shrine, perhaps imagined, perhaps seen through Stonehouse's window. According to the farmer who occupies the current incarnation of Stonehouse's hut, an adjacent structure is all that remains of a small temple that was destroyed during the Cultural Revolution.

8. According to China's oldest book of geography, the sun is said to set behind Mount Yen (*Shanhaiching:* Hsishan.4). Hence to live west of Mount Yen is to live in the wilderness. The realm of Amida Buddha is also west of the setting sun, the contemplation of which constitutes the first of sixteen visualizations used in Pure Land meditation. §The best tea leaves are those picked in spring. The same is true for bamboo shoots. §Civil service exams were discontinued in North China during most of the Yuan dynasty, but they were still held periodically in the provincial capital of Hangchou, which was sixty kilometers, or a two-day journey, south of Hsiamushan.

5. To glorify the Way what should people turn to
   to words and deeds that agree
   but oceans of greed never fill up
   and sprouts of delusion keep growing
   a plum tree in bloom purifies a recluse
   a patch of potatoes cheers a lone monk
   but those who follow rules in their huts
   never see the Way or get past the mountains

6. Movement isn't right and stillness is wrong
   and the realm of no-thought is confusion instead
   the Patriarch didn't have no-mind in mind
   any thought at all means trouble
   a hut facing south isn't so cold
   chrysanthemums along a fence perfume the dusk
   as soon as drifting clouds start to linger
   the wind blows them past the vines

7. Under the pines its doors are frozen open
   a gilt statue glows in blue light
   startled deer resume dreams in the clouds
   a falling monkey swings from a broken vine
   gazing at mountains I love mountains more
   without me searching the Way finds me
   it's been so long since I went to the gate
   the moss and lichen must be layers thick

8. More than twenty years west of Mount Yen
   I've never been cheated by a hoe
   in spring a garden of tea and bamboo
   in fall a few trees of chestnuts and pears
   when the moon lights the summit at night I sing
   when the clouds turn warm I walk along the stream
   with most of my friends still taking exams
   why do I leave my gate open

翠寶丹崖列四傍　茅菴恰好在中央
一身布衲衣裳煖　百念消融歲月忘
石瘦種來蒲葉細　土深迸出筍芽長
有時夜半聞鐘磬　知有招提在下方

莫謂山居便自由　年無一日不懷憂
竹邊婆子長偷筍　麥裡兒童故放牛
栗蠓地虀傷菜甲　野豬山鼠食禾頭
施為便有不如意　只得消歸自己休

菴住霞峰最上頭　嚴崖巉嶮少人遊
擔柴出市青苔滑　負米登山白汗流
口體無厭宜節儉　光陰有限莫貪求
老僧不是閒忉怛　只要諸人放下休

嘯月眠雲二十年　自憐衰老見時艱
烏來索飯上臺立　僧去化糧空缽還
蝦蜆人爭撈白水　鑊鉏我且斸青山
黃精食盡松花在　不著閒愁方寸間

9. A monk's robe is made of twenty-five patches, one for each of the twenty-five kinds of existence and the twenty-five kinds of understanding that liberate its wearer. §Thinner rushes make better mattresses and meditation cushions. §The large bell in a Buddhist temple is normally rung around four AM, when the monks and nuns file into the shrine hall for morning devotions.

10. Elders and children are often assigned the more marginal tasks in a farm family, like gathering medicinal herbs or wild plants in the hills and grazing the oxen or water buffalo.

11. On current maps, the mountain Stonehouse lived on is called Hsiamushan, or "Redcurtain Mountain." In addition to "Redcloud," he also calls it "Redfog" and "Redbank." The *hsia:red* in these various names refers to the color of clouds at dawn or sunset.

12. The *crows* conjure up the image of those who wear black monastic robes for the assurance of free food and lodging. According to his contemporaries, Stonehouse preferred not to beg. When he ran out of food, he survived on water. §The root of solomon-seal, or *Polygonatum cirrhifolium,* contains a significant amount of starch and is usually dug up in early spring. §Pine pollen is slightly sweet and also has nutritional value. It is gathered in late spring by placing a sheet under a pine tree and knocking the branches with a pole. §The *square-inch* is the mind.

9. Kingfisher gullies and cinnabar cliffs
   and a thatched hut right in the middle
   beneath a patched robe my body stays warm
   thoughts fade away I forget the date
   rushes grow thinner where the soil is rocky
   bamboo shoots grow longer where the soil is deep
   sometimes after midnight I hear a bell
   and realize there's a temple below

10. Don't think a mountain home means you're free
    a day doesn't pass without its problems
    old ladies steal my bamboo shoots
    boys lead oxen into the wheat
    grubs and beetles destroy my greens
    boars and squirrels devour the rice
    when what happens isn't what you expect
    forget it and turn to yourself

11. My hut is at the top of Redcloud Peak
    few visitors brave the cliffs and ravines
    I slip on the moss lugging firewood to market
    and drip with sweat hauling rice back up
    with no end to hunger less is better
    with limited time why be greedy
    I don't want to spoil your fun
    only make you let go

12. In tune with the moon and clouds for twenty years
    to find myself old is hard
    crows gather for food on the rocks
    a monk returns with an empty begging bowl
    others drag surf for clams and shrimp
    I swing a hoe in the mountains
    when solomon-seal is gone there is still pine pollen
    and one square-inch free of care

幽居自與世相分　苔厚林深草木薰

山色雨晴常得見　市聲朝暮罕曾聞

煮茶瓦灶燒黃葉　補衲嚴臺剗白雲

人壽希逢年滿百　利名何苦競趨奔

古今誰解輕浮世　獨許嚴陵坐釣臺

瓦灶通紅茶已熟　紙窗生白月初來

他非莫與他分辨　自過應須自翦裁

入得山來便學呆　尋常有口嬾能開

溪淺泉清見石沙　屋頭無角寄藤蘿

夜深月下長猿嘯　苔厚嚴前少客過

庭竹欹斜春雪重　嶺梅消瘦夜寒多

寥寥此道非今古　徒把磚來石上磨

白髮禪翁久住菴　衲衣風捲破襤毵

溪邊掃葉供爐灶　霜後苫茆覆橘柑

本有天真非造化　現成公案不須參

豁開戶牖當軒坐　盡日看山不下簾

13. In the biography of the T'ang poet Lu Kuei-meng, it is said that a small portable tea stove was among the necessary possessions of every recluse.

14. Lao-tzu says, "Those who seek learning gain every day / those who seek the Way lose every day" (*Taoteching*: 48). Lao-tzu also says, "Everyone has a goal / I alone am dumb and backward" (20). §Again, the windows are covered with oil-paper. §Yen Tzu-ling and Liu Hsiu were boyhood friends. When Liu led a rebellion that resulted in the restoration of the Han dynasty with himself as Emperor Kuang-wu, he invited his old friend to join him at court. But Yen declined and became a hermit on the Fuchun River south of Hangchou, where he spent his days fishing from a boulder. The boulder has since been submerged by the waters of a dam, and the nearby shore is now the location of a retreat for the wealthy and well-connected.

15. As Stonehouse tells us in poem 145, his hut had no gables because his roof was round with a central peak. §Once common throughout central China, gibbons and their eerie howls are now found in the wild only in a few nature reserves in the extreme south. §Huai-jang was the dharma heir of Hui-neng, the Sixth Patriarch of the Zen sect. After Hui-neng's death in 713, Huai-jang moved to Fuyen Temple on Hengshan in southern Hunan province. One day on the slope above the temple, he saw Ma-tsu meditating and asked him what he was doing. Ma-tsu said he was trying to become a buddha. Huai-jang picked up a brick and started grinding it on a boulder. When Ma-tsu asked what he was doing, Huai-jang said he was making a mirror (*Chuantenglu:* 5). The boulder is still there, not far from Huai-jang's grave, another hundred meters up the trail.

16. The region south of the Yangtze is the earliest-known home of not only the orange but also of such citrus fruits as the tangerine, the kumquat, and the pomelo. Hermits with the good fortune to inherit such trees from previous hermits, or with the patience to wait for saplings to bear fruit, receive enough income to support themselves for at least several months of the year. In North China, it's walnut trees. §During the preceding Sung dynasty, the koans, or recorded conversations, of previous Zen masters were compiled into books and used as subjects for meditation and aids to enlightenment.

13. My home is secluded far from the world
    the moss and woods are thick and the plants perfumed
    I can see mountains rain or shine
    all day I hear no market noise
    I light a few leaves to make tea on my stove
    to patch my robe I cut a cloud whisp
    lifetimes seldom fill a hundred years
    why bother chasing profit or fame

14. I entered the mountains and learned to be dumb
    I'm usually too tired to open my mouth
    I don't point out the mistakes of others
    my own faults are what I try to alter
    the tea is done the stove is red
    the moon is up the windows are white
    who sees through this illusory world
    Yen Tzu-ling sat alone on his rock

15. The stream is clear enough to see pebbles
    my ungabled hut sits among vines
    gibbons howl late at night when the moon sets
    few guests get past the moss below the cliffs
    bamboos in the yard bend with spring snow
    plum trees on the ridge are gnarled by winter nights
    the solitude of this path isn't old or new
    grinding a brick on a rock is a waste

16. A white-haired old monk at home in a hut
    the wind has torn my robe into rags
    at the edge of a stream I rake leaves for my stove
    after a frost I weave covers for orange trees
    what's basically real isn't created
    ready-made koans aren't worth a thought
    all day I sit by an open window
    looking at mountains not lowering the screen

臥雲深處不朝天　只在重巖野水邊
竹榻夢回窗有月　砂鍋粥熟灶無煙
萬緣歇盡非除遣　一性圓明本自然
湛若虛空常不動　任他滄海變桑田

下方田地雖平坦　難及山家無點埃
素壁淡描三世佛　瓦瓶香浸一枝梅
門前瀑布懸空落　屋後山巒起浪堆
岳頂禪房枕石臺　白雲飛去又飛來

大道從來無盛衰　未明大道著便宜
聖賢隱伏當斯世　邪法流行在此時
痛策諸根休自縱　常存正念莫他為
人身一失袈裟下　萬劫千生不復追

破屋蕭蕭枕石臺　柴門白日為誰開
名場成隊挨身入　古路無人跨腳來
深夜雪寒唯火伴　五更霜冷有猿哀
袈裟零落難縫補　收捲雲霞自剪裁

17. Hermits in South China sleep on cots of woven bamboo or hemp, while their colleagues in the colder north prefer brick beds with built-in ovens. §Only that which is not subject to cause and effect, and thus change, is real. §Silt carried by the Yellow River has extended its reach into the Pohai Sea more than two hundred kilometers over the past five thousand years. Hence the image of the sea turning into mulberry groves was a real one witnessed and recorded in historic times. By Stonehouse's time, the image had become a cliché for the impermanence of what seemed most permanent.

18. The three buddhas are Amida, Shakyamuni, and Maitreya, the buddhas of the past, the present, and the future. §*Dust* also refers to the dust of the senses.

19. In Buddhism, rebirth is conceived as taking place on a wheel, with one's next existence determined by one's actions in this and previous existences. Though existences on this wheel rise and fall, their illusory nature remains unchanged. §The monk's robe of twenty-five patches protects its wearer from twenty-five kinds of existence in the realms of Passion, Form, and Formlessness.

20. Admission to the civil service or military officer corps was based on a series of competitive examinations held at the local, the provincial, and the national levels. The examination hall for the region in which Stonehouse lived was in nearby Hangchou.

17. I lie down in the clouds no sign of the sky
    above high cliffs and wild streams
    I wake on a cot the moon in the window
    the porridge done the fire out
    all causes end without driving them off
    our nature's full light shines by itself
    transparent as space it never changes
    even if the sea becomes a mulberry grove

18. My hermitage leans against rocks at the summit
    clouds drift off and more clouds arrive
    a waterfall hangs beyond my door
    a mountain ridge rises like a wave in back
    on the face of a rock I drew three buddhas
    for incense I placed a plum branch in a jar
    the land below might be level
    but it can't match a home above the dust

19. The Way doesn't rise or fall
    those who are blind look for an advantage
    sages and wise men escape from this world
    where counterfeit truth prevails
    rein in your senses don't indulge them
    be ever mindful and nothing else
    lose your body beneath a patched robe
    and say good-bye to a thousand rebirths

20. My broken-down hut leans against rocks
    why does my gate stay open all day
    people line up for government exams
    no one sets foot on an ancient trail
    on snow-filled nights a fire is my companion
    on frost covered dawns I hear a gibbon howl
    my tattered robe isn't easy to mend
    I cut a new patch when clouds roll in

人壽相分一百年　有誰能得百年全
危如茅草郎當屋　險似風波破漏船
流俗沙門真可惜　貪名師德更堪憐
寥寥世道今非昔　日把柴門緊閉關

綠霧紅霞竹徑深　一菴終日冷沈沈
等閒放下便無事　著意看來還有心
古鏡未磨含萬象　洪鐘纔扣發圓音
本源自性天真佛　非色非空非古今

優游靜坐野僧家　飲啄隨緣度歲華
翠竹黃花閒意思　白雲流水淡生涯
石頭莫認山中虎　弓影休疑盞裡蛇
林下不知塵世事　夕陽長見送歸鴉

滿頭白髮瘦崚嶒　日用生涯事事能
木白秋分春白朮　竹筐春半曬朱藤
黃精就買山前客　紫菜長需海外僧
誰道新年七十七　開池栽藕種茭菱

21. In ancient China and India, people believed that the human lifespan once extended for thousands of years and that the limit of one hundred was recent and due to the degeneration of human morals. Buddhists say it is much easier to become enlightened as a monk or a nun than it is for a lay person beset with the cares of secular life. Hence, to waste such an opportunity on mediocrity or vanity is tragic.

22. Bamboo grows so thick on Hsiamushan, trails disappear as soon as they're made. §Until fairly recently, mirrors in China were made of bronze or brass, and they had to be kept polished in order to reflect. §Bodhidharma says, "To find a buddha all you have to do is see your nature. Your nature is the buddha" (*The Zen Teaching of Bodhidharma*: 13). §Avalokiteshvara says, "Form is emptiness, and emptiness is form" (*Heart Sutra*).

23. In the first line, Stonehouse contrasts the unstructured religious practice of hermits with that of monks in a monastery. §Line 5 apparently refers to the Tiger Hill Zen Sect, to which Stonehouse traced his spiritual ancestry through his teacher, Chi-an. The hill, which is in Suchou, was said to resemble a tiger. §In his biography in the *Chinshu*: 43, Yueh Kuang explains to a distraught guest that the image of a snake in his wine bowl is merely the reflection from a nearby painting. §The last two lines recall a line from Lu Yu's West Garden: "In the woods fading rays call the crows home."

24. The roots of mountain thistle, or *Atractylis ovata,* are used as a spleen and stomach tonic. §In poem 12, Stonehouse implies that solomon-seal was readily available on Hsiamushan. Apparently he ate all there was to find and was forced to buy more. §The *seaweed* was, no doubt, a present from the Korean monk Yu T'ai-ku (Korean: Taego Pou), who, in fact, visited Stonehouse in the summer of 1347 when the latter was going on seventy-seven. For more on their meeting and later exchange of letters, see J.C. Cleary's *A Buddha from Korea*. Since Stonehouse died at the age of eighty-one and wrote this poem when he was seventy-seven, he must have finished his *Mountain Poems* shortly before his death. §Lotus roots and water chestnuts are both nutritious starches that flourish in the watery regions south of the Yangtze.

21. A life lasts one hundred years
    but which of us gets them all
    precarious as a teetering thatched hut
    or a leaking boat in a storm
    mediocre monks are pathetic
    would-be masters are sadder still
    the world's empty ways aren't what they were
    some days I shut my old gate tight

22. Green mist red clouds a trail through bamboo
    and a hut where quiet lasts
    just let go and worries end
    stop to think and the mind reappears
    an unpolished mirror holds millions of shapes
    a bell doesn't ring until it is rung
    our original nature is the real buddha
    nothing solid or empty nothing old or new

23. A monk in the wild sits quiet and relaxed
    he survives all year on what karma brings
    bamboo and yellow flowers occupy his thoughts
    white clouds and streams simplify his life
    he doesn't mistake a rock for a tiger on a hill
    or the image of a bow for a snake in a bowl
    in the woods he knows nothing of the world's affairs
    at sunset he watches the crows return

24. I may be white-haired and mostly bones
    but I'm well-versed in daily survival
    I pound mountain thistles in a mortar in fall
    I sun-dry vine buds in a tray in spring
    I buy solomon-seal from a peddlar in the village
    and eat seaweed when a foreign monk arrives
    but who would have guessed at seventy-seven
    I would dig a pond for lotus roots and water chestnuts

卜得重嚴遠市朝　柴門半掩草蕭蕭
是誰白髮貧無諂　那箇朱門富不驕
急債莫於寬裡放　妄情須是靜中消
白雲也道青山好　夜夜飛來伴寂寥

風檐來往塞官塘　站馬如飛日夜忙
冒寵貪榮謀仕宦　貪生重利作經商
人間富貴一時樂　地獄辛酸萬劫長
古往今來無藥治　如何不早去修行

入此門來學此宗　切須仔細要推窮
清虛體寂理猶在　忖度心忘境自空
樹掛殘雲成片白　山銜落日半邊紅
是風動耶是幡動　不是旛兮不是風

客愛幽聞到竹籬　逢迎應恕禮全虧
滿頭白髮鬖鬆聚　一頂袈裟撩亂披
黃葉火殘終夜後　青猿聲斷五更時
擁衾相對蒲團坐　各自忘言契此機

25. The first line recalls the opening of the second poem in Cold Mountain's *Collected Poems*: "High cliffs were the home I chose / bird trails beyond the tracks of man."

26. The regions north and south of the Yangtze Delta are still the major producers of salt and silk in China. For many centuries, taxes on these two products provided the government with its major source of revenue, and trade was tightly controlled, with distribution taking place via the Grand Canal and the Yangtze. §The government also maintained an extensive network of horse-mounted couriers for transmission of documents. §Buddhists recognize a series of hells from which one is eventually reborn into another existence, though not necessarily a human one. Length of residence in these hells varies depending on one's karma. §A *kalpa* is a unit of time equivalent to the existence of a world, from its creation until its final destruction. §The reference to elixir was apparently aimed at Taoist alchemists, who sought to cheat death through the ingestion of various minerals and herbs.

27. The *gate* is the gate of Zen, and the *teaching* is the central teaching of Bodhidharma: "This mind is buddha." §One day in the seventh century, two monks were arguing in the courtyard of Fahsing (now Kuanghsiao) Temple in the southern Chinese city of Kuangchou. Pointing to a flag flapping in the wind, one monk said that the wind was moving. A second monk argued that the flag was moving. Having just arrived at the temple and overhearing their argument, Hui-neng said, "It's not the wind that's moving. And it's not the flag. The only things moving around here are your minds" (*Sutra of the Sixth Patriarch:* 1).

28. Either Stonehouse's visitor was a Confucian hermit, in which case some sort of headgear was called for, or a monk who had given up the monastic requirement of shaving one's head twice a month. §Here, the untied kasaya would belong to Stonehouse. §The *leaves* suggest Stonehouse used up whatever firewood he had on hand in the course of the night. And the sound of the gibbon announcing the dawn suggests the wilderness was not far off and that the monks in the local monastery were sleeping late. §Meditation cushions are normally filled with rice straw, and quilts usually include an inner layer of cotton wadding or silk cocoons.

25. I chose high cliffs far from town
     the sound of tall grass a half-open gate
     where's an old pauper who isn't deferential
     or a rich man who isn't vain
     emergency loans don't come without strings
     fantasies fade only in stillness
     clouds too say mountains are better
     returning at night they ease the solitude

26. Their zigzagging sails crowd government quays
     their relay mounts fly night and day
     officials seeking favor and glory
     merchants after comfort and gain
     but wealth and honor in the world soon pass
     while the pain of hell lasts ten-thousand kalpas
     and no elixir offers a cure
     why not practice while time remains

27. Who enters this gate and studies this teaching
     has to be thorough and push to the end
     empty the body and reason remains
     forget the mind and the world disappears
     cloud-covered trees form a landscape of white
     swallowing the sun the mountain turns red
     the flag moves or is it the wind
     it isn't the wind or the flag

28. A friend of seclusion arrives at my gate
     we greet and pardon our lack of decorum
     a white mane gathered in back
     a monk's robe worn untied
     embers of leaves at the end of the night
     howl of a gibbon announcing the dawn
     sitting on cushions wrapped in quilts
     words forgotten finally we meet

百歲光陰過隙駒　幾人於此審思惟
已躬下事未明白　生死岸頭真嶮巇
衲定線行嬌婦淚　飯香玉粒老農脂
莫言施受無因果　因在果成終有時

自入山來萬慮澄　平懷一種任騰騰
庭前樹色秋來減　檻外泉聲雨後增
挑薺煮茶延野客　買盆移菊送鄰僧
錦衣玉食公卿子　不及山僧有此情

是身壽命若浮漚　只好挨排過了休
事欲稱情常不足　人能退步便無憂
衰榮可喻花開落　聚散還同雲去留
我已久忘塵世念　頹然終日倚岑樓

自覺從前世念輕　老來任運樂閒情
芒鞋竹杖春三月　紙帳梅花夢五更
求佛求仙全妄想　無憂無慮即修行
松風昨夜烘然說　自是聾人不肯聽

29. A man was required to have his parents' permission to become a monk. His wife's approval was not necessary since she and their children lived with the man's parents. §For all their self-reliance, many hermits would starve without the generosity of nearby farmers. Charity is the first of the six *paramitas*, or "means to the other shore." §Religious alms are likened to seeds planted in a field of blessing, bringing benefit to both the giver and the receiver.

30. Although Stonehouse may have had Hsiamushan mostly to himself, line 6 suggests he was not alone. During the last decade of his life, which was the same period during which he composed most of these poems, a number of disciples moved to the summit and built a small shrine hall next to his hut. The small temple that resulted was only recently vacated during the Cultural Revolution. §Flowering in fall, chrysanthemums are a symbol of old age (their name is also a homophone for "old") and constitute an appropriate gift to an elderly person. Hospitality to strangers and generosity to friends remain among the virtues cultivated by Chinese of all classes. §The gentry included the propertied and educated elites both in the country and in town.

31. The *Diamond Sutra* ends with this gatha: "All dependent things / are dreams or illusions, bubbles or shadows / they're dew or they're lightning / regard them like this."

32. Shoes made of braided grass are still worn by farmers in less-developed areas of China. Elsewhere, they are also still used by relatives of the bereaved during a funeral. §The third line is indebted to Su Tung-p'o: "With grass shoes and a new bamboo staff / I set off on a hundred-coin journey." §*Paper curtains* refers to a kind of mosquito net that was hung over the bed during Stonehouse's day. It had a gauze top for ventilation, and the sides were made of paper printed with butterflies and plum blossoms. §While Buddhists seek the enlightenment of the Buddha, Taoists seek unity with the Immortal Tao. The fifth-century Taoist T'ao Hung-ching planted hundreds of pines around his hermitage in Hangchou in order to hear the wind in their branches. The *pine wind* also refers to the sound of a buddha's voice.

29. A hundred years flash by
    does anyone think this through
    if what you're doing isn't clear
    the edge between life and death is sheer
    stitches on a monk's robe are a loving wife's tears
    grains of sweet rice are an old farmer's fat
    don't think charity has no reward
    every seed bears fruit in time

30. Cares disappeared when I entered the mountains
    serene at heart I let the world go
    before my door the shade fades in fall
    the spring roars in back after a rain
    I offer tea and vegetables to a visiting farmer
    to a neighbor monk I give chrysanthemums in a pot from town
    the jaded life of the gentry
    can't match a mountain monk's with scenes like these

31. This body's lifetime is like a bubble's
    may as well let things go
    plans and events seldom agree
    who can step back doesn't worry
    we blossom and fade like flowers
    we gather and part like clouds
    earthly thoughts I forgot long ago
    withering away on a mountain peak

32. I've never treasured thoughts of success
    I welcome old age and enjoy being free
    grass shoes a bamboo staff the last month of spring
    paper curtains plum blossoms daybreak dreams
    eternal life and buddhahood are utter illusions
    freedom from worry and care is the practice
    last night the howling pine wind spoke
    this is something the deaf can't hear

逐日挨排過了休　明朝何必預先憂
死生老病難期約　富貴功名不久留
湖上朱門繁蔓草　澗邊遊徑變荒丘
所言皆是目前事　只是無人肯轉頭

分明空劫那邊事　一道神光自古今
百鳥不來山寂寂　萬松長在碧沈沈
消磨本有凡情執　析蕩全從聖量心
白髮頭陀老病侵　住來茅屋幾年深

競利奔名何足誇　清閒獨許野僧家
心田不長無明草　覺苑長開智慧華
黃土坡邊多蕨筍　青苔地上少塵沙
我年三十餘來此　幾度晴窗映落霞

我本禪宗不會禪　甘休林下度餘年
鶉衣百結通身挂　竹篾三條驀肚纏
山色溪光明祖意　鳥啼花笑悟機緣
有時獨上臺盤石　午後無雲月一天

33. The four afflictions are birth, illness, old age, and death. §The lakes of the Yangtze Delta were not resorts but centers of aquaculture and commerce and connected to the Grand Canal and the Yangtze River. The *trails* led upstream to retreats in the mountains.

34. One day the Fourth Patriarch, Tao-hsin, saw birds flocking around a distant mountain. Investigating, he found the birds gathered around a monk. Tao-hsin asked the monk what he was doing. The monk said he was meditating. Tao-hsin asked who was meditating and what was the subject of his meditation. Unable to answer, the monk stood up and bowed and introduced himself as Fa-yung. Later, when he became a disciple of Tao-hsin, the birds stopped coming (*Chuantenglu*: 4). §The kalpa of nothingness lasts from the destruction of one universe until the creation of the next. Thus, the light that Stonehouse sees is from the end of the last universe: Such is the power of karma. The phrase can also be applied to thoughts and in Zen is used to refer to one's original face.

35. Delusion is the worst of the three poisons, which also include desire and anger. §Fiddlehead ferns made up the diet of two of China's most famous recluses: Po-yi and his brother, Shu-ch'i, both of whom preferred to die of hunger on Shouyangshan rather than eat the produce of a realm ruled by an unfilial king. §In characterizing the decades of life, the Chinese usually quote Confucius: "Thirty and on one's own. Forty and no doubts" (*Lunyu*: 2.4). According to poem 170, Stonehouse was forty when he moved to Hsiamushan.

36. Bodhidharma is credited with bringing Zen to China in the late fifth century. But the transmission of the Zen tradition began a thousand years earlier when Shakyamuni held up a flower and Kashyapa smiled. §As evidence of his own enlightenment, Stonehouse told his master, "When the rain finally stops in late spring, the oriole appears on a branch." §From the flat-topped boulders at the summit of Hsiamushan, the view includes Lake Taihu to the north and the 1500-meter peaks of the Tienmu Mountains to the south.

33. Day after day I let things go
    why worry about tomorrow today
    the four afflictions are hard to predict
    wealth and honor don't last
    lakeside villas are swallowed by vines
    streamside trails disappear into weeds
    such things are easy for all to see
    but no one is willing to look

34. A white-haired monk afflicted with age
    living under thatch year after year
    I've exhausted my life on simple passions
    my movements all spring from the sacred mind
    when birds don't come the mountain is quiet
    ten thousand pines keep it dark green
    from the kalpa of nothingness it's clear
    a miraculous light still shines

35. What can you say about profit and fame
    to a solitary untroubled mountain monk
    weeds of delusion don't grow in the mind
    where flowers of wisdom bloom
    bamboo shoots and fiddleheads blanket the slopes
    dust seldom falls on moss-covered ground
    I was over thirty when I first arrived
    how many sunsets have turned my windows red

36. I was a Zen monk who didn't know Zen
    so I chose the woods for the years I had left
    a patched robe over my body
    braided bamboo around my waist
    mountain shade and stream light explain the Patriarch's meaning
    flower smiles and bird songs reveal the hidden key
    sometimes I sit on flat-topped rocks
    cloudfree afternoons once a month

四十餘年獨隱居　不知塵世幾榮枯

夜爐助煖燒松葉　午鉢充飢摘野蔬

坐石看雲閒意思　朝陽補衲靜工夫

有人問我西來意　盡把家私説向渠

蠆尾狼心滿世間　爭先各自使機關

百年能得幾回笑　一日曾無頃刻閒

車覆有誰知改轍　禍來無地著羞慚

老僧不是多饒舌　要與諸人揭蓋纏

鳥兔奔忙不暫停　嚴居忽爾到頹齡

水邊行道影偏瘦　松下看山眸轉青

紅葉旋收供瓦灶　黃花時採插銅瓶

勞生好飲利名酒　昏醉無由喚得醒

茅屋青山綠水邊　往來年久自相便

數株紅白桃李樹　一片青黃菜麥田

竹榻夜移聽雨坐　紙窗晴啟看雲眠

人生無出清閒好　得到清閒豈偶然

37. Stonehouse lived as a hermit for thirty-five years on Hsiamushan, but he also lived for three years with Kao-feng on Tienmushan's West Peak and six years with Chi-an on Langyashan near Chienyang. §Although the practice was never as widespread in China as it was in India, monks were encouraged to restrict themselves to a noon meal, which they ate following their morning begging rounds. §One of the most common koans asked by Zen masters is: "Why did Bodhidharma come east?" The student's answer is expected to express the essence of Zen rather than supply the Patriarch's presumed motivation.

38. One of the first measures enacted by the First Emperor when he unified China in 221 BC was to standardize the axle length of carts so that all tracks would be the same width. §The Five Obstacles include desire, anger, tiredness, anxiety, and doubt. And the Ten Chains include shamelessness, insensitivity, envy, meanness, regret, laziness, over-activity, self-absorption, hate, and secretiveness.

39. According to Chinese mythology, the sun is the home of a crow, and the moon is the abode of a hare. The moon is yin and represents Earth, hence its symbol is an animal of the land; the sun is yang and represents Heaven, hence its totem is a creature of the air. §Stonehouse's *blue eyes* could refer to the Zen eyes of Bodhidharma, the "blue-eyed barbarian," who brought Zen to China. But they could also refer to cataracts. Ironically, cataract surgery was introduced to the Chinese by Indian monks about the same time that Bodhidharma arrived, but the technique had been lost by Stonehouse's time. §While Stonehouse used chrysanthemums for his altar, others infused them in their wine.

40. Etiquette requires paying a return visit to someone else who visits. Apparently Stonehouse no longer held up his side of such relationships. Perhaps he didn't look forward to a long hike with a town at the end of it. Or, more likely, he didn't like leaving his hut. §As previously noted, windows were usually covered with oilpaper.

37. More than forty years I've lived as a hermit
    out of touch with the world's rise and fall
    a stove full of pine needles keeps me warm at night
    a bowl of wild plants fills me up at noon
    I sit on rocks and watch clouds and let thoughts wander
    I patch my robe in sunlight and cultivate silence
    until someone asks why Bodhidharma came east
    and I list all my possessions

38. Scorpion tails and wolf hearts overrun the world
    everyone has a trick to get ahead
    but how many smiles in a lifetime
    how many moments of peace in a day
    who knows a toppled cart means try another track
    when trouble strikes there is no time for shame
    this old monk isn't just talking
    he's trying to remove your obstacles and chains

39. The crow and the hare race without rest
    living in the cliffs suddenly I'm old
    my reflection looks thin when I walk beside a stream
    my eyes have turned blue viewing mountains through pines
    I gather red leaves to burn in my stove
    I pick yellow flowers to put in a vase
    toiling away for the wine of success
    others get drunk and can't be revived

40. A thatched hut blue mountains green streams
    visits by now are up to me
    two or three peach trees and plum trees in bloom
    green and yellow fields of vegetables and wheat
    I sit all night in bed listening to rain
    I open my paper window and doze off watching clouds
    nothing is better than being free
    but getting free isn't luck

古人為道入山中　日用工夫在已躬
添石墜腰舂白米　攜鋤帶雨種青松
擔泥拽石何妨道　運水搬柴好用功
韓懶借衣求食者　莫來相伴老禪翁

萬物生成感宿根　已長彼短不須論
一團猛火利名路　三尺寒冰佛祖門
草莽荊榛狐窟宅　雲霄蓬島鶴乾坤
滿頭白髮居嚴谷　幾度憑欄到日嚧

嚴居我本為修行　不許人知每自評
道性淳和餘習盡　覺心圓淨照功成
種松鉏菜一身健　補衲翻經兩眼明
世異事殊真好笑　避秦亦得隱山名

歷遍乾坤沒處尋　偶然得住此山林
茅菴高插雲霄碧　蘚逕斜過竹樹深
人為利名驚寵辱　我因禪寂老光陰
蒼松怪石無人識　猶更將心去覓心

41. Although Buddhist monasteries in China were non-profit, many depended on income from rent on land donated by wealthy patrons. And some monasteries became so rich, the monks did little or no work. This was rarely the case at temples in the mountains. At these more remote religious centers the emphasis was on meditation and manual work, and the monastic rules of Pai Chang prevailed, chief of which was "no work, no food."

42. *Roots* refers to past actions whose karmic fruit we reap today. §When Taoist adepts finally succeed in transforming themselves through yoga and alchemy into pure spirit, they turn into cranes and fly off to the Island of Penglai, which is the dwelling place of the immortals and which is still said to appear from out of the mist off the northern coast of the Shantung Peninsula. §The last line suggests that there are not many visitors on the path of solitude and simplicity.

43. In his *Peach Blossom Spring,* T'ao Yuan-ming tells the story of a group of people fleeing the oppressive rule of the Ch'in dynasty, which unified China in 221 BC. In the course of their flight, these refugees discovered a hidden valley. When a fisherman stumbled onto their sanctuary several hundred years later, he found a peaceful farming community. Eventually the fisherman returned to his own village and told others about his discovery. But the refugees obliterated the traces he left to mark his route, and their valley was never found again.

44. In the last two lines, Stonehouse recalls the Zen monk who sees beyond the mountains but who has not yet seen beyond the emptiness with which he has replaced them.

41. The ancients entered mountains in search of the Way
    their daily practice revolved around their bodies
    they tied heavy stones to their waists to hull rice
    they carried their hoes in the rain to plant pines
    it goes without saying they moved dirt and rocks
    and never stopped hauling firewood and water
    the slackers who wear a robe to get food
    don't hang around an old Zen monk

42. Everything's growth depends on old roots
    why argue about who's tall or short
    the road to success is a tunnel of fire
    the door to buddhahood is a wall of ice
    my hut sits alone among brambles and weeds
    the cloudy Isle of Penglai is a crane's universe
    my hair has turned white in the cliffs and gorges
    how often have I leaned on a fence rail till dark

43. I moved to the cliffs in order to practice
    I didn't need others to judge my faults
    when natures are simple old habits end
    when thoughts are pure awareness arises
    planting pines and weeding have strengthened my body
    reading sutras and sewing have sharpened my sight
    the world's anomalies are funny indeed
    the refugees of Ch'in are called hermits too

44. I searched creation without success
    by chance I found this forested peak
    my thatched hut pokes through clouds and sky
    the moss-slick trail cuts through bamboo
    favor and shame arouse the ambitious
    I grow old on the stillness of Zen
    dark pines and strange rocks remain unknown
    to those who look for mind with mind

年老心閒身亦閒　埽除一榻臥松間
嚴肩幽寂自為喜　世路崎嶇人轉頑
風煖野禽聲瑣碎　日斜花藥影闌珊
藜羹粟飯家常有　不用持盂更下山

清晨汲水啟柴門　看見天空四歛氣
黃獨火香思懶殘　碧桃花謝悟靈雲
林閒猿鶴慣曾見　世上衰榮杳不聞
幾度坐來苔石煖　好山直看到斜曛

白雲深處結茅廬　隨分生涯樂有餘
未死且留煨芋火　息機何必絕交書
湛然凝寂通三際　廓爾圓明裡十虛
菴內不知菴外事　幾番花落又還敷

細把浮生物理推　輸贏難定一盤棋
僧居青嶂閒方好　人在紅塵老不知
風颭茶煙浮竹榻　水流花瓣落青池
如何三萬六千日　不放身心靜片時

45. Lines 5 and 6 are from Ou-yang Hsiu's *Liuyishihhua,* except that Ou-yang has the sun high and the flower shadows heavy. Although the peony is the showiest of China's summer flowers, it requires the sun for its glory. §The green leaves of pigweed, or *Chenopodium album,* are eaten fresh as salad greens in Europe but are usually cooked in China. Pigweed has been a metaphor for simple fare ever since Confucius had nothing but this to eat for ten days while traveling through an inhospitable region. §Millet is usually boiled in water with a dash of arrowroot added as a thickener to make a gruel. §Although monks all have a large bowl they use for begging, the hermits I've met coming down the mountain invariably carry an empty sack and leave their bowls at home. Stonehouse was known for his refusal to beg for food.

46. The *sky's four moods* refers to the four seasons. §The T'ang dynasty official Li Mi heard about Lazy Scrap (Lan-ts'an) and decided to pay him a visit. When Li arrived, Lazy Scrap offered the official part of a sweet potato he was roasting and advised him: "Don't talk too much, and you'll last ten years as prime minister" (*Kaosengchuan*). Li did, in fact, become prime minister, but his readiness to criticize kept him in and out of favor. §Magic Cloud (Ling-yun) was enlightened while watching peach petals falling, after which he composed this gatha: "For thirty years I expected a sword / scattering leaves I unsheathed another branch / then I discovered peach blossoms / and haven't had any more doubts" (*Wutenghuiyuan:* 4). The reference to gibbons and cranes recalls a story recorded in Ko Hsuan's *Paoputzu* in which an army is said to have entered the mountains of South China around 1000 BC. The soldiers turned into insects and sand, while the officers turned into gibbons and cranes.

47. Lines 5 and 6 recapitulate the two stages of meditation known as *chih-kuan: stilling* (thoughts) and *illuminating* (one's nature). §Temporal boundaries separate the past, the present, and the future. The ten directions include the eight points of the compass as well as the sky above and the earth below.

48. The Chinese play two kinds of chess: *wei-ch'i,* which the Japanese call *go,* and *hsiang-ch'i,* which is similar to Indian or Western chess. Both have been played in China for more than three thousand years. Here, the former is meant. §Dust is a necessary accompaniment of roads and marketplaces. In Buddhist parlance, it also refers to the world as perceived by the senses. §The *tea smoke* is from the small clay brazier Stonehouse used for heating tea water.

45. I'm old but my body and mind are at peace
    I've cleared a place to lie in the pines
    the seclusion of a mountain home makes me happy
    the world's rough roads make others perverse
    when the air turns warm the birds all chatter
    when the sun declines peony shadows fade
    as long as there's millet and pigweed soup
    why should I take my bowl down the mountain

46. I open my door at dawn to fetch water
    and examine the sky's four moods
    sweet potatoes roasting recall Lazy Scrap
    peach petals falling woke up Magic Cloud
    I often see gibbons and cranes in the forest
    but hear no news of the world
    how many days have I warmed moss-covered rocks
    gazing at mountains till twilight

47. I built a thatched hut deep in the clouds
    and find enough joy in what life brings
    I manage to keep a potato fire burning
    and still write letters despite a lack of schemes
    clear and still as ice I transcend the bounds of time
    open and full of light I encompass the ten directions
    but I don't know what happens outside my door
    how many times has spring followed fall

48. Study the patterns of transient existence
    the outcome of a game of chess isn't fixed
    a monk in the mountains needs to be free
    people in the dust grow old unaware
    wind blows tea smoke over my bed
    the stream drops petals into a pool
    with thirty-six thousand days
    why not spend a few being still

恁麼徹底恁麼去　放下從頭放下來

兩片脣皮堆白釀　一條古路長蒼苔

雲邊木馬飛如電　海底泥牛吼似雷

雪覆萬峰晴月夜　暗香春信到寒梅

清貧長樂道人家　日用頭頭自偶諧

昨夜西風吹古木　天明滿地是乾柴

霞飄素練粘丹壁　露滴真珠綴綠崖

活計從來隨現定　不勞辛苦去安排

了了常知似不知　儼然如兀又如癡

旋嵐倒獄鎮長靜　一念萬年終不移

有耳聽聲風過樹　無心應物月臨池

休言我獨能明了　此事人人盡可為

計拙慚虧應世才　聰明無分占癡呆

自言境物皆虛幻　誰解資財盡倘來

黃葉隨流聞去住　白雲橫谷謾徘徊

雙眸合卻方纔好　為愛青山又放開

49. The third and fourth lines refer to people who talk about the truth without knowing it for themselves, and the fifth and sixth lines summarize koans in which the wooden horse and the clay ox represent the liberated mind free of feelings and thoughts. As for the second of these metaphors, Tung-shan once asked Lung-shan what he had learned while living in the mountains. Lung-shan answered, "I saw two clay oxen plunge into the sea, and up until now I haven't heard any news" (*Chuantenglu:* 8). §The last two lines recall Lin Ho-ching's famous couplet about plum blossoms: "Their hidden scent rides the wind / the moon shines through the mist."

50. Not only Taoists, but Buddhists and Confucians also use the word *Tao:Way* to describe their path of spiritual practice. §The west wind blows in autumn and is usually the mildest of China's seasonal breezes.

51. Hurricanes (called "typhoons") are common in summer along the southeastern coast, while windstorms are usually confined to the arid regions of the northwest.

52. Confucius says, "The wise love water. The kind love mountains" (*Lunyu:* 6.21). While wisdom is the basis of enlightenment, compassion is the basis of liberation.

49. To get to the end the very end
    let it all go let it go
    saliva builds up on the lips
    moss grows thick on an ancient road
    a wooden horse flashes through the clouds
    a clay ox thunders beneath the sea
    a moonlit night on a thousand snowy peaks
    a hidden scent says spring has reached the winter plum

50. I'm poor but happy a man of the Way
    all my needs are satisfied by chance
    last night the west wind downed an old tree
    at daybreak firewood covered the ground
    gauze silk clouds adorned red scarps
    dew drop pearls bejeweled green cliffs
    what's present has always decided my living
    why should I burden myself with plans

51. You know very well yet seem not to know
    speechless like a dunce or a fool
    you keep still while storms flatten mountains
    not a thought moving for ten thousand years
    with ears you hear the wind in the trees
    with no-mind you mirror the moon above a pond
    but don't think you alone understand
    this is something anyone can do

52. The shame of dumb ideas is suffered by the best
    but lack of perception means a fool for sure
    among those who say it's all an illusion
    who sees that wealth is due to luck
    leaves in the stream move without a plan
    clouds in the valley drift without design
    once I closed my eyes everything was fine
    I opened them again because I love mountains

圓顱方服作沙門　便見牟尼佛子孫

止惡防非調意馬　忘機息見制心猿

鍊磨道性真金淨　涵養靈源美玉溫

把手牽他行不得　為人自肯乃方親

紅日東升夜落西　黃昏鐘了五更雞

乾坤老我一頭雪　歲月消磨百甕虀

寄言世上傷弓羽　好向深山擇木棲

借地栽松將作棟　喫桃吐核又成蹊

禪邊大有閒情緒　收拾乾柴向地爐

法道寥寥不可模　一菴深隱是良圖

門前養竹高遮屋　石上分泉直到廚

猿抱子來崖果熟　鶴移巢去澗松枯

浮世光陰有幾何　誰能挈挈又波波

廚空旋去尋黃獨　衲破方思藊綠荷

塵尾罷拈言語斷　佛經忘看蠹魚多

可憐身在袈裟下　趣境攀緣事如麻

53. Although Shakyamuni didn't cut his hair, his disciples began the custom of shaving their heads to distinguish themselves from members of other sects. They also wore the simplest possible garment made of a square piece of cloth, which they hung over one shoulder, and they took the Buddha's family name of Shakya as their own. §In regards to the residents of a Zen monastery, Stonehouse treats slouches and fanatics with equal disdain. §Compared to other stones, jade is relatively warm to the touch.

54. The Chinese eat pickles with nearly every meal as an accompaniment to steamed rice or porridge. For those who can't afford much else, pickled vegetables are sometimes the main course. Of the dozens of varieties available, pickled cucumbers remain the favorite. §The *Chankuotse* says, "When a bird that has been previously shot at hears a bow-string, it flies away as fast as it can" (Chutse). While Stonehouse's advice is not without merit, hunters also string nets between trees to capture thrushes and other song birds.

55. The *spring* still flows from the rocks behind the current incarnation of Stonehouse's hut. §Among the fruits I've been surprised to find in the cliffs of China are gooseberries and passion fruit, loquats and dragon eyes.

56. The Chinese yam, or *Dioscorea japonica,* is usually dug up in fall, when its large winged seeds make it easy to distinguish among the many plants that normally conceal its leaves and tendrils. §Lotus leaves retain their leathery appearance through the summer but become dry and brittle as fall approaches. Hence, they only provide temporary attire. §The whisk is an abbot's symbol of authority and consists of a handle to which the tail of an elk or deer or ox is attached. Stonehouse put down his whisk and stopped giving sermons in 1339 after serving as abbot of Pinghu's Fuyuan Temple for eight years.

53. A round head and square robe constitute a monk
    behold a descendant of Shakyamuni Buddha
    stopping wrongs and evils taming the horse of will
    banishing thoughts and schemes caging the monkey mind
    refining his true nature until it's pure as gold
    keeping the mystic source warm as jade
    give him a pull but he won't budge
    only when he's willing is he friendly

54. The sun climbs in the east and goes down in the west
    the bell rings at dusk the rooster crows at dawn
    yin and yang have turned my head to snow
    meanwhile I've gone through a hundred crocks of pickles
    I plant pines for beams wherever I find room
    I spit out peach pits and make a peach-tree trail
    tell the bow-wary birds of the world
    head for the mountains and choose any tree

55. The path of the Buddha is too singular to copy
    but a well-hidden hut comes close
    I planted bamboo in front to make a screen
    from the rocks I've led a spring into the kitchen
    gibbons bring their young when cliff fruits are ripe
    cranes move their nests when gorge pines turn brown
    lots of idle thoughts occur in Zen
    the deadwood I gather for my stove

56. There isn't much time in this passing life
    why spend it running around
    when my kitchen is bare I go look for yams
    when my robe needs a patch I think of lotus leaves
    I've put down the elk tail and stopped giving sermons
    my long-forgotten sutras are home to silverfish
    how sad to hide beneath a monk's robe
    and still have so many goals and ties

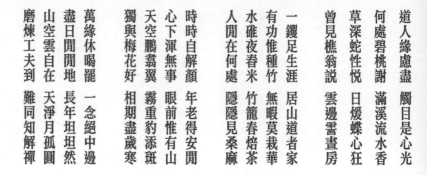

道人緣慮盡　觸目是心光
何處碧桃謝　滿溪流水香
草深蛇性悦　日煖蝶心狂
曾見樵翁説　雲邊畫畫房

一钁足生涯　居山道者家
有功惟種竹　無暇莫栽華
水碓夜舂米　竹籠春焙茶
人間在何處　隱隱見桑麻

時時自解顏　年老得安閒
心下渾無事　眼前惟有山
天空鵬翯翼　霧重豹添斑
獨與梅花好　相期盡歲寒

萬緣休喝罷　一念絕中邊
盡日閒閒地　長年坦坦然
山空雲自在　天淨月孤圓
磨煉工夫到　難同知解禪

57. The term *tao-jen,* which I've rendered "man of the Way," was at first applied to Taoists, then also to Buddhists, and eventually to Buddhists alone. §The fisherman who discovered the hidden valley mentioned in poem 43 did so by following peach petals upstream to a spring that flowed from a cleft in the rocks.

58. Timber bamboo remains a major product of the hills south of Huchou, though Stonehouse was probably more interested in harvesting the edible shoots of the smaller varieties that still cover the slopes of Hsiamushan. §Tea leaves picked in spring are generally the best. The different kinds of green and red teas are produced by varying the exposure of the leaves to heat. §Mulberry and hemp usually grow on land unsuitable for rice, hence at the margins of farming communities.

59. The P'eng is the great bird in the first chapter of *Chuangtzu,* where it is used as a symbol of transcendence. It is so big it must climb ninety thousand miles into the sky before it has room to turn south. §In the *Yiching:* 49, the leopard that can change its spots is used as a metaphor for the person who succeeds in eliminating his vices through the cultivation of virtue. The P'eng represents the goal of Taoist practice, while the spotless leopard represents the goal of Confucian cultivation. §The flowering plum, meanwhile, is China's symbol of perseverance in the face of hardship, blossoming during the coldest period of the year.

60. The phrase used here for religious practice, *mo-lien:grinding-firing,* recalls the story of grinding a brick to make a mirror, for which see poem 15 and the accompanying note.

57. Men of the Way are done with reason
    all they see is the light of the mind
    somewhere peach trees shed their bloom
    their fragrance fills the stream
    overgrown slopes are bliss for a snake
    sunshine is butterfly heaven
    once I heard a woodcutter mention
    a lean-to in the clouds

58. A hoe provides a living
    for a man of the Way in the mountains
    usually busy planting bamboo
    he doesn't have time to grow flowers
    a water wheel hulls his rice at night
    he dries spring tea in a bamboo tray
    where is the world of men
    their hemp and mulberry appear in the haze

59. Most of the time I smile
    old men can relax
    my mind is free of troubles
    nothing but mountains meet my eyes
    the P'eng soars into the sky
    a leopard blends into mist
    I'm more like the flowering plum
    I wait for the year-end cold

60. Reasoning comes to an end
    a thought breaks in the middle
    all day nothing but time
    the whole year undisturbed
    on a pristine mountain clouds float free
    in a clear sky the moon is a lonesome o
    even if physical discipline worked
    it wouldn't match knowing Zen

深山僧住處　端的勝蓬萊　地上並無草　園中卻有梅　聞多諸想滅　靜極自心開　一頂破禪衲　和雲曬石臺

何人能似我　無事亦無為　平澹忘懷處　蕭然絕照時　紙窗開竹屋　瓦灶爇松枝　屈曲黃泥路　團團紫槿籬

山路歌聲絕　樵歸煙火村　溪光晴瀉遠　野色晚來昏　唐代高僧寺　宋朝丞相墳　嚴臺舒野望　依約見松門

欲窮窮不到　一虎笑嚴臺　本自無形段　如何有去來　撼他林木動　吹我竹門開　一陣從何起　颼颼遍九垓

61. *Pine Gate* is apparently another name for Lone Pine Pass, about forty kilometers southwest of Hsiamushan. §Just beyond the pass was Lingfeng Temple, which dates back to the end of the T'ang dynasty. §I have no idea which Sung-dynasty prime minister is meant, but in the vicinity of Lone Pine Pass are several stupa cemeteries and pagodas that date back to the Sung. §The headwaters of the West Fork of the Sha River also begin at the pass and flow west of Hsiamushan on their way to Taihu Lake.

62. The hibiscus is native to most of south China, where it is commonly grown as a hedge. §Lao-tzu says, "I change nothing / and the people transform themselves / I stay still / and the people adjust themselves / I do nothing / and the people enrich themselves / I want nothing / and the people simplify themselves" (*Taoteching: 57*).

63. Penglai is the ethereal abode of immortals and thought to be located off the coast of the Shantung Peninsula in North China. §As elsewhere, *dust* refers to the world of sensation. §The plum blooms during the harshest time of the year and has been the friend of recluses throughout Chinese history.

64. In the last line some editions have "a tiger roars." The words for *laugh* and *roar* are homophones, both being pronounced *hsiao*. While *roar* would seem more appropriate, I think Stonehouse was being playful. An early Chinese belief recorded in the *Hanshu* says, "When a tiger roars, the wind rises. When a dragon stirs, the clouds gather" (*Biography of Wang Pao*).

61. A view of the wild unrolls from the cliffs
    Pine Gate is there as always
    a monastery from the T'ang
    a Sung prime minister's grave
    stream light flows into the distance
    the wilderness turns dark at dusk
    singing fades from mountain trails
    as woodcutters head for village smoke

62. A winding muddy trail
    an immense hibiscus hedge
    a paper-window bamboo hut
    stove-blackened pines
    a humble place free from care
    quiet untroubled days
    who can do as well
    nothing to do or change

63. A hermitage deep in the mountains
    leaves Penglai in the dust
    the ground is free of weeds
    plum trees fill the garden
    thoughts dissolve there's so much time
    it's so quiet the mind appears
    a monk's ragged robe
    dries on the rocks next to a cloud

64. Where did that gust come from
    whistling through the sky
    shaking the whole forest
    blowing open my bamboo door
    without any arms or legs
    how does it move around
    I'd track it down but can't
    from the cliffs a tiger laughs

霞霧山頭頂　雲邊闢小房
夏涼窗近竹　冬煖閣朝陽
繭紙衣裳軟　山田粥飯香
此生隨分過　無可得思量

一鑊足生涯　長年飽水柴
有山堪寓目　無事可干懷
嵐氣溼茅屋　苔痕上土階
任緣終省力　渾不用安排

山廚修午供　泉白似銀漿
羹熟筍鞭爛　飯炊粳米香
油煎清頂蕈　醋煮紫芽薑
百味皆難及　何須説上方

真空如湛海　微動即成漚
縱受形骸報　便懷衣食憂
識情奔野馬　妄念走狂猴
不悟空王旨　輪迴卒未休

65. Hsiawushan, or "Redfog Mountain," is another variant of Hsiamushan, or "Redcurtain Mountain." Stonehouse's hut was on the southern slope just below the summit. §People who couldn't afford cloth wore clothes made of a heavy grade of mulberry paper. During the winter they added a lining of cotton wadding or of silk cocoons that proved unsuitable for making silk cloth.

66. Thatch is the most common roof covering in the mountains, although hermits who can afford them use earthenware tiles. §If there is one element of Chinese culture that most Westerners find incomprehensible, if not exasperating, it's the Chinese glorification of acceptance. But acceptance provides the basis for transcendence, while struggle keeps us enslaved to the dialectic of opposites. At the end of his *Taoteching,* Lao-tzu says, "The Way of the sage / is to act without struggling" (81).

67. As previously noted, the *spring* was next to Stonehouse's hut. §In stews, thin bamboo shoots that have been preserved in salt are preferred over of the larger, fresh shoots. §*Hard-grain rice* refers to a non-glutinous variety rather than the softer rice most Chinese prefer. §I'm not sure what kind of mushrooms Stonehouse had in mind. The *violet cortinarius* and the *indigo lactarius* are both edible. Meanwhile, some editions have "clear-cap" in place of "blue-cap."

68. At the end of the *Diamond Sutra,* the Buddha says, "All composite things are like a dream, an illusion, a shadow, a bubble." §Lao-tzu says, "The reason we have disaster / is because we have a body / if we didn't have a body / we wouldn't have disaster" (*Taoteching*: 13). §*The Lord of Emptiness* is the Buddha. §The motive force that moves the Wheel of Rebirth is the Three Poisons: Delusion, Desire and Anger. And chief among these is Delusion.

65. From the top of Hsiawushan
     my hut peeks through the clouds
     cool in summer beside bamboo
     warm in winter facing the sun
     cocoon-paper clothes feel soft
     mountain-grown rice smells fine
     I take what this life brings
     nothing else is worth my time

66. A hoe provides a living
     the water and wood last all year
     mountains soothe my eyes
     no troubles burden my mind
     swirling mist soaks through thatch
     a trail of moss climbs dirt steps
     accepting saves my strength
     no need to arrange a thing

67. Lunch in my mountain kitchen
     the spring provides the perfect sauce
     behold a stew of preserved bamboo
     a pot of fragrant hard-grain rice
     blue-cap mushrooms fried in oil
     purple-bud ginger pickles
     none of them heavenly dishes
     but why should I cater to gods

68. Perfect emptiness is a transparent sea
     where the faintest breath makes foam
     as soon as we have a body
     we have worries about food and clothes
     runaway racehorse perceptions
     uncaged monkey delusions
     until you understand the Lord of Emptiness
     the Wheel of Rebirth rolls on

山家八月天　時物自相便
豈莢新垂隴　稻花香滿田
割茅修舊屋　斫竹覓清泉
世上誰知我　優遊樂晚年

茆庵竹樹間　塵世不相關
門對一池水　窗開四面山
煙熏茶灶黑　塵蒸布裘斑
不悟空王法　緣何得此聞

紅日半銜山　柴門便掩關
綠蒲眠褥軟　白木枕頭彎
松月來先照　溪雲出未還
迢迢清夜夢　不肯到人間

扶杖出松林　聞行上翠岑
鶴群衝鶴散　樹影落溪沈
野果棘難採　藥苗香易尋
澹煙斜日暮　紅葉半巖陰

69. The eighth month of China's lunar calendar is roughly equivalent to September in the Gregorian calendar. §Farmers often take advantage of the hiatus that occurs during this period, when weeding and watering are no longer necessary and harvesting has not yet begun, to make repairs to their homes and irrigation systems. §In areas where fields are terraced, farmers often grow beans and melons on the banks separating levels. §Bamboo canes are prepared for use as water pipes by dropping hot coals into one end and allowing them to burn through the junctures.

70. The *pond* also appears in poem 24, and Stonehouse's portable tea stove is first mentioned in poem 13. §As in poem 68, *the Lord of Emptiness* refers to the Buddha, whose teaching on the subject is often summarized by the phrase that is the focus of the *Heart Sutra:* "Form is emptiness, and emptiness is form."

71. In poem 27, the mountain swallows the sun: Is it the mountain or is it the sun? §Until recently, the Chinese preferred to sleep on hard pillows designed to cool the brain. In addition to wood, porcelain was also used.

72. When Buddhist monks or nuns venture into the mountains, they carry a six-foot staff with rings on the top that jangle to announce their presence to wild animals. There is also a spade on the bottom for negotiating slippery slopes and for digging up the odd root. §*Leaving the pines* suggests climbing beyond the treeline, but it also refers to leaving monastic life.

69. The Eighth Month in the mountains
    the perennial fruits are at hand
    pea pods hang on terraced banks
    rice-flower perfume fills the fields
    I cut tall grass to patch my hut
    I chop bamboo to channel the spring
    I wonder if anyone knows
    how much I enjoy old age

70. A thatched retreat among bamboo
    beyond the world of dust
    a pond before the door
    mountains out every window
    a tea-stove black with soot
    a hemp robe streaked with dirt
    if I didn't understand the Lord of Emptiness
    how did I end up here

71. When the red sun swallows the mountain
    I shut my makeshift door
    my new grass mattress gives
    my lacquered wooden pillow curves
    and when the pine moon shines
    before mountain clouds return
    clear night dreams go far
    but not to the world below

72. I grabbed my staff and left the pines
    I wandered up an emerald peak
    a flock of cranes chased a hawk
    tree shadows darkened the streams
    thorns protected the wild fruit
    their scent made herbs easy to find
    a veil of smoke in fading light
    crimson leaves on a cliff in shade

好山千萬疊　屋占最高層
減塑三尊佛　長明一碗燈
鐘敲寒夜月　茶煮石池冰
客問西來意　惟言我不能

取捨與行藏　人生各有方
乾坤容我嬾　名利使他忙
背日鷗眠埠　營窠燕遶梁
情迷隨物轉　不得悟空王

結草便為菴　年年用覆苫
紙窗松葉暗　竹屋蘚華粘
麥飯惟饒火　藜羹不點鹽
生涯隨分過　誰管世人嫌

淒淒茅舍新秋夜　白荳花開絡緯啼
山月如銀牽老興　閒行不覺過峰西

73. The Buddhist trinity is usually represented by Amida, Shakyamuni, and Maitreya, the buddhas of the past, the present, and the future. §A small handbell is used while chanting. §At the end of the fifth century, Bodhidharma left his home in southern India and brought Zen to China. Originally, the word *dhyana:zen* meant "meditation." Following Bodhidharma's arrival, it was also used to refer to his technique of "pointing directly to the mind." Eventually, it was also applied to the sects that emphasized this teaching. "Why did Bodhidharma come east?" was a favorite koan of Chinese Zen masters as it demanded the student "come east" himself.

74. Heaven and Earth represent the basic dialectic of yin and yang. §*The Lord of Nothing* (or Emptiness) is the Buddha, who teaches that because all things depend on other things for their existence none of them is real.

75. Although mosses are non-flowering plants, their spore capsules are sometimes borne on long stems that suggest the stem of a flower. §Wheat-bran gruel is made by grinding wheat together with its husk and boiling the resulting mixture. §For *pigweed soup* see my note to poem 45. Wheat-bran and pigweed are among the survival foods of the poor. §Lao-tzu says, "The best are like water / bringing help to all / without competing / choosing what others avoid / hence approaching the Tao" (*Taoteching*: 8).

76. This poem was apparently written on the Moon Festival, when the Chinese celebrate the harvest. Next to New Year, it is the most important festival of the year, and family members go to great lengths to be together on this night, which is the full moon night of the eighth lunar month.

73. On a ten-thousand-story-high mountain
    my hut sits at the very top
    I shaped three buddhas from clay
    and keep an oil lamp burning
    I ring a bell cold moonlit nights
    and brew tea with pond ice
    but ask me why Bodhidharma came east
    and I can't say a word

74. Take it or leave it do it or don't
    everyone has his own path
    Heaven and Earth let me be lazy
    profit and fame keep others at work
    gulls sleep on piers with their backs to the sun
    swallows build nests above roof beams
    seduced by passion controlled by things
    people aren't aware of the Lord of Nothing

75. I built my hut out of grass
    every year I add more thatch
    pine trees shade paper windows
    moss flowers line bamboo walls
    wheat-bran gruel only needs fire
    pigweed soup requires no salt
    I live on whatever comes my way
    why should I avoid what others hate

76. A thatched hut is lonely on a new fall night
    with white peas in flower and crickets calling
    mountain moon silver evokes an old joy
    suddenly I've strolled west of the peak

滿山筍蕨滿園茶　一樹紅花間白花

大抵四時春最好　就中猶好是山家

有人問我何年住　坐久總方省得來

門外碧桃親手種　春光二十度花開

厭煩勞役愛安閒　箇樣如何居得山

百丈已前嚴穴士　生涯全在钁頭邊

年老安居養病身　日高猶自未開門

怕寒起坐燒松火　一曲樵歌隔塢聞

童子未曾歸動火　水雲早已到投齊

山菴喜免征徭慮　賸種青松只賣柴

玉堂銀燭笙歌夜　金谷羅幃富貴家

爭似道人茅屋下　一天晴月曬梅花

77. Fiddleheads have been standard fare among hermits ever since Shu-ch'i and Po-yi tried to survive on the blameless diet of ferns and deer milk around 1100 BC. §Spring is also the best time to pick tea leaves. In its natural state the tea tree can grow to over thirty meters in height, but in tea orchards it is usually kept waist-high. §The second line suggests a peach tree in a grove of plum trees. Normally the peach blooms a month or more after the plum, but elsewhere Stonehouse links the flowering of both trees. Apparently Stonehouse planted varieties whose flowering overlapped.

78. If, as Stonehouse tells us in poem 170, he moved to Hsiamushan in 1312, this poem would have been written in 1332. But Stonehouse left to become abbot of Pinghu's Fuyuan Temple in 1331. Hence, Stonehouse must be rounding off the years or counting some springs twice.

79. Pai-chang was the eighth-century Buddhist monk who established the basic monastic rules used in Zen temples, which he summarized by "no work, no food." He spent the latter part of his life among the cliffs of Paichangshan, about one hundred kilometers west of Nanchang in Kiangsi province.

80. The cold has driven Stonehouse to consider a fire of branches and logs as opposed to his normal fire of leaves and twigs. §In China, woodcutters sing to accompany the rhythm of their work. Stonehouse may also be alluding to the eleventh-century hermit-poet Chu Tun-ju who titled his collected poems *Woodcutter Songs*. Chu retired to Chiahsing Prefecture, the next prefecture to the east and where Stonehouse served as abbot from 1331 to 1339.

81. Before persons can be ordained, they must spend several years as a novice under the guidance of a senior monk or nun. Once ordained, monks and nuns are allowed to wander at will and stay at any temple where they can find room. §During the Yuan dynasty, monks were exempt from *corvée*, or forced labor on state projects. §In addition to firewood, hermits sell or barter herbs and wild fruits to obtain such necessities as salt, rice or flour, cooking oil, lamp oil, and cloth.

82. The appellation "jade hall" was at first applied to the imperial palace and in particular the women's apartments. However, by Stonehouse's day the term was reserved for the Hanlin Academy, which housed the country's most prestigious scholars. §In the fourth century, Shih Ch'ung held ostentatious banquets at a place called Gold Valley not far from Loyang. It was said that anytime a guest failed to drain his cup, Shih had one of the serving girls beheaded.

77. Mountain of fiddleheads orchard of tea
    one tree of pink among the white
    of all the seasons spring is the best
    this is when a mountain home shines

78. Someone asked what year I arrived
    I sat until the answer came
    the peach tree I planted outside the door
    has flowered in spring twenty times

79. If you hate hard work and like to loaf
    you won't survive in the mountains
    Pai-chang lived in the cliffs long ago
    his life depended completely on a hoe

80. Old and retired I nurse a sick body
    long after sunrise my door is still closed
    shivering I get up to light a pine fire
    over the next rise I hear a woodcutter's song

81. Novices don't stay to stir the fire
    wandering monks prefer free meals
    but hermits at least avoid *corvée* and taxes
    they plant more pines and sell more wood

82. Jade-hall silver-candle nights of song
    gold-valley silk-curtain homes of the rich
    can't compare with a hermit's thatched hut
    where plum blossoms shine in unclouded moonlight

相逢盡説世途難　自向安中討不安

除卻淵明賦歸去　更無一箇肯休官

山廚寂寂斷炊煙　凍鎖泉聲欲雪天

面壁老僧無定力　又思乞食到人間

種了冬瓜便種茄　勞形苦骨做生涯

眾人若要廚堂好　須是園頭常在家

粥去飯來何日了　日生月落幾時休

都來與我無干涉　空起許多閒念頭

屋後青松八九樹　門前紫芋兩三畦

山居道者機關少　家火從頭説向人

此事誰人敢強為　除非知有莫能知

分明月在梅花上　看到梅花早已遲

83. T'ao Ch'ien (Ta'o Yuan-ming) lived in the early fifth century and is revered as one of China's greatest poets. Finding the demands of government service not to his liking, he resigned his post and retired to his old farmstead at the foot of Lushan. He celebrated his decision in his *Ode to Retirement*: "O let me retire / let socializing end and traveling stop / let the world and me say good-bye."

84. The most distinctive sound of a traditional Chinese kitchen is that of the bellows, which is built into the side of the stove with a handle that can be pumped whenever more heat is needed. §The *spring*, as noted elsewhere, is next to Stonehouse's kitchen. §The practice of "wall contemplation" is associated with Bodhidharma, who is said to have spent nine years sitting in a cave near Shaolin Temple before transmitting his understanding of Zen to Hui-k'o. §According to his contemporaries, Stonehouse preferred to survive on water rather than beg from others.

85. Winter melon, *Benincasa cerifera*, and Chinese eggplant, *Solanummel longcana*, both bear their fruit well into the fall — at least they do in South China. Neither requires much effort to grow, and both are easily preserved, the former with heat or vinegar and the latter with ashes.

86. Rice porridge is usually eaten in the morning, while steamed rice is the staple at lunch and dinner in South China. The only difference between the two is the amount of water used in cooking. However, rice porridge is much easier to digest. Hence it is preferred by those who are old or sick.

87. Taro, *Colocasia esculenta* or the "purple potato," is one of the principle starches of hermits south of the Yangtze, where it thrives on the warmer weather and the more abundant summer rainfall.

88. Buddhists often liken the teaching of buddhas and patriarchs to a finger pointing to the moon: Once you've seen the moon, you don't need to look at the finger. Here, Stonehouse replaces the finger with plum blossoms but finds their more delicate light difficult to let go.

83. Everyone I meet says the world's ways are hard
    even where it's peaceful they can't find peace
    except for T'ao Ch'ien's *Ode to Retirement*
    no one else mentions resigning

84. My cookstove is quiet the smoke has stopped
    the spring is frozen the sky says snow
    facing a wall my concentration gone
    again I think about begging in town

85. I plant winter melon then eggplant
    I wear myself out staying alive
    but someone who wants a decent kitchen
    needs his own garden at home

86. Will porridge and rice ever end
    will the sun and moon ever stop
    either way I remain unconcerned
    so many thoughts occur in vain

87. Eight or nine pines behind his hut
    two or three patches of taro in front
    a mountain recluse doesn't have many plans
    all he talks about is his fire

88. It's something no one can force
    besides knowing it's there there's nothing to know
    the moon shines bright above the flowering plum
    but who can look past the blossoms

過去事已過去了　未來不必預思量
只今便道即今句　梅子熟時梔子香

一日打眠三五度　也消不得許多閒
循環數遍琅玕竹　又出青松望遠山

攀緣起倒易消停　卒急難除是愛憎
我笑青山高突兀　青山嫌我瘦崚嶒

真空湛寂惟常在　不覺良由妄所朦
真性何曾離妄有　花開花落自春風

天湖水湛琉璃碧　霞霧山圍錦幛紅
觸目本來成現事　何須叉手問禪翁

89. In South China, plums ripen and gardenias bloom in the fifth lunar month. This is also when "plum rains" arrive and weeding normally begins. Ripe plums also recall the story of Ta-mei, whose name means "Big Plum." When Ta-mei visited Ma-tsu, he asked, "What is a buddha like?" Ma-tsu said, "This mind is the buddha." Ta-mei left and built a hut deep in the mountains. Some years later, when Ma-tsu heard of Ta-mei's whereabouts, he sent a monk to inquire after him. The monk asked Ta-mei, "What truth did you discover that made you move to this mountain?" Ta-mei said, "Ma-tsu taught me 'this mind is the buddha.' That's why I moved here." The monk said, "Ma-tsu's teaching is different now." Ta-mei asked, "How is it different?" The monk said, "Now he teaches 'that which isn't the mind isn't the buddha.'" Ta-mei said, "That old man still isn't done confusing people. He can have his 'that which isn't the mind isn't the buddha.' I'll stick with 'this mind is the buddha.'" When the monk returned and reported this coversation, Ma-tsu said, "The plum is ripe" (*Chuantenglu: 7*).

90. The kind of jade mentioned here is an iridescent variety found in the Kunlun Mountains of myth, where many plants are made of precious stones. §The *pines* were between Stonehouse's hut and the summit, from which the main peaks of the Tienmu Mountains are visible to the south.

91. Love, hate, and delusion make up the Three Poisons that turn the Wheel of Rebirth. Stonehouse's point is similar to that of Hui-neng: "Suffering is enlightenment" (*Sutra of the Sixth Patriarch: 2*).

92. The phrase *true emptiness* is used to characterize the Theravada notion that nirvana is empty of all characteristics. But it is also used by followers of the Mahayana, who hold that true emptiness is also empty of emptiness and thus includes all things. Hence nirvana includes hell. The same holds for our true nature: Life includes death.

93. According to the sutras of the Pure Land sect, the ground of Amida's Western Paradise is made of aquamarine, which ranks first among the gemstones that comprise the Seven Jewels. §Silk brocade remains among the most famous products of the Hangchou area. §*Sky Lake* was the name Stonehouse gave to the spring next to his hut. §*Hsiawu*, or "Redfog," is one of several variants Stonehouse used for Hsiamu, or "Redcurtain," which is the name in use on current maps.

89. What's gone is already gone
    and what hasn't come needs no thought
    now for a right-now line
    plums are ripe and gardenias in bloom

90. Three or four naps every day
    still don't exhaust all my free time
    I circle the jade bamboo once or twice
    and gaze at far mountains from above the green pines

91. The tide of attachment is easy to stop
    but it's hard all at once to end love and hate
    I laugh at the mountain for towering so high
    and the mountain calls me thin as a ridge

92. True emptiness is silent but always present
    masked by delusion for reasons unknown
    our true nature never leaves unreal existence
    flowers bloom and fall when the spring wind blows

93. Sky Lake is a pool of aquamarine
    Redfog Peak is a brocade screen
    regarding what appears before your eyes
    why bow your head and ask an old monk

年老氣衰真箇㑲　晨朝更不見和南
客來無語相抵對　辛苦空勞到草菴

老去一身都是嬾　閒來百念盡成灰
與兄相見略彈指　無奈人情強接陪

山地無塵長不埽　柴門有客扣方開
雪晴斜月侵詹冷　梅影一枝窗上來

茅屋低低三兩間　團團環遶盡青山
竹床不許閒雲宿　日未斜時便掩關

禪兄何事到煙蘿　老我生涯苦不多
嚴下木樨香滿樹　園中菜甲綠成窠

一片無塵新雨地　半邊有蘚古時松
目前景物人皆見　取用誰知各不同

94. Among the dozens of Buddhist and Taoist hermits I've encountered in China, I've never met one who didn't conduct some sort of daily ceremony at dawn and again in the evening involving chanting and meditation. §The *folded hands* refers to the traditional mode of greeting, either with hands pressed together, as if in prayer, or with one hand folded inside the other. No doubt Stonehouse is being facetious here. Despite living as a recluse, he attracted many visitors toward the end of his life, including representatives of the imperial court.

96. When expecting guests, it is customary to sweep the path in front of one's house and to leave the gate ajar. Here, Stonehouse receives some unexpected visitors that require no such preparation.

97. The width of structures in a Buddhist monastery is still measured in terms of one-meter-wide straw mats, even though such mats have long since gone out of fashion in China.

98. The *smoke* is that of temple incense burners, and the *tangles* are those of koans used for instruction and meditation. Stonehouse contrasts these with the fragrance of wild plants and the logic of his garden.

99. Lao-tzu says, "Existence makes something useful / but nonexistence makes it work" (*Taoteching*: 11). Pointing to a huge gnarled oak tree, Chuang-tzu says, "It's because its wood is useless that it has lived to such great age" (*Chuangtzu*: 4.6).

94. Old and exhausted I'm truly lazy
    no more folded hands at dawn
    guests arrive and I face them speechless
    their trek to my hut ends up a waste

95. Now that I'm old I'm utterly lazy
    a hundred idle thoughts all turn to ash
    but when a friend suddenly arrives
    inescapable feelings force me up

96. There isn't any dust to sweep on a mountain
    guests have to knock before I open my gate
    after a snowfall the setting moon slips through the eaves
    the shadow of a plum branch reaches the window

97. My hut is less than three mats wide
    surrounded by mountains on every side
    my bamboo bed couldn't hold a cloud
    I shut the door before sunset

98. Why do my Zen brothers choose smoke and tangles
    this life of mine isn't hard
    gardenias perfume the trees above the cliff
    the shoots in my garden form patches of green

99. A clean patch of ground after it rains
    an ancient pine half-covered with moss
    such scenes appear before us all
    but how we use them isn't the same

萬境萬機俱寢息　一知一見盡消融

閑閑兩耳全無用　坐到晨雞與暮鐘

嚴房終日寂寥寥　世念何曾有一毫

雖著衣裳喫粥飯　恰如死了未曾燒

新縫紙被烘來煖　一覺安眠到五更

聞得下方鐘鼓動　又添一日在浮生

門前枯木似人立　屋後好山如浪堆

老我為人無可說　高高雲路賺兄來

山形凹凸路高低　石占雲頭屋占蹊

地窄栽來蔬菜少　又營小圃在橋西

百年日月閒中度　八萬塵勞靜處消

綠水光中山影轉　紅爐焰上雪花飄

100. The bell announcing the end of the monastic day is normally rung between 9 and 10 PM.

101. Although most Chinese consider burial more filial, as it returns the body intact from whence it came, during the Yuan dynasty cremation became so popular and wood sufficiently scarce that the government was compelled to issue a decree forbidding the practice, except in the case of monks and nuns. Unlike the Indians, who cremate their dead in the open on top of a pyre, the Chinese prefer to place the corpse inside a wooden box and the box inside a brick structure designed especially for cremation.

102. As previously noted, those who couldn't afford cloth used a heavy grade of mulberry paper. §Temple bells are rung just before dawn.

104. The second line is intended as a pun on Stonehouse's name. Stonehouse built his hut adjacent to the trail that led up the southern slope of Hsiamushan. The summit was another two hundred meters beyond his hut. §I'm not sure which bridge Stonehouse had in mind. There are two villages with the word *bridge* in their names at the foot of the next mountain to the west.

100. A myriad worlds and forces have crumbled
    all that I've known and seen has vanished
    my two fine ears are no good at all
    I sit past the cockcrow and the evening bell

101. My home in the cliffs is like a tomb
    barren of even one worldly thought
    although I eat food and wear clothes
    I look like a corpse not yet cremated

102. I heat a new paper quilt by the stove
    and sleep all night until dawn
    when I hear a bell somewhere below
    add one more day to a passing life

103. There's a snag in front like a standing man
    a ridge in back like a gathering wave
    this old monk couldn't be the reason
    it's the road through the clouds that lures friends here

104. Sawtooth mountain up-and-down road
    stone in the clouds house on the trail
    land is too scarce to grow much
    I even farm west of the bridge

105. A hundred years slip by when you're free
    ten thousand cares dissolve when you're still
    a mountain image shimmers on sunlit water
    snowflakes swirl above a glowing stove

西方有路不肯去　地獄無門門要過

金閣銀臺仙子少　鑊湯爐炭罪人多

著意求真真轉遠　擬心斷妄妄猶多

道人一種平懷處　月在青天影在波

要求作佛真箇易　唯斷妄心真箇難

幾度霜天明月夜　坐來覺得五更寒

萬緣脫去心無事　諸有空來性坦然

幾度夜窗虛吐白　月和流水到門前

一事無心萬事休　也無歡喜也無憂

無心莫謂便無事　尚有無心箇念頭

於事無心風過樹　於心無事月行空

風聲月色消磨盡　去卻一重還一重

106. In the Western Paradise of Amida Buddha everything is made of gold, silver, aquamarine, crystal, coral, carnelian, and nacre (the iridescent lining of the giant clam): the entire array known as the seven jewels. §Buddhists recognize a number of hells, some of which are hot but others of which are cold.

107. In Seng-ts'an's long poem on the practice of Zen, the Third Patriarch says, "When the mind is serene / things disappear by themselves" (*Believing in the Mind*: 10).

108. Yung-chia's *Song of Enlightenment* begins: "Does no one else see / the idle follower of the Way / who neither acts nor studies / who neither ends delusions nor seeks the truth?"

109. *Conditions* are what the mind uses to link things together. §Buddhists recognize twenty-five kinds of existence: fourteen in the realm of desire, seven in the realm of form, and four in the realm beyond form. §Stonehouse channeled the spring that flowed from the rocks next to his hut into a pond that he dug in his front yard.

110. According to the second of the Buddha's Four Noble Truths, passion is the cause of sorrow. §Here *no mind* refers to the fourth and highest state of meditation, which is devoid of all thought but which is still subject to karma and thus impermanence.

111. Our false mind is an illusion, and our true mind can't be grasped. Hence Buddhists sometimes call our true mind "no mind." "No mind in work, no work in mind" is a saying attributed to the ninth-century Zen master Te-shan.

106. There's a road to the West that nobody takes
     people want out but Hell has no gate
     jeweled pavilions and terraces are empty
     cauldrons and ovens are full

107. Look for the real and it becomes more distant
     try to end delusions and they just increase
     followers of the Way have a place that stays serene
     when the moon is in the sky its reflection is in the waves

108. Trying to become a buddha is easy
     but ending delusions is hard
     how many frosty moonlit nights
     have I sat and felt the cold before dawn

109. Stripped of conditions my mind is blank
     emptied of existence my nature is bare
     often at night my windows turn white
     the moon and the stream visit my door

110. Work with no mind and all work stops
     no more passion or sorrow
     but don't think no mind means you're done
     the thought of no-mind still remains

111. No mind in my work the wind through trees
     no work in my mind the moon through space
     windsound and moonlight wear away
     one layer then another

新年頭了舊年尾　明日四兮今日三

道業未誠空白首　大千無處著羞慚

白髮催人瘦入肩　住來茅屋已多年

禪無腰帶褲無口　一領褊衫沒半邊

一軸楞伽看未周　夕陽斜影水東流

雲歸自就茅簷宿　一日光陰又早休

茅簷雨過日頭紅　瞬息陰晴便不同

況是死生呼吸事　黃昏難保聽朝鐘

明明見了非他見　了了常知無別知

記得去秋煙雨裡　猿來偷去一雙梨

半窗松影半窗月　一箇蒲團一箇僧

盤膝坐來中夜後　飛蛾撲滅佛前燈

112. Line 2 refers to the third and fourth days of the year, when the new moon first becomes visible. *Fourth* and *third* also recall a story that appears in the second chapters of *Chuangtzu* and *Liehtzu*. It seems that a group of monkeys were dissatisfied with their diet of three acorns in the morning and four in the evening. When the trainer agreed to change this to four in the morning and three in the evening, the monkeys ceased their objections. §The Chinese calculate their ages not from their birthdays, but from New Year's Day. Hence, the holiday often reminds people of the ephemeral nature of life.

113. In the last line, Stonehouse is refering to the *kasaya,* which is worn like a toga over one shoulder and thus covers only half as much of the upper body as a regular robe. Although it is standard attire in India and Southeast Asia, it is usually reserved for begging and temple ceremonies in China.

114. Hermits all have their favorite text that they read or chant every day. Among Buddhists, it's now the *Lotus* and *Titsang* sutras. Fifteen hundred years ago, the *Lankavatara* was the only sermon of the Buddha that Bodhidharma thought suitable for students of Zen. It is, however, not that easy to read and would be hard to finish in the course of a day. In the introduction to his English translation, D.T. Suzuki notes that its profundities "are presented in a most unsystematic manner." §The subduction of the Indian Plate beneath the Asian Plate has raised the elevation of Tibet far above that of China. As a result – east of the area of impact, and this includes most of Tibet and all of China – all rivers flow east.

116. The last line calls to mind a story about the Han-dynasty Taoist Tung-fang Suo, who stole three magic peaches that conferred immortality during a visit to the legendary court of the Queen Mother of the West.

112. The new year comes the old year goes
the fourth tomorrow the third today
still unenlightened I have aged in vain
where in the world can I express my shame

113. My hair has turned white my body is gaunt
I've lived in a hut more years than I can count
my shorts have no drawstring my pants have no legs
and half of my robe is missing

114. Before I can finish the *Lankavatara*
sunset shadows flow east with the rivers
clouds return and I retire to my hut
another day's passage ends early again

115. Rain soaks my hut then the sun shines
weather can change in the blink of an eye
but not as fast as the breath of existence
at dusk you can't hear the morning bell

116. No one else sees what I see clearly
no one else knows what I know well
I recall one misty day last fall
a gibbon came by and stole two pears

117. Half the window pine shadow the other half moon
a single cushion a single monk
sitting cross-legged after midnight
when a moth puts out the altar lamp

長年心裡渾無事　每日菴中樂有餘
飯罷濃煎茶喫了　池邊坐石數遊魚
飯炊五合陳黃米　羹煮數莖青薺苗
淡薄自然滋味好　何須更要著薑椒
移家深入亂峰西　煙樹重重隔遠溪
年老心閒貪睡穩　猒聞鐘響與雞啼
山風吹破故窗紙　片片雪花飛入來
添盡布裘渾不煖　拾枯深撥地爐灰
半窗斜日冷生光　破衲蒙頭坐竹床
枯葉滿爐燒焰火　不知屋上有寒霜
幾樹山花紅灼灼　一池春水綠漪漪
衲僧若具超宗眼　不待無情為發機

118. The Chinese prefer their tea strong and unadulterated. Its ability to allay hunger and thirst and to clear the senses without overstimulating them has made it the drink of choice among those who meditate.

119. *Old rice* refers to rice left over from the last harvest, and *a handful* suggests Stonehouse was rationing it out until the new harvest was in.

120. Stonehouse's hut on Hsiamushan was ten kilometers west of the East Fork of the Sha River.

121. A robe with a lining of cotton wadding is still the normal winter attire for monks and nuns. Over time, the wadding tends to shift to the bottom and requires periodic replacement or refurbishing.

122. Stonehouse is being facetious. Burning leaves in his tea stove as the winter night approaches suggests he has no wood.

123. *A few trees in bloom* refers to peach trees.

118. Not one care in mind all year
     I find enough joy every day in my hut
     and after a meal and a pot of strong tea
     I sit on a rock by a pond and count fish

119. I steam a handful of old rice for dinner
     I boil a few sprouts for a soup
     bland but natural flavors are fine
     who needs to add ginger or spice

120. I moved west deep into the mountains
     put trees and mist between me and the river
     old and untroubled I like to sleep late
     I hate to hear roosters or bells

121. Mountain wind ripped out my old paper windows
     snowflakes swirl inside
     my once padded robe isn't padded anymore
     with a stick I probe the ashes

122. The setting sun's cold light half fills my window
     I sit here in bed beneath a ragged robe
     the stove ablaze with dry leaves
     who would guess there's frost overhead

123. A few trees in bloom radiant red
     a pond in spring rippling green
     a monk with eyes that see beyond Zen
     doesn't have to be dead to use them

雲未歸時便掩扃　柴床眠穩思冥冥

山家不養雞和犬　日到茅簷夢未醒

粥去飯來茶喫了　開窗獨坐看青山

細推百億闇浮界　白日無人似我閒

黑霧濃雲撥不開　忽然去了忽然來

任他伎倆自磨滅　紅日依前照石臺

一天紅日曉東南　自拔青苗插瘦田

布裰半沾泥水溼　歸來脫曬竹房前

喫桃吐核核成樹　樹大花開又結桃

春去秋來知幾度　爭教我不白頭毛

茅屋方方一丈慳　四簷松竹四圍山

老僧自住尚狹窄　那許雲來借半閒

125. Watered-down rice is eaten at breakfast and steamed rice at other meals. In the case of monks and nuns who adhere to the letter of the precepts, the noon meal is their last meal of the day. Tea is drunk to aid digestion and also to dispel fatigue. §*Jambu* is the short form of the Sanskrit *Jambudvipa*. Ancient Buddhist geography divided the world into four continents, with Jambudvipa comprising all of Asia.

126. "To push away the clouds in order to the see the sun" is an old saying the Chinese use when someone is trying to remove insurmountable obstructions from their path. §Stonehouse is referring to the outcrop of flat-topped boulders at the summit not far from his hut.

127. As the days of fall and winter become shorter and darker, the place where the sun rises moves progressively southward, and clouds take the place of clear skies. The sun's reappearance in a cloudless sky on the southeastern horizon marks the advent of spring. §The *sprouts* could be those of young rice plants, but wheat would be more appropriate on marginal ground.

128. The peach is native to China and appears in the archaeological record of the Hangchou area as early as five thousand years ago. In poem 78, Stonehouse dates his arrival on Hsiamushan by the peach tree he planted twenty years earlier outside his door.

129. The "ten-foot chamber" originally referred to an abbot's room and was later extended to include the adjacent room in which he met privately with visitors and students.

124. I shut my door before clouds return
     and sleep on a cot my thoughts obscure
     hermits don't raise dogs or chickens
     sun hits the roof and I still dream

125. After porridge after rice after drinking tea
     I sit by a window and gaze at the mountains
     during the day throughout Jambu
     is anyone more idle than me

126. Dense fog and clouds you can't push apart
     suddenly appear and suddenly depart
     clever people can wear themselves out
     sun lights the rocks the same as before

127. When the red sun lights the southeast sky
     I transplant sprouts into barren fields
     my robe of patches soaked and muddy
     I take off and dry in front of my hut

128. I eat a peach spit out the pit the pit becomes a tree
     the tree grows and flowers and bears another peach
     spring ends and fall begins how many times
     how can I keep my hair from turning white

129. My hut isn't quite ten feet on a side
     surrounded by pines bamboo and mountains
     an old monk hardly has room for himself
     much less for a visiting cloud

臨機切莫避刀鎗　拌死和他戰一場

打得趙州關子破　大千無處不皈降

有限光陰一百年　幾人得到百年全

縱饒百歲終歸死　只是相分後與前

一大藏經閒故紙　一千七百葛藤窠

誰能去討他分曉　起箇念頭猶是多

溪邊黃葉水去住　嶺上白雲風往來

爭似老僧常不動　長年無事坐嚴臺

霞霧山高路又遙　菴居從葡蔲三條

郤嫌住處太危險　落賺多人登陟勞

老覺形枯氣力衰　客來勉強出支陪

自憐不解藏綜跡　松食荷衣憶大梅

130. One day when Chao-chou was working alone in the monastery kitchen, he shut the door and let the room fill with smoke. Then he cried, "Fire!" When the other monks came running, he said, "Say the word, and I'll open the door!" But none of the monks could think of anything to say. When Abbot Nan-ch'uan arrived, he handed him a lock through a window, and Chao-chou finally opened the door (*Chuantenglu*: 10). Chao-chou and his teacher Nan-ch'uan were among the most reknowned Zen masters of the ninth century.

132. Among the 1440 works listed in the Buddhist Canon in Stonehouse's day was a series of five Sung-dynasty works (the *Chuantenglu* and its companion volumes) that included some seventeen hundred koans. §Vines were used in the production of paper.

134. Hsiawushan, or "Redfog," is one of several names Stonehouse uses for Hsiamushan, or "Redcurtain." Its summit is four hundred meters higher than the surrounding countryside, which is only ten meters above sea level.

135. Pine nuts have kept many recluses from starving and have provided a rare treat for others. Lotus-leaf attire is not entirely imaginary, though it is usually associated with immortals: "A lotus-leaf robe and a belt of vines / suddenly he appears and suddenly departs" (*Nine Songs: Lesser Lord of Long Life*). §Big Plum, or Ta-mei, was a disciple of Ma-tsu. Following his enlightenment, he moved so far into the mountains people thought he had died. Then one day, a monk who had lost his way stumbled into a clearing and discovered him sitting in front of a hut. Not long afterward, Ta-mei had more disciples than he knew what to do with (*Chuantenglu*: 7).

130. Don't run from his knife when he strikes
    make it a fight to the death
    break down Chao-chou's door
    and the universe will fall at your feet

131. Our time is confined to one hundred years
    but which of us gets them all
    hundred-year-olds die too
    it's only a matter of sooner or later

132. The Canon is full of old paper
    seventeen-hundred tangled vines
    who can see through the mess
    one thought is still too many

133. Leaves on the shore are swept downstream
    clouds on the ridge are blown back and forth
    neither can match an old monk who stays still
    sitting in the cliffs doing nothing all year

134. Redfog is high and the trail is long
    my hut is made of bamboo and vines
    people prefer to stay where it's safe
    but many are fooled into making the climb

135. Old and withered my strength is gone
    but visitors force me up
    I regret not learning to hide my tracks
    but pine nuts and lotus clothes recall Big Plum

道人屋冷四簷竹　長者門高買尺牆
屋冷道人心愈靜　門高長者日多忙

盡道凡心非佛性　我言佛性即凡心
工夫只怕無人做　鐵杵磨教作線鍼

南北東西去復還　陸行車馬水行船
利名門路如天遠　走殺世間人萬千

居山那得有工夫　種了冬瓜便種瓠
設使一毫功不及　許多田地盡荒蕪

離眾多年無坐具　入山長久沒袈裟
單單有箇鐵鐺子　留待人來煮瀑花

布衣破綻種青麻　糧食無時刈早禾
辛苦做來牽補過　復身免得報檀那

136. Repressed by the Confucian values of earlier governments, merchants were given unprecedented freedom and power during the Yuan dynasty, when the Mongols made extensive use of their services in collecting taxes and financing state projects.

137. Buddhists agree that we all possess the potential to become buddhas but differ as to how the realization of buddhahood takes place. While most sects say it is realized in stages and through moral discipline and meditation, the Zen sect prefers the radical approach of Bodhidharma: "If you can find your buddha nature apart from your mortal nature, where is it? Beyond this nature, there is no buddha" (*The Zen Teaching of Bodhidharma:* 16–17). Thus, when pointing to the buddha, Zen masters point to the everyday-mind.

138. Long before the Grand Canal was completed, an extensive system of small canals and natural waterways enabled people to do much of their long-distance traveling by boat. The system of roads was even more extensive and was maintained by the government to assure its continued control over the territory it administered.

139. For *winter melon,* see my note to poem 85. Gourds, or *Lagenaria vulgaris,* are grown for their use as containers and utensils as well as for food.

140. This poem refers to a straw-filled meditation cushion and a patched begging robe. §This particular iron pot had three feet and was small enough to fit on the portable brazier normally used for heating tea water. Its primary use, however, was for heating wine, here replaced by freshly drawn water from Stonehouse's spring. The precepts under which monks and nuns live forbid the drinking of alcoholic beverages.

141. The stalk of the blue hemp plant is used for making string and rope. §According to his contemporaries, Stonehouse refused to beg for alms.

136. A hermit's hut is empty encircled by bamboo
a merchant's gate is high with hundred-foot-long walls
in his empty hut a hermit finds peace
behind his high gate a merchant finds none

137. Others say everyday-mind isn't our buddha nature
I say our buddha nature is simply everyday-mind
afraid that no one will do any work
they tell us to grind iron rods into needles

138. East and west and north and south and back again
by cart and horse and boat on land and water
the gate to fame and fortune is more remote than Heaven
yet mortals by the million perish on the road

139. What sort of practice takes place in the mountains
planting winter melons then planting gourds
and if your effort falls a bit short
most of your fields end up beneath weeds

140. Too long out of temples I don't have a cushion
too long in the mountains I don't have a robe
all I have is an iron pot
to entertain guests with fresh boiled water

141. When seams come apart I plant blue hemp
when food runs out I harvest green rice
I pull myself through with effort
and when things are better it's not thanks to alms

飯香麥炒和松粉　菜好藤花雜筍鞭
我已盡形無別念　任他作佛與生天

山居活計钁頭邊　衣食須營豈自然
種稻下田泥沒膝　賣柴出市擔磨肩

钁頭添鐵屋頭懸　健即鋤雲倦即眠
紅日正中黃獨熟　甘香不在火爐邊

團團一箇尖頭屋　外面誰知裡面寬
世界大千都著了　尚餘閒地放蒲團

草菴盤結長松下　面面軒窗盡豁開
目對青山終日坐　更無一事上心來

深秋時節雨霏霏　蘚葉層層印虎蹄
一夜西風吹不住　曉來黃葉與階齊

142. Pine meal is made by grinding sun-dried or roasted pine nuts. §I'm not sure what kind of vine Stonehouse gathered his buds from, perhaps a relative of the morning glory. At a monastery in Taiwan where I lived for several years, we dined throughout the summer on tiger lily buds, picked a day or two before they were due to open and stir-fried in oil.

143. Hermits usually need to sell something in order to buy the few things they can't produce themselves. If it isn't firewood, it's usually herbs or other mountain products. One Buddhist nun I met in the Chungnan Mountains got by on the harvest from four walnut trees.

144. The Chinese yam, unlike its cousins in the sweet potato family, is not especially thick and needs all the help it can get. Elsewhere, Stonehouse says he turned to it when there was nothing else to eat.

145. In poem 15, Stonehouse says his hut has no gables. Apparently, this is why. §Buddhists say the universe contains a billion worlds, and yet all billion were able to fit inside Vimilakirti's hut, in the sutra of the same name, with room to spare for Manjushri and a host of other bodhisattvas and celestial beings. §*Zazen* means to "do zen," hence to meditate. I've used the Japanese pronunciation, which comes closer to the original T'ang-dynasty pronunciation than does the modern Mandarin.

147. The South China tiger, which is now rarely seen, is much smaller than its Bengal or Siberian cousins. The Chinese associate the tiger with the wind, which rises when it roars. §For more on the steps in front of his hut, see verse 157.

142. A steaming pot of parched wheat and pine meal
     a fragrant dish of bamboo shoots and vine buds
     when I'm exhausted I think of nothing else
     let others become gods or buddhas

143. Life in the mountains depends on a hoe
     food and clothes don't come by themselves
     I'm knee-deep in mud planting rice in the fields
     or my shoulders are raw from hauling wood to town

144. I fix my hoe and let my hut lean
     I farm the clouds and sleep when I'm done
     yams turn ripe from overhead sun
     their flavor doesn't come from the stove

145. Standing outside my pointed-roof hut
     how much space do you think is inside
     all the worlds of the universe are there
     with room to spare for a zazen cushion

146. Beneath tall pines I built a hut
     windows open on all four sides
     I sit all day facing mountains
     nothing else comes to mind

147. Late autumn rain is a rain of mist
     tiger tracks appear in the moss
     the west wind doesn't stop all night
     by dawn yellow leaves are up to the steps

團團紅日上青山　竹屋柴門尚閉關
白髮老僧眠未起　勞生磨蟻正循環

山舍清幽絕點塵　心閒與世自相分
不知何處碧桃放　幽鳥銜來遶竹門

老來無事可千懷　竹榻高眠日枕斜
夢裡不知誰是我　覺來新月到梅花

禪餘高誦寒山偈　飯後濃煎谷雨茶
尚有閒情無著處　攜籃過嶺採藤花

僧因產業致差科　官府勾追恥辱多
我有山田三畝半　盡情回付與檀那

楮閣安爐種炭團　床鋪新薦被新棉
一冬煖活如何說　夢想不思兜率天

148. The image of ants marching around the inside of a stone mortar was made famous as a simile for the movement of astronomical bodies in the *Chinshu*. They reminded Stonehouse of his fellow humans working their various treadmills.

149. As in poem 2, there is so little going on in Stonehouse's dwelling that birds living in a more remote part of the forest think his hut deserted and bring wild peach twigs to build nests.

150. Obviously, a short and a light sleep. The faint glow of the new moon is briefly visible at sunset. However faint and brief, Stonehouse tells us in poem 59 that he has a special sensitivity for the plum.

151. Cold Mountain, or Han-shan, was a Buddhist poet who lived in the latter half of the eighth century in the Tientai Mountains near the Chekiang coast. His three-hundred-odd poems have been translated into English by several people, including myself. §A *gatha* is a four-line poem with three, five, or seven syllables to the line. Its original function was to summarize preceding materials in a Buddhist sutra, but it was adapted by Chinese Buddhists as a stand-alone poem. §For chanting, Cold Mountain's poem 302 would be a good choice: "The mountain I live on / nobody knows / here in the clouds / it's always deserted." §Again, *zazen* means "to meditate." §Most varieties of tea benefit from frequent mist, but not heavy rain. §Vine buds, which also appear in poem 142, are a mountain delicacy.

152. During various periods in Chinese history, monks were issued a small piece of land from which they supported themselves by farming or by renting it to others. During the Yuan dynasty, a special office was set up to handle monk affairs, and it was to this office that monks were required to apply. Ironically, Stonehouse was appointed head of this office for the entire province in 1331 when he became abbot of Fuyuan Temple. However, the office was eliminated three years later.

153. Tushita Heaven is the highest of the Buddhist heavens in the realm of desire where all needs are satisfied and where bodhisattvas are reborn before their final rebirth.

148. When the sun comes over the mountain
     the door of my hut stays closed
     ants begin their rounds in the mortar
     the white-haired monk sleeps on

149. My hut is secluded beyond the dust
     my empty mind is out of touch with the times
     somewhere a peach tree is blooming
     unfamiliar birds deck my door with twigs

150. Now that I'm old nothing disturbs me
     I'm asleep on my cot before the sun sets
     dreaming unaware who I am
     until the new moon lights the plum blossoms

151. I chant a Cold Mountain gatha after zazen
     after dinner I sip valley-mist tea
     and when something lingers I can't express
     I cross the ridge to gather a basketful of vine buds

152. For property monks apply at an office
     but government snares and insults abound
     I own a half acre of mountain land
     they can have back as alms when I die

153. I put mulberry logs in the stove to make charcoal
     new cotton in my quilt a new mat on the bed
     what can I say about staying warm all winter
     I don't dream about Tushita Heaven

去年家火缺支持　家火今年用不虧
田裡多收三斗穀　門前添得一方池

白雲影裡尖頭屋　黃葉堆頭折腳鐺
漏笊籬撩無米飯　破砂盆擣爛生薑

修行豈得不成佛　水滴年深石也穿
不是頑皮鑽不破　惟人只欠自心堅

獨坐窮心寂杳冥　箇中無法可當情
西風吹盡擁門葉　留得空階與月明

玉蝶梅花香滿樹　水池洗菜綠浮科
錦衣公子如知得　定是移家入薜蘿

逆順未嘗忘此道　窮通一味信前緣
是他了達虛空性　不動纖毫本自然

寒披荷葉衣裳煖　飢食松花餅餌香
不比世人營口體　奔南走北一生忙

154. Stonehouse's pond also appears in poem 24.

155. A bowl with ridges on the inside surface is used for mashing and extracting juice from spices, herbs, and roots.

156. In *Choosing a Friend,* the T'ang poet Meng Chiao wrote, "If you want to be like the immortals / your mind must be as hard as iron."

158. The Hangchou area is still famous for its silk brocade.

159. Buddhists define reality as that which is independent of all else, including the dimensions of space and time and thus change.

160. The use of lotus leaves for clothing is also mentioned in poem 135. However, by the time the weather turns cold in fall, they are too dry and brittle to be of any use as clothing. Perhaps the cold weather here is that of early summer, when lotus leaves first appear and not long after which pine pollen is gathered.

154. Last year my food supply failed me
     this year I can't use it all
     I've gathered three bushels of grain too many
     and filled what once was a pond

155. A pointed-roof hut in the shade of the clouds
     a broken-legged pot on a pile of dry leaves
     a strainer with holes that doesn't strain rice
     and to mash fresh ginger a busted ridge-bowl

156. You're bound to become a buddha if you practice
     if water drips long enough even rocks wear through
     it's not true thick skulls can't be pierced
     a person just needs a hard enough mind

157. I meditate alone·in the quiet and dark
     where nothing comes to mind
     I sweep the steps when the west wind is done
     I make a path for the moonlight

158. Jade-winged plum blossoms perfume-filled trees
     pond-washed vegetables floating stems of green
     if the silk-clad young lords knew about this
     they would move into the wild for sure

159. Good and bad fortune never lose their way
     success and failure both depend on karma
     realize both are empty at heart
     and what doesn't change is real

160. A lotus leaf robe keeps me warm when I'm cold
     pine pollen cakes smell good when I'm hungry
     I'm not like those who chase food and clothes
     running north and south busy all their lives

新縫紙被煖烘烘　黃葉堆頭火正紅
閒夢不知誰喚醒　五更聽得下方鐘

旋斫青柴逐把挑　擔頭防脫莫過腰
今朝未保來朝日　且了寒爐一夜燒

今年難測是寒喧　一日陰晴變幾番
簷下紙窗乾又溼　門前石逕溼還乾

峰頂團團盡是松　茅蘆著在樹陰中
天風一陣來何處　吹起波濤響半空

黃羅直裰紫伽梨　出入侯門得意時
爭似道人忘寵辱　松鍼柳線補荷衣

春歸暑退一秋涼　日晷如梭夜漸長
盡把工夫閒雜話　幾曾回首暫思量

我見時人日夜忙　廣營屋宅置田莊
到頭一事將不去　獨有骷髏葬北邙

161. This appears to be a second version of poem 102.

162. A late spring cold wave finds Stonehouse short of wood and reduced to cutting new growth. The most common means of carrying things in China is still a length of bamboo broad enough not to cut into the shoulder and notched at either end to hold ropes to which loads can be attached.

163. The Tienmu Mountains receive a meter of rain annually, with most of it falling between April and September.

164. The *waves* were probably those of Lake Taihu, China's fourth-largest body of fresh water, visible from the summit behind Stonehouse's hut. Buddhists often use waves as a metaphor for reality, which we erroneously separate into distinct forms only to watch them rejoin the water from which they arose.

165. Monks chosen by the emperor to head the office in charge of monastic affairs were allowed to wear the imperial colors of purple and yellow and were given special access to imperial quarters.

167. Peimang was the name of a long, low ridge of hills between the ancient capital of Loyang and the Yellow River. It was used as a cemetery by the wealthy and powerful as early as the Chou dynasty more than three thousand years ago. A popular description of the perfect life goes: "To be born in Hangchou / to be buried on Peimang."

161. I warm my new paper quilt by the stove
     where a pile of dry leaves glows red
     I wonder who will wake me from my dream
     just before dawn I hear a bell below

162. I chop green wood and lift a load
     I try to keep it above my waist
     what exists today won't exist tomorrow
     I stoke a cold stove and burn it all night

163. It's hard to say if the year is hot or cold
     sunlight and shade change throughout the day
     my hut's paper windows are dry then wet
     the stone steps in front are wet then dry

164. Around the summit I only see pines
     and a thatched hut set in their shade
     where does that gust of wind come from
     stirring up waves echoing through space

165. Sewing purple robes with fine yellow silk
     they reach the heights through back doors
     unlike a hermit beyond praise and blame
     mending lotus clothes with willow floss and a pine needle

166. Spring is gone summer is gone autumn was cool
     the days are like a shuttle the nights are getting long
     people whine and chatter even while they work
     how often do they stop and think

167. The people I meet are invariably busy
     enlarging their houses and fields
     until the day it all comes apart
     and all they possess are bones on Peimang

箇箇聞知有死生　聞知何不早修行

堂堂大道無人到　開眼明明入火阬

三塗一報五千劫　出得頭來是幾時

盡説修行不在遲　今年還有後年期

山名霞幕泉天湖　卜居記得壬子初

山頭有塊臺盤石　宛如出水青芙藥

更有天湖一泉水　先天至今何曾枯

就泉結屋擬終老　田地一點紅塵無

外面規模似狹窄　中間取用能寬舒

碧紗如煙隔金像　彫盤沉水凌天衢

蒲團禪椅列左右　香鐘雲板鳴朝哺

瓷甖土種吉祥草　石盆水養龍湫蒲

飯香粥滑山田米　瓜甜菜嫩家園蔬

得失是非都放卻　經行坐臥無相拘

有時把柄白塵拂　有時持串烏木珠

有時歡喜身舞蹈　有時默坐觜盧都

168. The *fiery pit* includes the three lower rebirths: the various hells, the realm of hungry ghosts, and the world of beasts.

169. *Below* refers to the three lower rebirths mentioned in the previous note. Buddhists say it is rare to be born a human and rarer still to hear the Dharma.

170. Spirit grass, or *Reineckia carnea,* is a member of the lily family. Its ability to flourish in vases indoors has made it a common sight in shrine halls. §For the deer-tail whisk see my note to poem 56. §Beads are used as a rhythmic or mnenomic device in chanting.

168. Everyone knows about death and rebirth
     they know but they don't change
     instead of taking the wide-open Way
     they enter the fiery pit clear-eyed

169. People all say there's time to change
     there's always another year
     but headed for five-thousand kalpas below
     they won't get another chance soon

170. To Redcurtain Mountain and Sky Lake Spring
     I moved in the spring of 1312
     there's a flattopped rock near the summit
     like a blue lotus rising from a pool
     and a spring I call Sky Lake
     flowing since the world began
     beside the spring I built a hut for my old age
     my fields don't have a speck of worldly dust
     my home looks cramped from outside
     but inside there's room for all my things
     a gilt statue veiled by emerald silk
     a carved bowl filled with water to the sky
     a straw mat on the left a bookstand on the right
     incense gong and bell to mark the dusk and dawn
     I planted spirit grass in a porcelain pot
     and dragontail rushes in a rocky pool
     there's mountain-grown rice to steam or boil
     vegetables and melons from my garden
     but no right or wrong no profit or loss
     walking sitting sleeping no ties
     sometimes I pick up my white deer whisk
     sometimes I finger black wooden beads
     sometimes I feel like dancing
     sometimes I sit like a dunce

懶舉西來祖意説　甚東魯詩書
自亦不知是凡是聖　他豈能識是牛是驢
客來未暇陪説話　拾枯先去燒茶爐
紅香旖旎春花開敷　清陰繁茂夏木翳如
嚴桂風前喚回山谷　梅花雪裡清殺林逋
人間無此真樂　山中有甚凶虞
也不樂他輕與高蓋　也不樂他率眾匡徒
也不樂他西方極樂　也不樂他天上淨居
心下常無不足　目前觸事有餘
夜籟合樂　曉天昇鳥　戲魚翻躍
好鳥相呼　路通玄以幽遠境
超世而清虛　騷人盡思吟不成句
丹青極巧畫不成圖　獨有淵明可起矛解道
吾亦愛吾盧　山中居沒閒時
無人會惟自知　逸山驅竹筧寒水
擊石取火延朝炊　香粳旋舂柴旋斫
砂鍋未滾涎先垂　開畬未及種紫芋
鉏地更要栽黃耆　白日不得手腳住

170. (contintued) §Bodhidharma brought Zen to China in the late fifth century, and by the seventh century Zen masters were using his arrival as the subject of one of their most popular koans. §*The Book of Odes* and the *Spring and Autumn Annals* are among the works all scholars and would-be officials were expected to know by heart. Both are attributed to Confucius, who spent most of his life in his native state of Lu. §*Shan-ku* was the pen name of the Sung-dynasty poet Huang T'ing-chien, who memorialized cassia flowers in his poems. §Lin Pu, or Lin Ho-ching, also lived in the early Sung as a recluse just outside the walls of Hangchou. Lin was one of China's most famous lovers of plum blossoms, which he immortalized in his poetry. §The *crow* refers to the sun, for which see poem 39. §T'ao Yuan-ming, or T'ao Ch'ien, was China's most famous country poet, and he extoled the virtues of the retired life in his verse.

too lazy to explain why Bodhidharma came east
not to mention the histories or odes of Lu
I don't know if I'm a fool or a sage
or if others are oxen or donkeys
when guests arrive there's no time to chat
I gather dry wood and light the tea stove
fragrant pink flowers appear in spring
the cool shade of summer is gone too soon
cassias on the wind call Shan-ku to mind
plum blossoms in the snow purified Lin Pu
true joys like these aren't found in town
evil doesn't thrive in the mountains
I don't want a fancy carriage
I don't want a flock of disciples
I don't want a Buddhist paradise
I don't want a Taoist heaven
my mind never fails to find enough
my eyes have plenty to see
the sounds of the night are music
at dawn the crow flies
fish swim and jump in play
birds call and sing for joy
on the road to the dark and distant
in the realm of transcendence and void
inspired poets are speechless
master artists can't paint
only Yuan-ming would know what I mean
I happen to love my hut too
in the mountains I'm never idle
but I've learned what others don't know
how to channel a spring across a slope
how to start the morning fire with rocks
how to hull mountain rice and chop wood
before the pot boils I drool
on half-cleared land I plant taro
and where I've hoed deep I plant beans
I don't stop moving all day
long before sunset I'm done

黃昏未到神思疲　歸來洗足上床睡
困重不知山月移　隔林幽鳥忽喚醒
一團紅日懸松枝　今日明日也如是
來年後年還如斯　春草離離夏木葳
秋雲片片冬雪霏　虛空落地須彌碎
三世如來脫垢衣

晴明無事登霞峰　伸眉望極開心胸
大湖萬頃白瀲灩　洞庭兩點青濛茸
初疑仙子始綰角　碧紗帽子參差籠
又疑天女來獻花　玉盤捧出雙芙蓉
明知此境俱幻妄　對此悠然心未終
徘徊不忍便歸去　夕陽又轉山頭松

乾鵲傍簷鳴鵲咤　烏鴉遶屋聲鴉啞
西菴道者來送果　東鄰稚子去偷瓜
吉凶占相既有驗　罪福果報應無差
道人若有此見解　青銅鏡面生痕瑕
懶融一見四祖後　白鳥更不來御花

170. (continued) §Mount Sumeru is at the center of the universe and is as many miles high as there are grains of sand in the Ganges. §The *dirt* is not only the dust of the senses but includes emptiness as well.

171. Stonehouse is standing above his hut at the summit of Hsiamushan and looking northeast across Lake Taihu. Covering more than twenty-five hundred square kilometers, Taihu is China's fourth-largest fresh water lake. About fifty kilometers from Hsiamushan on the other side of the lake are an island and adjacent peninsula known as West Tungting and East Tungting. Both are about one hundred square kilometers in area and rise to a height of three hundred meters. §The last three lines suggest the scene may have also reminded Stonehouse of his hometown of Changshu, another seventy kilometers beyond the twin "islands."

172. The Chinese consider magpies good luck and crows bad luck. §Bronze mirrors were polished on one side and inscribed with designs and phrases on the reverse side. Some mirrors were said to reveal their reverse-side inscriptions to the viewer and were prized by fortune tellers. §Tao-hsin was the Fourth Patriarch of Zen, and Fa-yung was called "lazy" because he never stood up or bowed to greet visitors. One day from his hermitage near Nanking, Tao-hsin saw birds flocking around a distant mountain. When he went to investigate, he found not only birds but the footprints of wolves and tigers around a monk who was sitting on the ground meditating. The monk was Fa-yung. When Tao-hsin feigned fright, Fa-yung said, "There is still this in you?" Tao-hsin responded by drawing the character for "buddha" on the ground in front of Fa-yung. When Fa-yung expressed embarassment, Tao-hsin said, "There is still this in you?" Fa-yung became a disciple of Tao-hsin and a great Zen master in his own right. But after this meeting, the birds and wild animals no longer visited him (*Chuantenglu*: 4).

back home I wash off my feet and sleep
too tired to notice the mountain moon's passage
birds wake me up from a distant grove
the red sun's disc shines through the pines
today and tomorrow don't differ
the years are all the same
in spring plants sprout
in summer woods flourish
in autumn clouds gather
in winter snow flies
take emptiness off and Sumeru shatters
buddhas don't wear dirty clothes

171. A clear sky and nothing planned I climbed Hsia Peak
gazing into the distance I opened my heart
Taihu's expanse was sparkling white
Tungting's two dots were green velvet buds
at first I imagined a young immortal's top-knots
his silk cap with uneven sides
then I saw a deva bringing flowers
two lotuses rising from a plate of jade
I knew such scenes were illusions
but facing the horizon my mind wouldn't stop
until I couldn't bear it and walked back down
I turned again at sunset toward the summit pines

172. Magpies talk magpie outside my hut
crows talk crow circling my roof
a monk to the west brings me fruit
a boy to the east steals my melons
once you know how to tell fortunes
good and bad shouldn't differ
a monk who attains such understanding
can read the back of a mirror
after Lazy Yung met Tao-hsin
birds stopped bringing him flowers

林木長新葉　遠屋清陰多
深草沒塵跡　隔山聽樵歌
自耕復自種　側笠披青簑
好雨及時來　活我新栽禾
遊目周宇宙　物物皆消磨
既善解空理　不樂還如何

寒山曾有言　吾心似秋月
我亦曾有言　吾心勝秋月
秋月非不明　有圓復有缺
安得如我心　圓明常皎潔
有問心如何　教我如何說

月來照我門　風來吹我襟
勸君石上坐　聽我山中吟
玄鬢化為雪　朝光成夕陰
萬事草頭露　豈得長如今

飯飽拂石睡　睡足起閒行
囂囂孟夏景　新樹鳴黃鶯
俯仰瓻時物　散誕暢吟情
只此是真樂　何必求虛名

173. Most farmers south of the Yangtze wear a hat with a framework of bamboo strips and an outer covering of bamboo leaves. And until recently, the standard raincoat in South China consisted of layers of coir cloth, which is made from the bark of trees in the coconut family. §Stonehouse is refering to the "plum rains," which normally arrive in early June with the plums and the summer monsoon. §The first of the Buddha's Four Noble Truths is: "All is sorrow," which itself is based on the realization that all things are impermanent and hence empty.

174. The fifth poem among Cold Mountain's three-hundred-plus poems is a favorite among Buddhists: "My mind is like the autumn moon / clear and bright in a pool of jade / nothing can compare / what more can I say."

175. Loosening the lapels of one's robe and exposing one's chest is a metaphor for revealing one's innermost thoughts and feelings. §The penultimate line recalls an ancient folksong known as "Dew on the Leek": "Dew on the leek / how quickly it dries / it dries and tomorrow falls once again / when a man dies does he return?"

176. Stonehouse is referring to the flat-topped boulders beyond his house at the summit. §Confucius is reported saying, "*The Book of Odes* says, 'The twittering oriole / it rests at the top of the hill.' When it rests, it knows where to rest. Is it possible man is inferior to this bird?" (*Tahsueh:* 3:2)

173. The forest grows new leaves
surrounding my hut with more cool shade
tall grass hides a dusty trail
across the next ridge a woodcutter sings
I plough and I plant
my coircloth coat and leaf hat askew
the rain is in time
my rice sprouts are saved
I've scanned the whole world
everything fades
emptiness is easy
but what about sorrow

174. Cold Mountain has a line
my mind is like the autumn moon
I have a line of my own
my mind outshines the autumn moon
not that the autumn moon isn't bright
but once it's full it fades
how unlike my mind
always full and bright
as to what the mind is like
tell me what to say

175. The moon lights up my door
the wind blows open my robe
sit down on a rock my friend
hear my mountain song
black hair turns to snow
dawn to evening shade
everything is dew on the grass
how can anything last

176. After I eat I dust off a boulder and sleep
and after I've slept I like to walk
a cloudy late summer scene
an oriole sings in an unfamiliar tree
enjoying the passing season
happy to sing out its heart
true joy is right here
why chase empty fame

山中一雨滋　原上百物好
手種三畝薯　亦可延昏早
咄哉世間人　名利常關抱
頭上雪紛紛　胃中塵浩浩

種豆兩三畦　離離覆原上
不知陽和功　惟言土力壯
老兔伏崖根　心心欲希望
果能息汝貪　我寧不食醬

小不讀佛書　大不識玄旨
焉知百萬門　只在方寸裡
終日恣貪嗔　幾時念生死
一朝老病來　懊惱亦徒爾

結屋荒山巔　隨緣度朝夕
賣柴糴米歸　煮粥做飯喫
雖是勞形骸　且免當戶役
説妙與談玄　箇卻曉不得

177. The sutras of the Buddha say there are a million doors to the truth, and you only need to walk through one. §Buddhists often refer to the mind as the "one square-inch." §Love and hate, along with delusion, comprise the Three Poisons that keep us turning on the Wheel of Rebirth.

178. The Chekiang Plain begins a few kilometers east of Hsiamushan and encompasses more than a thousand square kilometers of rich farmland. §Apparently, the rabbit is waiting for the tendrils to reach beyond the plain to his burrow at the bottom of the cliff, while Stonehouse is even more patient, waiting for them to reach the summit. §The *sauce* of the last line is, no doubt, soy sauce, made from the beans grown on the plains.

179. The maze of waterways that irrigate the fields of the Chekiang Plain depends on the rainfall of the Tienmu Mountains, of which Hsiamushan is among the northernmost spurs. §As elsewhere, *dust* refers to sensation.

180. The government required every household with able-bodied males to provide a certain number of day's labor on government construction projects or service in local militias. But since monks were no longer members of a household, they were exempt from such duties.

177. If you don't read sutras when you're young
     you won't know what they mean when you're old
     you won't know a million doors
     are in your infinitesimal mind
     indulging all day in love and hate
     how often do you think about life and death
     one day old age will surprise you
     and remorse will be too late

178. Someone plants a few patches of beans
     suddenly tendrils cover the plain
     people forget the sunshine and sweat
     they say it's due to the soil
     an old rabbit hides at the base of the cliff
     expectation filling his thoughts
     if he would give up his greed
     I would give up my sauce

179. Whenever the mountains enjoy a good rain
     everything flourishes down on the plain
     planting an acre of yams
     can wait for another time
     but worldly people alas
     never stop thinking of fortune and fame
     their heads become mountains of snow
     their hearts become seas of dust

180. I built my hut on a lonely peak
     and pass my days in karma's wake
     I sell wood to buy grain
     and live on porridge and rice
     even though I'm always tired
     at least I avoid *corvée*
     but talking about the dark and distant
     that is something I can't do

放下全放下　佛也莫要做
動念即成魔　開口便招禍
飲啄但隨緣　只麼閒閒過
執法去修行　牽牛來拽磨

破屋三兩椽　住在千峰上
雲散天宇清　放目聊四望
世界空裡花　起滅皆虛妄
日落山風寒　閉門燒火向

結屋霞峰頭　耕鉏供日課
山田六七坵　道人三兩箇
開池放月來　賣柴糴米過
老子少機關　家私都說破

兩箇窮道人　三間弊漏屋
開得一坵田　收得半櫓穀
煮粥儘有餘　做飯卻不足
也勝利名人　奔南又走北

181. Buddhists recognize an infinite number of demons, or *maras*, one for every thought, word, and deed. The sole purpose of these demons is to obstruct those who seek liberation from understanding the true nature of reality. §*Dharma* is the Buddhist word for that which is held to be real, especially the Buddha's teaching. §As early as the T'ang and Sung dynasties, Chinese monks used the ox as a metaphor for their untamed minds. Among the most famous examples of such use was P'u-ming's series of ten oxherding pictures with accompanying verses describing the stages of Zen training.

182. The distance between three rafters was the space allotted to each monk in the meditation hall. Normally, this was equivalent to three feet. During the Yuan dynasty, structures were measured by the number of rafters used in their construction, and taxation of householders was attempted on this basis — though unsuccessfully. In poems 97 and 184, Stonehouse says his hut was two or three mats wide, a mat being equivalent to three feet. And in poem 129, he says his hut wasn't quite ten feet on a side.

184. These last two poems suggest Stonehouse shared his hermitage with several other monks. No doubt they included Chih-jou, the monk whose name appears as the editor of Stonehouse's *Mountain Poems* and *Zen Talks*.

181. You have to let everything go
buddhahood has to go too
each thought becomes a demon
opening your mouth invites trouble
accept what karma brings
and live your life in freedom
use the Dharma for your practice
lead your ox to the mill

182. My broken-down hut isn't three rafters wide
perched above a thousand peaks
clouds unveil an empty sky
the horizon extends in all directions
the world is a flower in space
its bloom and decay are illusions
after sunset the wind turns cold
I close my door and face the fire

183. I built my hut on Redcloud Peak
ploughing and hoeing make up my day
half-a-dozen terraced fields
two or three men of the Way
I made a pond for the moon
and sell wood to buy grain
an old man with few schemes
I've told you all about me

184. A couple of impoverished monks
living in broken-down huts
we clear mountain fields
and harvest baskets of chaff
enough to make porridge
but not enough for rice
still we outdo the rich and famous
hurrying north and south

石屋禪師偈讚

送東林院主歸華亭

參禪人　須猛烈　吹毛劍　佛來與祖來

拈起當頭截　雲中木馬驚嘶　山上鯉魚出血

萬仞崖頭奉凱歸　等閒踏破華亭月

送慶侍者回里省師

汝師年老中山寺　朝暮無人可瞻侍

不歸掃灑執巾瓶　師資禮法合也未

汝母兼又年紀高　除汝一人更無二

望斷秋風未見歸　倚門日日長垂淚

籬師棄母入山來　所圖畢景成何事

安貧樂道固所難　住箇茆菴豈容易

也要種竹栽松　也要鉏山攟地　也要運水搬柴

也要澆蔬灌芋　也要行道諷經　也要攝心除睡

蔡羹黍飯塞飢瘡　淡虀薄粥通腸胃

人生皆為口體忙　我亦未免形骸累

These verses were collected by Stonehouse's disciple Chih-jou from poems that Stonehouse wrote for visitors on Hsiamushan or at Fuyuan Temple. Thus, their focus is less personal and more instructional than the Mountain Poems. Most were written in the four-line gatha form that came to China from India along with Buddhist sutras.

1. *Huating* is an old name for Sungchiang, which is about forty kilometers northeast of Pinghu, the town where Stonehouse served as abbot for eight years. Tunglin Temple was on a small hill in Sungchiang. §The student of Zen undertakes the seemingly impossible mission of finding his mind, here suitably represented by such anomalous creatures as an animated wooden horse and an amphibious carp. And when he does find his mind, he destroys it on sight.

2. The position of *shih-che:attendant* was filled in rotation from among the lower ranking monks in the meditation hall. His primary duty was to wait on the abbot.§Circumambulation as a form of meditation is practiced at most Zen temples in conjunction with sitting. §Pigweed, *Chenopodium album,* is a member of the goosefoot family and synonymous with "survival food."

BOOK TWO
GATHAS

1. *For the Abbot of Tunglin Monastery Returning to Huating*

A student of Zen
has to be fierce
a sword that splits hairs
into shimmering snow
let buddhas and patriarchs come
cut them in two on the spot
a wooden horse neighs in the clouds
a carp on the mountain bleeds
return to the towering cliffs a hero
step right through the Huating moonlight

2. *For Attendant Ch'ing Going Home to See His Teacher*

Your teacher grows old at Chungshan Temple
with no one to lean on from dawn to dusk
unless you return to serve and attend him
how can he maintain a teacher's decorum
your mother too is advanced in years
with nobody left but you
her hopes of old age are fading without you
her tears fall every day at her gate
leaving your mother and teacher for the mountains
what did you hope to achieve
to rejoice in the Way and poverty is hard
to live in a thatched hut isn't easy
you have to plant pines and bamboo
you have to hoe slopes and dig ditches
you have to haul water and wood
you have to tend taro and greens
you have to walk circles and chant
you have to sit still and not sleep
with pigweed soup and millet for your hunger
watered-down rice and gruel for your stomach
people all work for food and clothes
I'm trapped too by burdens of the body

自家心地如未明　業識茫茫無本據
水邊林下暫經過　吾汝皆非久居計
月江和尚有書來　勉汝歸寧有深意
開緘未讀便抽身　不負來音全孝義
有言孝為百行先　在俗在僧誰不然
侍師奉母名敬田　何須入眾拜參禪
忽然思敬又嫌喧　短策不妨閒往還

海都寺求語

急急做工夫　單提狗子無　脊梁高豎起
屹似須彌盧　翻來覆去看　要了此公案
瞥然妄念生　便逐他使喚　精進不懈怠
坐立道可待　懶惰又昏沉　驢年也未在
若也放得下　無可無不可　千七百葛藤
盡是敲門瓦

留進菴主

丹陽進禪人　隨我住有日　雖立志參禪
未曾有所入　菴中諸事務　渾不憚勞役
口體甘淡薄　身心頗真實　一朝拜我前

2. (continued) §*Karmic awareness* refers to the constantly changing consciousness created by the effects of our past deeds. §The saying about filial piety comes from the Paihu Tungyi: "Filial piety is the most beautiful of virtues and first of all duties" (20). §The last line suggests the monk to whom this poem was addressed was from a family of means.

3. A monk once asked Chao-chou if a dog possessed the buddha-nature. Chao-chou's *wu:no* became one of Zen's most famous koans and begins the collection known as the *Wumenkuan,* or *Gateless Gate.* On a later occasion, however, Chao-chou told another monk, *Yu:yes.* See the *Wutenglu:* 4 for the full account. §Mount Sumeru is located at the center of the universe and is as many miles high as there are grains of sand in the Ganges. §The donkey is not among the animals of the Chinese twelve-year cycle. Hence a donkey-year is not part of the natural order. §Seventeen hundred is the approximate number of koans in the *Wutenglu,* or *Record of the Five Lamps,* from which later koan collections were compiled. §Chinese temple gates can be quite thick. Using a brick to gain the attention of those inside is an old metaphor for using learning as a tool to gain admission to the inner sanctum. But once inside, the brick no longer has any value and is better tossed aside.

4. Nowadays, *an-chu:abbot* means "abbotess," but in Stonehouse's day the term was restricted to the chief monk of a small temple or hermitage. §Tanyang is a town on the Grand Canal just south of where it intersects the Yangtze.

unless we fathom the ground of our mind
karmic awareness provides no support
the woods and streams are a temporary home
neither of us should plan a long stay
a letter arrived from Master Yueh-chiang
asking you back between the lines
you left before you finished
unable to bear a whole letter about duty
but filial duty comes first they say
among laymen among monks it's the same
parents and teachers are fields of devotion
you don't need to be a monk and practice Zen
one day your thoughts will turn away from noise
a riding crop won't slow occasional visits

3. *For the Monks at Haitu Temple*

Straining at your practice
focused on what a dog doesn't have
backbones held erect
lofty as Sumeru
checking one side then the other
trying to understand this koan
suddenly delusion rises
just as fast you send it off
working hard never resting
sitting standing always ready
laziness and stupidity
and donkey years don't apply
but if you can just let go
no is fine so is yes
seventeen-hundred tangled vines
so many bricks to bang on the gate

4. *For Abbot Chin*

Zen monk Chin from Tanyang
here with me awhile
you resolved to practice Zen
but never got the chance
a temple has its share of work
from which you've never shied
content with meager food and clothes
honest in both thought and deed
now today you come to me

請語為法則　我寫此數言　助汝進道力
只就我山居　隨緣度朝夕　莫學野盤僧
東西與南北　尋常動用中　精勤莫放逸
剔起眉毛看　畢竟是何物　看破看底人
大事方了畢

示鐵壁劉居士

見性成佛無別佛　古人說話最條直
當頭坐斷沒纖毫　切忌隨他言語覓
縱饒虛妄百千般　究竟還歸一真實
老僧吐露真實情　寄與雲間劉鐵壁

山中四威儀

山中行　信步慢騰騰　攀蘿去　又上一崚嶒
山中住　幾度朝還暮　手栽松　陰涼成大樹
山中坐　飄飄黃葉墮　沒人來　閉門燒餕火
山中臥　松風穿耳過　沒來由　好夢都吹破

5. The emphasis in Zen on seeing one's nature began with Bodhidharma: "Whoever sees his nature is a buddha; whoever doesn't is a mortal. But if you can find your buddha nature apart from your mortal nature, where is it? Our mortal nature is our buddha nature. Beyond this nature there is no buddha. The buddha is our nature. There is no buddha besides this nature. And there is no nature besides the buddha." (*The Zen Teaching of Bodhidharma*: 16-17)

6. Buddhist rules governing moral behavior are summarized under these categories, known as the Four Postures: walking, standing, sitting, and lying down. §As he tells us in his *Mountain Poems*, Stonehouse's *big fire* was usually one of leaves and twigs rather than logs.

asking for instruction
I write down these lines
to help you on the Path
try this mountain life of mine
pass your days in karma's wake
don't be like the monks who wander
east and west and north and south
in your ordinary actions
be alert don't relax
trim your eyebrows back and look
what exactly do you see
see through the one who sees
then your task is done

5. *For Layman Ironwall Liu*

See your nature become a buddha there is no other buddha
the ancients said it best
then you grab but nothing is there
don't be misled by words
despite the million kinds of fiction
all lead back to a single truth
this old monk is writing it down
addressing it *Ironwall Liu in the Clouds*

6. *Four Mountain Postures*

Walking in the mountains
unconsciously trudging along
grab a vine
climb another ridge

Standing in the mountains
how many dawns become dusk
plant a pine
a tree of growing shade

Sitting in the mountains
zig-zag yellow leaves fall
nobody comes
close the door and make a big fire

Lying in the mountains
pine wind enters the ears
for no good reason
beautiful dreams are blown apart

重巖之下十首

重巖之下　火種刀耕　有粟有蔬　可煮可烹
了我目前　樂我餘生　坐眄庭柯　幾度衰榮

重巖之下　希古為儔　徹證本根　一了便休
紛紛玄徒　念死話頭　待兔守株　求劍刻舟

重巖之下　草莽日交　人影不來　黃葉飄飄
谷鳥晚啼　山月夜高　松露鶴飛　濕我禪袍

重巖之下　蛇虎為鄰　我心既忘　彼性亦馴
人生在世　各具天真　含齒戴髮　胡為不仁

重巖之下　未透本根　觸境遇緣　擾擾紛紛
應須悟理　超越見聞　久久自然　左右逢原

7.1 The slash-and-burn technique of preparing forested land for farming is still used by a number of hill tribes in Southwest China, most notably the Aini near the Burma border. Once cleared, a field is used for three years and then allowed to lie fallow for three years.

7.2 There once was a farmer in the state of Sung who saw a rabbit break its neck when it accidentally ran into a stump. The farmer dropped his hoe and waited beside the stump for another rabbit. But no more rabbits came, and he became the laughing stock of Sung (*Hanfeitzu*: 49). §In the state of Ch'u, a man was crossing a river when he dropped his sword into the water. He promptly made a mark on the side of the boat where the sword disappeared. When the boat reached the other side, he got out and looked in the water below the place he had marked, but without success. The boat had moved, but the sword had not (*Lushih Chunchiu:Ts'ai-chin*).

7.3 The crane and pine are symbols of immortality and transcendence.

7.4 The South China tiger is much smaller than its Siberian and Indian cousins but can be just as deadly when threatened or surprised on the trail. The cobra, the banded krait, and the bamboo snake kill people every year south of the Yangtze.

7.5 The last line is from *Mencius*: 4B.14.

7. *Below High Cliffs — ten poems*

1. Below high cliffs
   I slash and I burn
   there's vegetables and grain
   to boil and steam
   to satisfy the present
   to brighten old age
   looking at a tree in the yard
   I count its falls and springs

2. Below high cliffs
   my companions are the ancients
   having reached the source
   here I rest
   others of more mystic persuasion
   study koans to death
   wait beside stumps for rabbits
   notch boats to find lost swords

3. Below high cliffs
   all day I see plants
   no sign of people
   yellow leaves in the wind
   birds call at dusk from the valley
   the mountain moon rises at night
   a crane takes flight from a pine
   and showers my robe with dew

4. Below high cliffs
   tigers and snakes are my neighbors
   once I forgot my mind
   their natures suddenly became tame
   people born in this world
   all have something divine
   mouths of teeth heads of hair
   why can't they be kind

5. Below high cliffs
   unaware of the source
   wherever you turn is karma
   chaos and confusion
   in order to see the truth
   look beyond your senses
   it's always been this way
   the spring flows all around you

重嚴之下　靜默自居　三際不來　心如境如

斜月半窗　殘火一爐　嗟彼睡夫　蝶夢邅邅

重嚴之下　幡然一隻　掇兮無邊　禈兮無口

夜入禪那　晝勤隴畝　道在其中　別更何有

重嚴之下　目對千山　一根返源　六處皆閒

白雲飄飄　綠水潺潺　動靜自忘　別是人間

重嚴之下　不修形骸　木食草衣　布幟筍鞋

竹密暗窗　苔深覆階　蕭焉忘情　寂爾虛懷

重嚴之下　飽飯熟眠　縱情放逸　歲月虛延

老病時臨　眾苦交煎　臨渴掘井　熱悶徒然

7.6 The last line refers to Chuang-tzu's story in which he dreams he is a butterfly. On waking, he wonders if he isn't a butterfly dreaming he is a man (*Chuangtzu*: 2.11).

7.7 For Stonehouse's legless pants, see also verse 113 of his *Mountain Poems. Zazen* means "meditation."

7.8 In addition to the eyes, the ears, the nose, the mouth, and the skin, Buddhists recognize the mind as the sixth and most important of our senses. As Kuan-yin discovered in the *Surangama Sutra,* any of the six can lead to enlightenment. §The last line is from Li Pai's *Answering a Question in the Mountains:* "You ask me why I chose these hills / lost in thought I smile and don't answer / peach petals in the stream lead into the distance / there's another world beyond the world of man." Li Pai's peach petals allude to T'ao Yuan-ming's story about a hidden world known as Peach Blossom Spring.

7.10 The penultimate line is part of an old Chinese saying directed at those who wait until it's too late to act. It comes from the *Huangti Suwen:* "To treat an illness after it appears is like digging a well after you're thirsty or forging weapons after a war begins." §The *heat* of the last line also refers to that of hell.

6. Below high cliffs
   serene in solitude
   not visited by time
   the mind creates the world
   the window holds a setting moon
   the stove contains a dying fire
   pity the sleeping man
   startled from his butterfly dream

7. Below high cliffs
   a white-haired old man
   his robe with no hem
   his pants with no legs
   practicing zazen at night
   working his fields by day
   herein lies the Path
   where else could it be

8. Below high cliffs
   I face a thousand mountains
   one sense finds the source
   all six relax
   white clouds drift
   green water ripples
   beyond movement and stillness
   there's another world

9. Below high cliffs
   I don't dress up my body
   I eat roots and wear plants
   my socks are hemp my shoes are sedge
   dense bamboo shades my windows
   thick moss covers the steps in front
   desires die in the quiet
   cares disappear it's so still

10. Below high cliffs
    you eat and sleep your fill
    indulge desire and lethargy
    idle away the months and years
    until old age and illness arrive
    and a thousand pains afflict you
    digging a well when you're thirsty
    you endure heat in vain

次韻送智西堂歸靈隱

一榻平分鑑古軒　爐薰相對坐忘眠
山林禮樂無今昔　時節因緣有變遷
樹影高低深夜月　猿聲長短五更天
兩冬不得梅花信　又約梅花到冷泉

會趙初心提舉

老來腳力不勝鞋　竹杖扶行步落花
待月伴雲眠蘚石　尋梅陪客過鄰家
粥香瓦缽山田米　雪汎瓷甌水磨茶
今日為翁時薦出　此心長只在煙霞

別南山經室

屋借雲邊兩載居　晴原無事便攜鉏
和香採得鄰家菊　趁嫩挑來自種蔬
秋殿寂時山磬歇　夜窗虛處野煙疏
明朝又向他山去　何日重來讀梵書

8. The *hsi-t'ang:senior instructor* was in charge of teaching the monks in the west, or meditation, hall of a Zen monastery. §Linyin Temple is still one of the most famous sights of Hangchou. §During the T'ang dynasty, the poet Lin Ho-ching planted hundreds of plum trees around his hermitage on Kushan Island at the edge of what eventually became Hangchou's West Lake. The area around the lake is still famous for its plum blossoms. §*Cold Spring* was the old name for the stream that flows along the rock face opposite the entrance to Lingyin Temple.

9. Although the bureau that Chao Ch'u-hsin headed is not specified, during the Sung and Yuan dynasties the title of *t'i-chu:commissioner* was limited to officials in charge of granaries, the salt monopoly, and the tea monopoly. My guess is the tea monopoly. §In Stonehouse's day, tea leaves were ground into powder and the powder pressed into cakes. Slices from the cakes were then boiled in water and whisked into a froth. The *floating snow* refers to the resulting froth of bubbles in the tea cup.

10. There are dozens of temples named South Mountain in China. Although his biography makes no mention of it, this poem suggests Stonehouse spent a few years on an extended pilgrimage. During the Yuan dynasty, a temple of this name in southern Fukien province was famous for its library. §The library is usually on the second floor above one of the shrine halls, and it usually includes a few rooms for visiting scholars or monks. §Monastic activity slows in fall, while many resident monks or nuns use the break between summer and winter meditation sessions to visit other temples and masters. §The *Vyakarana* is the first sutra delivered at the beginning of a new kalpa by Brahma, Lord of Creation. Originally a million stanzas in length, it was reduced to a very manageable three hundred by the Indian grammarian, Panini.

8. *To Senior Instructor Chih on his Return to Lingyin Temple – to his rhyme*

On my humble thought-worn cot
facing stove smoke we forget sleep
the rites and music of the woods are timeless
seasonal conditions change and disappear
a tree's jagged shadow in the moon's setting light
a gibbon's wavering howl in the pre-dawn sky
two winters now no plum flower news
their blossoms are probably at Cold Spring again

9. *On Meeting Commissioner Chao Ch'u-hsin*

My old legs can't keep up with my shoes
I need a staff to help me walk across the petals
I rest on mossy rocks with the moon and the clouds
I show a guest the plum blossoms beyond a neighbor's hut
a clay bowl of fragrant gruel made from mountain rice
a porcelain cup of floating snow brewed from stream-milled tea
today for you I've made a brief appearance
usually this mind stays inside the mist

10. *On Leaving South Mountain Sutra Library*

For two years I've borrowed a room from the clouds
I grabbed a hoe when time and rain permitted
I gathered the perfume of a neighbor's flowers
and picked the products of my garden
mountain music fades when autumn halls are still
forest mist slips in where window panes are missing
tomorrow I'm leaving for another mountain
when will I return to read the *Vyakarana*

秋日秦川道中

處處西風葉落頻　偶歸湖寺蹔容身
故人十有幾人在　世事萬無一事真
擾擾勞生同作夢　明明果報各由因
余諳此理能消遣　終不隨他自損神

偶作

今年七十七顏齡　血氣潛消老病增
踏雪探梅知腳重　挑雲度嶺覺肩疼
光陰別去忙如箭　世念休來冷似冰
卻憶向時遊獄洞　兩三回上最高層

冬至

作宵冬至一陽生　萬物欣欣盡向榮
鐵樹花開紅朵朵　石田筍出綠莖莖
人間化日縈添綠　竹外幽禽便轉聲
白髮老僧窗下坐　爐香多誦兩行經

11. The Chin River flows from Maoshan northwest into the Yangtze at Nanking and parallels the route between Nanking and Huchou. In number 68 of his *Zen Talks,* Stonehouse refers to Pinghu's Fuyuan Temple as Lake Temple. Here, however, the reference must be to Huchou's Wanshou Temple on Taochangshan, where Stonehouse lived for a time with his teacher, Chi-an. The last line recalls *Chuangtzu:* "Though he has a body, he doesn't harm his mind" (6.12).

12. The Chinese still delight in finding the year's first plum blossoms, as they signify the end of winter and the beginning of spring. §Although I haven't been able to render the full import of line 7, the Chinese indicates that the cave was on one of China's five sacred mountains. My guess is Sungshan, on whose Lesser Peak Bodhidharma's cave is located.

13. In addition to the calendar of twelve lunar months, the Chinese divide the year into twenty-four solar periods. During the solar period prior to the winter solstice, the power of yin is at its greatest and is represented by the six broken yin lines of the hexagram *K'un:Earth*. On the evening of the solstice, *K'un* is replaced by *Fu:Return,* with its solitary yang line at the bottom. §Iron trees are said to bloom upon a bodhisattva's death, but here the expression is euphemistic and refers to the black branches of deciduous trees. §The *stitch* refers to a peculiarity of the old Chinese solar calendar, to which stitches of red string were added as the sun began to lengthen its arc. §A short hymn is sung at the beginning of ceremonies involving the burning of incense.

94

11. *Autumn on the Chin River Road*

Everywhere the west wind rains down leaves
chance led me back to Lake Temple's shelter
among those I knew how many remain
of a thousand worldly cares not one of them is real
all of life's turmoil turns out to be a dream
clearly every harvest depends upon the seed
knowing this truth has helped make me free
I've never followed those who harm their minds

12. *Occasional Poem*

I'm fading this year at seventy-seven
my energy is waning my ills are on the rise
I trudge out of breath through snow to find plum blossoms
I shoulder a cloud across the ridge in pain
daylight and darkness vanish like arrows
thoughts of the world lie frozen in ice
I recall visiting the great cave long ago
was it two or three times I climbed the peak

13. *Winter Solstice*

A yang line appeared last night on the solstice
everything turns with joy toward the light
iron trees bloom in scarlet profusion
barren fields blossom in patterns of green
the transforming sun adds a stitch to the world
hidden birds sing beyond the bamboo
a white-haired old monk sitting below his window
chants an extra verse of the incense hymn

卻南州提舉再招

自憐業繫在娑婆　一度尋思一嘆嗟
世上多逢人面虎　山中少見佛心蛇
禦寒補衲裁荷葉　遣睡煎茶煮瀑花
老拙背時酬應懶　不能從命出煙霞

雪中示徒

六出飄飄入夜多　洒窗相似撲燈蛾
山家富貴銀千樹　漁父風流玉一蓑
深徑絕無樵子語　陰崖卻有獵人過
菴前黃歇無尋處　唯見寒梅數朵花

送皐侍者

侍者參得禪了也　萬兩黃金也合消
世上豈無千里馬　人間難得九方皐

送漆匠

裡面盡情灰得了　外頭方始好揩磨
雖然本有靈光在　也要工夫發用他

14. As in gatha 9, the title of commissioner was restricted to the chief of special government agencies concerned with the storage, transport, and supply of certain foodstuffs, including grain, tea, and salt.

15. The *six-petaled flower* is the snowflake and contrasts here with the five-petaled plum blossom. §The yam is among the foods a hermit turns to when nothing else is available.

16. A thousand-mile horse can run for a thousand miles without stopping. §Chiu-fang Kao appears in *Liehtzu*: 8, where he is noted for his ability to recognize a great horse despite being unable to distinguish its color or sex.

17. The resin used to make lacquer is taken from the lacquer tree, *Rhus verniciflua*. While lacquer itself is clear, the jet black patina common to most lacquerware is the result of adding lampblack, which is collected by scraping the inside of a metal hood hung over burning oil lamps. Lacquerware utensils and furniture are made by applying a dozen or more layers of lacquer varnish, each of which is sanded and rubbed before the next is applied.

14. *On Commissioner Hsi Nan-chou's Second Invitation*

We mourn our karmic ties to the world
to stop and think is to sigh
human-faced tigers roam the towns
buddha-hearted snakes are rare in the mountains
to keep warm I patch my robe with lotus leaves
to stay awake I boil spring water for tea
old and out of touch I'm socially inept
I can't obey requests to leave the mist behind

15. *For a Disciple in the Snow*

Six-petaled flowers filled the night
beating against my window like moths against a lamp
a forest of silver makes a hermit wealthy
a raincoat of jade turns a fisherman into a prince
the trails are barren of woodcutter talk
below dark cliffs a hunter passes
before my hut no sign of yams
just a few early plum blossoms

16. *For Attendant Kao*

For an attendant to understand Zen
a ton of gold would be a fair price
the world doesn't lack thousand-mile horses
but a Chiu-fang Kao is hard to find

17. *For a Lacquer Worker*

You sweat on the inside gathering soot
then on the outside you rub
although potential to shine exists
it takes work to bring it to light

送真藏主禮育王

鴈宕天台華頂峰　鄮山乳寶接天童
遍遊元不離雙足　盡在摩尼一點中

送就禪人禮祖

人人有具黃金骨　何必諸方禮塔頭
堪笑丹陽就禪者　春深猶自浙東遊

送松江深上人

參方禮祖外邊事　一著工夫在己躬
親觀阿師秋已半　樹彫葉落露金風

18. After uniting most of India in the third century BC, Ashoka became a Buddhist and ordered his officials to erect stupas containing the Buddha's relics throughout the four quarters. When foreign invaders later laid waste to Buddhist sites in India, the contents of several of these stupas made their way to China. Thus, at the end of the third century AD, a piece of the Buddha's skull reached the port of Ningpo, where it is still housed inside a temple named for the great Indian monarch. §The place names mentioned in the poem are all south of Ashoka Temple: Mount Ma is known for its limestone caves; Mount Tientung ("Heaven's Child") was one of China's greatest Zen centers during Stonehouse's day; Mount Tientai and its Huating Peak were the seat of the Tientai sect of Buddhism; and farther south, Mount Yentang was associated with Nikula, the fifth of Buddhism's Sixteen Arhats, who entered nirvana there after arriving from India in the fourth century AD. §The magic pearl, or mani jewel, grants to its possessor whatever is asked for.

19. The patriarchs of the Zen sect include Bodhidharma and his five successors as well as the founders of the lineages that flourished in the T'ang dynasty. §When the body of one who cultivates a religious life is burned, small crystalline relics are found. I have never seen gold ones, but I have seen Shakyamuni's in the Lintung Museum east of Sian, and they resemble hundreds of small diamonds. §Tanyang is just south of where the Grand Canal intersects the Yangtze. §During the Yuan dynasty, East Chekiang included the coastal prefectures. In his *Mountain Poems,* Stonehouse tells us that spring is the best season in this part of China, and he wonders why anyone would trade it for the dust of the trail.

20. Sungchiang was the prefecture northeast of the Chiahsing-Huchou area. During the Yuan dynasty, it was a major trading center, while nearby Shanghai was barely on the map. §In ancient times, nobles were required to pay their respects to the emperor at mid-autumn, and this custom was later observed by students and teachers. §The Chinese analysis of matter associates earth with the center, water with the north, wood with the east, fire with the south, and metal with the west, which is where the wind blows from in autumn in this part of China.

18. *For Librarian Chen on his Way to Worship Ashoka*

Yentang Tientai Huating Peak
Mount Ma's Nipple Cave nursing Heaven's Child
wherever you go you can't leave your feet
they're all inside a single magic pearl

19. *For Zen Monk Chiu on his Way to Worship the Patriarchs*

Everyone has gold bones
why go around worshipping stupas
Zen monk Chiu from Tanyang you're crazy
leaving East Chekiang in late spring

20. *For Monk Shen of Sungchiang*

Worshipping patriarchs is superficial
focus your practice on yourself
visit your teacher before autumn ends
before the metal wind strips the trees bare

送椿上人禮寶陀

寒潮日夜吼雷音　耳聽何如眼聽親
小白花嚴觀自在　頻伽聲裡現全身

示禪上人

古今無法可傳流　只要愉心死便休
大抵是他人自肯　福源不會按牛頭

送雪峰維那

留香堂裡十聲佛　驚倒江西馬簸箕
八十四人扶不起　維那歸去莫教遲

送人遊五臺

去去臺山最上層　文殊合掌笑相迎
嚴前有箇金獅子　顛倒騎歸輿老僧

21. Putuo Island is in the Chushan Archipelago off the Chekiang coast north of Ningpo. Since the T'ang dynasty it has been recognized as the residence of Avalokiteshvara, or Kuan-yin, the Bodhisattva of Compassion. §In Chinese, her name means "Seer of Sounds." In the *Surangama Sutra,* she reveals her enlightenment was achieved by merging her other senses with her sense of hearing. §The *white flower* is the *mandarava.* Meaning "to bring joy," it is one of the four celestial flowers. §This spot is at the southeast corner of the island at a place where the tide roars through an opening in the rocks and showers the cliff with seafoam. §The *kalavinka* is a bird of Himalayan valleys noted for its melodious voice.

22. The first line is from the *Wumenkuan: 27,* where it is said that the Dharma isn't taught, only learned. §Fuyuan Temple was Stonehouse's responsibility from 1331 until 1339. §As in P'u Ming's *Oxherding Pictures and Verses,* the ox was often used as a metaphor for the unruly mind, although not all Zen masters agreed about the extent to which it required training.

23. The Pure Land sect teaches devotees that chanting the name of Amida Buddha ten times will assure them of rebirth in his Western Paradise. §The *Kiangsi horse* refers to Ma-tsu, or Patriarch Ma, whose temple was in Kiangsi province and whose name means "horse" in Chinese. Ma-tsu was the originator of such unconventional teaching methods as the shout and the slap and presumably would have been displeased to have Pure Land devotees in his meditation hall. §The winnow is a basket used for separating grain from chaff. §Of the one hundred thirty-nine disciples to whom Ma-tsu transmitted the Dharma, eighty-four became teachers in their own right.

24. Mount Wutai is the sacred residence of Manjushri, the Bodhisattva of Wisdom, and is located in North China, a long day's bus ride southwest of Peking. §Pilgrims often encounter Manjushri during their visits to Wutaishan, though he appears in many guises and is not usually recognized until the pilgrim reflects on the encounter afterward. When I met him, he was carrying rocks to rebuild a temple that had been destroyed by the Red Guards. §The lion symbolizes courage and wisdom and is the traditional mount of Manjushri. Buddhist wisdom is the reverse of that of the world in that it comprises no knowledge or view, truth or doctrine.

21. *For Monk Ch'un on Pilgrimage to Putuo Island*

   Night and day the cold tide roars
   eyes can hear it better than ears
   Avalokiteshvara of the White Flower Cliff
   reveals herself in the kalavinka's voice

22. *For a Zen Monk*

   There is no Truth anyone can teach
   try to please yourself before you die
   others can do what they want
   Fuyuan monks don't restrain their ox

23. *For Meditation Master Hsueh-feng*

   There's a ten-tongued buddha lighting incense in the hall
   the Kiangsi horse panics and kicks the winnow over
   eighty-four people can't pick it up
   meditation master go home while there's time

24. *For a Traveler Bound for Wutai*

   Hurry to Wutai's highest peak
   to the smile and blessing of Manjushri
   below the cliffs is a golden lion
   ride it backward back here to me

送針工

手攜刀尺走諸方　線去針來日日忙
量盡別人長與短　自家長短幾曾量

示真副寺坐圓覺期

百日期中痛著鞭　工夫到處話頭圓
多生業障俱消滅　佛境分明在目前

送實監寺回大覺

楊岐骨格氣雄雄　一夏相忘寂寞中
秋至思歸天目去　竹房閒掩聽松風

送恕上人回鄉

孤身行腳緣何事　策杖歸鄉有底忙
白業不修禪不會　可憐空過好時光

送德都寺回里

德雲不在妙峰頂　卻向別山相見來
從此罷休行腳念　坐看心地覺花開

25. Here the tailor is a lay devotee who has come to the temple to make ceremonial robes for the monks. Lay Buddhists often offer their services to monastic communities in hopes of accruing merit for a better rebirth for themselves or their loved ones.

26. The *Complete Enlightenment Sutra* was one of the few texts used for instruction at Zen temples. Here, however, it lends its name to a three-month meditation retreat. It was customary during these periods for monks to focus on koans chosen by the meditation master.

27. Ta-chiao was probably the abbot of Shihchien Temple. §Yang-ch'i was a disciple of the eleventh-century Zen master Tz'u-ming. §A three-month summer retreat is held at most Zen monasteries. §Chuang-tzu says, "When springs dry up, fish find themselves in puddles, spraying water on each other to keep each other alive. Better to be in a river or lake and oblivious of each other" (6.5). §The Tienmu Mountains form the western border of Chekiang province and were home to thousands of recluses and dozens of temples and hermitages during the Sung and Yuan dynasties.

28. It was common for Zen monks to wander for several years from temple to temple and from master to master cultivating the practice of detachment from impermanence. §Stonehouse implies that Monk Chien was leaving the Order and returning to lay life.

29. *Cloud of Virtue* also appears in gatha 63. I suspect this is another name for Manjushri, whose residence is on Wutaishan, two hundred fifty kilometers southwest of Peking. In Sanskrit, *manjushri* means "wondrous virtue." §Wonder Peak, or Miaofeng, is forty kilometers northwest of Peking. During the Sung and Yuan dynasties, there were a number of monasteries built on Miaofeng, and during the Ming and Ch'ing dynasties it became a center for the worship of the Taoist divinity, Pi-hsia Yuan-chun. My guess is that Tetu was among its Buddhist temples.

25. *For a Tailor*

You rush around waving scissors and tape
busy all day with needle and thread
when you're done measuring others
do you ever measure yourself

26. *For the Monks of Chenfu Temple during the Complete Enlightenment Period*

Crack the whip for a hundred days
koans become clear when you practice long enough
smash the karmic walls of your past
before you lies the buddha realm

27. *For a Monk from Shihchien Temple Returning to Ta-chiao*

The bones of Yang-ch'i the will of a hero
oblivious all summer you sat here in silence
then fall arrived and thoughts of Tienmu
a bamboo hut an open door the sound of pine wind

28. *For Monk Chien Returning Home*

Why do some monks wander alone
while others hurry home with their staffs
forgetting good karma unclear about Zen
to waste such a chance is a shame

29. *For a Monk Returning to Tetu Temple*

Cloud of Virtue isn't on Wonder Peak
he's visiting another mountain instead
don't make any more pilgrimage plans
just watch awareness bloom in your mind

送真侍者

幾年入眾為參禪　三喚機緣未倒邊
再去諸方重請益　卻來這裡喫粗拳

送福上人禮祖

祖師塔是鶴崙磚　只在山邊與水邊
一一從頭巡禮遍　草鞋依舊自還錢

示來上人

看水看山何日了　奔南走北幾時休
可憐身在裂裳下　道業未成先白頭

送淨髮待詔二首

結緣待詔到山中　廊下諸僧盡整容
方丈老人何不剃　要留白髮過隆冬
剃了又長長又剃　一年幾度遠煩過
大夫只管來求福　我福如何有許多

送圓上人

妙淨圓明全體現　不須來問我如何
正因行腳禪和子　知解何曾有許多

30. Through his teacher, Chi-an, Stonehouse was a member of the lineage that began with Ma-tsu, the Zen master who introduced the shout and the slap as means of instruction.

31. When Bodhidharma died in 528, his remains were interred in a stupa on Hsiungershan at the headwaters of the Lo River. The site is outside the county seat of Lushih, two hundred kilometers southwest of Loyang. Three years after Bodhidharma died, an official met him walking in the mountains of Central Asia. He was carrying a staff from which hung a single sandal, and he told the official he was going back to India. Reports of this meeting aroused the curiosity of other monks, and they finally agreed to open Bodhidharma's stupa. But all they found inside was the missing sandal. §The custom of walking around the site of a holy relic, with or without prostrations between steps, is practiced in a clockwise direction. Three circuits are normal, but multiples of twenty-seven are also common.

32. Some Zen monks never stop looking for the perfect master and the perfect residence.

33. It is customary among Buddhist monks and nuns to shave each other's heads on the days of the new and full moon. §This poem must have been written while Stonehouse was abbot of Fuyuan Temple. If so, the mountains and the effort of the trip must be euphemistically meant. §Merit is acquired by both parties involved in any selfless deed. However, attachment to merit results in no merit.

34. Elsewhere, Stonehouse expresses similar sentiments regarding the practice of wandering from temple to temple looking for something the wanderer already has in his bag.

30. *For Attendant Chen*

How many years have you practiced Zen
three perfect shouts didn't knock you down
off you went seeking further instruction
now you're back for a slap in the face

31. *For Monk Fu Going to Worship the Patriarch*

The patriarch's stupa is a pile of bricks
next to a mountain next to a stream
walk around one step at a time
straw sandals still cost money

32. *For Monk Lai*

Visiting mountains and rivers without end
hurrying north and south without rest
pitiful body beneath a monk's robe
not yet enlightened and already old

33. *For a Barber — two poems*

A barber enters the mountains for merit
below the shrine hall he shaves all the monks
why is the old abbot exempt
he needs his hair for the winter

Shave it it grows back shave it again
how many trips do you make every year
all the way here for the merit
how much do you think we get

34. *For Monk Yuan*

It's pure and bright and totally present
why ask me what it's like
among you buddha-bound wandering monks
how many ever understand

送問上人歸大乘

一句明明向汝道　冷如猛火熱如冰
上人若不信我說　急急回歸問大乘

送人之五臺

短策輕包上五臺　銀樓金閣正門開
文殊相見喫茶了　收取玻璃盞子來

送聞上人

夏在大乘堂裡住　冬初來扣福源門
莫嫌老我無言說　一曲漁歌隔岸聞

送明道者

工夫不到不方圓　心若堅時石也穿
不見頭陀老迦葉　意根滅盡領金襴

送大維那省母

桶箍爆處見根源　熟路重行三月天
日暖北堂萱草綠　對娘莫説老婆禪

35. *Tacheng* was the name of a temple fourteen kilometers northeast of Pinghu. It was first built in 1315, or three years after Fuyuan Temple, and was famous for its spring-fed pond. As often happened, the abbot assumed the name of the temple.

36. Apparitions of Manjushri in many guises are reported by pilgrims who visit Wutaishan. §Wutai's five "peaks" are actually grassy knolls and easily reached on horseback – and now by car or bus. §The Pure Land of Amida also includes silver towers and gold pavilions, but here they refer to the transformed appearance of the white dagobas and the yellow-tiled roofs of the temple complexes that still cover the mountain. §The main gate is also the gate to the Buddha's Middle Path. §The traditional Chinese outer garment, whether full- or half-length, included spacious sleeves that were used as pockets.

37. The monk to whom this poem is addressed is not the same as the one in gatha 35. This monk's name means "hear," while the name of the monk in gatha 35 means "ask." Stonehouse uses their names in the last lines of both poems. §Pinghu's Fuyuan Temple was on the west shore of East Lake and Tacheng was beyond the north shore. The fisherman's song might refer to that of the fisherman in Ch'u Yuan's poem of the same name in which the fisherman chides Ch'u Yuan for insisting on moral integrity over flexibility. Or it might refer to Chang Chih-ho, who lived in the same region as Stonehouse, but during the T'ang dynasty, and who fished without bait (for his mind was not bent on catching fish) and who accompanied himself by composing short songs.

38. When Kashyapa responded to Shakyamuni's flower sermon with a smile, the Buddha gave him his robe, thus initiating the transmission of the Zen patriarchship. §Again, Stonehouse plays with the monk's name. *Ming* means "bright," and the Buddha's robe is golden.

39. An old saying reminds people: "Tasting the water, think of the source." §Ostensibly, the trail between the nunnery and the stream is meant, but the walkway used for circumambulation in the meditation hall also comes to mind. §*North hall* is a euphemism for one's mother, while *lily grass* refers to a son.

35. *For Monk Wen Returning to Tacheng*

> Here's a line that explains it clearly
> it's cold as fire and hot as ice
> if you don't believe my words
> hurry home and ask Ta-ch'eng

36. *For a Traveler Going to Wutai*

> Climb Wutai with a light pack and whip
> past the main gate to gold tiles and silver bricks
> after your tea with Manjushri
> drop that crystal cup in your sleeve

37. *For Monk Wen*

> All summer long you stay at Tacheng
> then winter comes and you knock on our gate
> don't blame me for not responding
> across the water I hear a fisherman's song

38. *For Monk Ming*

> It has no shape until you apply it
> your mind can slice rocks when it's hard
> remember that old ascetic Kashyapa
> he cut the root of thought and won a golden robe

39. *For Meditation Mistress Sheng*

> A crack in the bucket betrays the water's source
> back on the trail in late spring
> sun warms the north hall and lily grass is green
> don't use Old Lady Zen on young girls

示茂道者

作佛生天容易事　最難是做頭陀
勞神枯骨安閒少　運水搬柴普請多

示道人

自遠相尋到鵡湖　慇懃請問做工夫
老僧真實為人說　出處伽陀一字無

送勤上人

勤求警策做工夫　散亂昏沉盡掃除
後夜黑雲消散盡　長天如水月輪孤

示禪人二首

終日騎牛不識牛　何須辛苦外邊求
只消驀鼻牽來看　便是尋常這一頭

參得趙州無字透　玄關金鎖盡開通
三更月下泥牛吼　八面玲瓏海日紅

英上求語

客冒春寒訪隱肩　衲衣猶綴雪花輕
坐來出示諸方語　錦軸未開先眼明

40. In addition to normal monastic duties, the abbot ordered communal work whenever the occasion demanded. Such occasions included sunning books and bedding, working in monastery fields, constructing temple buildings, and preparing for a religious festival.

41. Parrot Lake, or Wuhu, is another name for Tunghu, or East Lake. And East Lake is synonymous with the town of Pinghu, just as West Lake calls Hangchou to mind. §*Gatha* means "song" in Sanskrit and refers to a four-line poem. In India, it was used in sutras to summarize sections of prose, but it could also stand alone. In China, its primary purpose was instructional, and it became part of every Zen master's repertoire.

42. At Zen monasteries, the term *ching-ts'e:warning-switch* refers to a long flat piece of wood used to strike dozing monks on the shoulder in the meditation hall.

43.1 Ta-an asked Pai-chang to describe someone searching for the buddha. Pai-chang said, "That would be like riding an ox while searching for an ox." Ta-an asked, "And what about after he finds it?" Pai-chang said, "That would be like someone returning home on the ox" (*Chuantenglu:* 9). In China, the ox was used as a metaphor for the mind as early as the T'ang dynasty and was represented in pictures as well as poems.

43.2 One day a monk asked Chao-chou, "What is Chao-chou's one word?" Chao-chou answered, "I don't even have half a word." The monk asked, "But Master, don't you exist?" Chao-chou replied, "I'm not a word" (*Chuantenglu:* 10). §The *gold lock* refers to the precepts and the *dark gate* to monastic life. §A monk once asked Lung-shan what he had learned while living in the mountains. Lung-shan answered, "I saw two clay oxen plunge into the sea, but up until now I haven't heard any news" (*Chuantenglu:* 8).

40. *For Monk Mao*

To be a god or a buddha is easy
the hardest thing to be is a monk
always exhausted never enough rest
if it's not wood or water it's temple work

41. *For a Monk*

People come a long way to reach Parrot Lake
anxious to ask about practice
this old monk tells them the truth
the gatha that frees you has no words

42. *For Monk Ch'in*

Find a switch to use in your practice
to drive daydreams and sleep far away
late at night when dark clouds vanish
the sky is an ocean the moon shines alone

43. *For a Zen Monk – two poems*

All day on an ox unaware of the ox
why endure hardship searching elsewhere
just pierce its nose and pull it around
guess who it is afterall

To get past Chao-chou's wordless riddle
open the gold lock and dark gate
the clay ox roars when the moon sets at midnight
the horizon turns red from the ocean-born sun

44. *For Monk Ying*

Braving spring cold you found my hidden door
your robe still flecked with snow
sit down and tell me the news of the realm
but open your eyes before you unroll your scroll

送維那之江西

上人壯志出叢林　一寸光陰一寸金
莫把世間閑學解　等閒埋沒祖師心

送凌侍者回淨慈

十里湖光浸六橋　到時須著眼頭高
斷是風暖楊花落　不是鳥窠吹布毛

送觀侍者

放下身心返自觀　略無毫髮許相瞞
雲收霧捲乾坤闊　月上青山玉一團

示勤道者

一片荒田一把鋤　翻來覆去下工夫
一鋤翻得春風轉　也有瓜茄也有瓠

示眾

念未生時猶妄覺　瞥興一念便傷他
工夫到此切須記　枯木巖前蹉路多

45. Here *patriarch* refers to Ma-tsu. It was Ma-tsu, more than any other monk, who freed Zen from its focus on meditation as the means to enlightenment. Ma-tsu's stupa is at Paofeng Temple in Kiangsi province sixty kilometers northwest of Nanchang.

46. Chingtzu Temple was located on the south shore of Hangchou's West Lake and has recently been rebuilt. §The three-kilometer-long dike that created West Lake includes six bridges that permit small boats to pass underneath. §The dike is still lined with willows that veil its rock facade with a haze of white willow fuzz in spring. §While the Hangchou area is known for its orioles, its most famous product remains silk brocade.

47. Stonehouse uses Attendant Kuan's name, which means "look," in the first line.

48. Monk Ch'in's name means "work" or "diligence." The phrase *spring wind* refers to the powers of rebirth and growth. §Melons, eggplants, and gourds are among the last vegetables to be harvested in fall, and some are left behind to germinate the following spring.

49. *Dead Tree Cliff* is a euphemism for the absence of thought and feeling. Someone who sits up all night in the meditation hall and never lies down is called "a dead tree."

45. *To a Meditation Master Leaving for Kiangsi*

So you've decided to leave this temple
every inch of time is an inch of gold
don't analyze what the world calls knowledge
just go bury the patriarch's mind

46. *For Attendant Ling Returning to Chingtzu Temple*

Three miles of lakelight flood the six bridges
when you arrive lift up your eyes
willow fuzz swirls in the dike's warm breeze
or is it down or silk from the bird nests

47. *For Attendant Kuan*

Let the self go and look back inside
don't let a single hair blind you
clouds disperse and the world is wide
rising from the mountain is a moon of jade

48. *For Monk Ch'in*

An overgrown field and a hoe
turn it all over let's see some work
every swing uncovers spring wind
and melons and eggplants and gourds

49. *For the Assembly*

Before a thought stirs it's already false
the moment a thought appears kill it
remember when you reach this stage
from Dead Tree Cliff lead many dead ends

行盡東西南北州　如今能得此心休
俱眠只在山中住　受用天籠一指頭

跋淨首座血書法華報親
父是誰兮母是誰　胸藏五逆是男兒
看他義斷情忘處　紅荇莟花三四枝

常侍者血書金剛經
此經在處皆有佛　不勞心力更施功
抵園秋晚霜葉重　樹葉紅於血染濃

寄魁書記
僧住城隍佛祖訶　先賢多是隱嚴阿
山泉流出人間去　清水自然成濁波

寄淨慈平山和尚二首
年老心孤憶弟兄　中峰且喜過南屏
潺潺一派雙溪水　流入西湖更好聽

50. Chu-shih was enlightened when T'ien-lung held up a finger. Later, whenever Chu-shih was asked about Zen, he said nothing and only held up his finger. When he was about to die, he said, "Ever since I obtained this One Finger Zen from T'ien-lung, I haven't been able to exhaust it (*Chuantenglu:* 11). T'ien-lung was also fond of saying, "I hold up this finger, and the whole universe moves with it."

51. Writing a sutra with one's own blood is done to gain merit for others. My first Buddhist master, the venerable Shou-yeh, spent more than a decade writing the *Avatamsaka Sutra* in blood and never fully recovered his health. §Among the five heinous acts that doom a person to rebirth in Hell are killing one's father, one's mother, or an arhat, shedding the blood of a buddha, or destroying the harmony of the congregation. Stonehouse implies that drawing one's own blood violates the first four of these prohibitions. §In the seventh of the eight cold hells, the flesh of sufferers is said to burst open like red lotus flowers. In drawing one's own blood for writing, the fingers are normally used.

52. The first line is from the *Diamond Sutra:* 12, which extols the emptiness of the six practices known as *paramitas:means to the other shore,* the first of which is *charity.* §The Buddha preached the *Diamond Sutra* in Jetavana, which was a forested park just outside the city of Sravasti. It was donated to the Assembly for their exclusive use by Anathapindaka.

54.1 Chingtzu Temple is on the south shore of Hangchou's West Lake and at the foot of Nanping Mountain. §Chung-feng (d. 1337) was one of the most eminent monks of the Yuan dynasty and, like Stonehouse, studied with Kao-feng in the Tienmu Mountains west of Hangchou. His Zen talks have also been preserved. P'ing-shan (Lin-t'ung) and Stonehouse were both enlightened while staying with Chi-an, hence their relationship as "dharma brothers." §Between Nanping Mountain and Phoenix Mountain to the east, two streams separate from the same source and flow side by side only to rejoin just before entering the southeast corner of West Lake.

50. *For a Follower of the Way*

    Now that you've toured every state in the realm
    why not let your mind rest
    Chu-shih spent his life in the mountains
    and all he needed was T'ien-lung's finger

51. *To Rector Pa-ching Writing the Lotus Sutra in Blood to Repay His Parents*

    Who was his father who was his mother
    who is this son planning heinous deeds
    behold his resolve and detachment
    the red lotus flowers blooming from his hands

52. *To Attendant Ch'ang Writing the Diamond Sutra in Blood*

    Wherever you find this sutra is a buddha
    why strain your heart for charity
    Jetavana's late autumn leaves are heavy
    with a red much darker than blood

53. *To Secretary K'uei*

    The patriarchs disapproved of monks who lived in town
    the sages of the past retired to the hills
    once a mountain stream enters the city
    its pure water soon turns muddy

54. *To Monk P'ing-shan of Chingtzu Temple – two poems*

    Old and alone I recall my elder brother
    crossing Nanping with Chung-feng for pleasure
    two streams of water babbling in one river
    entering West Lake the sound was even better

領破蹄穿五百牛　南屏寺裡一欄收
皮毛換得光生了　拽耙拖犁再起頭

寄友人二首

山舍無聊夜臥遲　因君記得去年時
豆花棚下曾分榻　月落松梢尚詠詩

萬松影裡三間屋　枯木嚴前一箇僧
十二三年如此過　肯將清德換虛名

古樵

空劫已前無影樹　撐天柱地赤條條
新州有箇賣柴漢　收拾將來一檐挑

無岸

舉頭四望白瀰瀰　南北東西竟莫知
不用篙篙撐到底　回頭便是上船時

54.2 Five hundred was the number of arhats in attendance at many of the Buddha's sermons and also the number who gathered after the Buddha's Nirvana to recite what they had heard. Their clay figures are often seen in the larger Buddhist monasteries in China. §*Nanping Temple* was another name for Chingtzu Temple, which was located at the foot of Nanpingshan.

55.1 No doubt the scene is the eighth full moon, or Mid-Autumn Festival, when families spend at least part of the night together outside. In fact, throughout the middle and lower reaches of the Yangtze, many people sleep outside during the height of summer to enjoy the cool air. See also 76 of the *Mountain Poems*.

55.2 The expression *k'u-mu:dead trees* also refers to those who spend all their time meditating.

56. The empty kalpa is the period of time between the destruction of one universe and the creation of the next one. §Hsinchou (now Hsinhsing) is one hundred kilometers southwest of Kuangchou and is the Sixth Patriarch's hometown. After receiving the patriarchship from the Fifth Patriarch, Huineng spent a number of years living with hill tribes in the mountainous regions of northern Kuantung province.

57. The Dharma is often likened to a raft that can be used to reach the far shore of liberation. But why exhaust yourself poling or rowing across when there's a favorable wind?

Five hundred oxen toothless and lame
crowd the corral of Nanping Temple
their once hairy hides now bare
they keep looking up from their ploughs

55. *To a Friend – two poems*

My hut is so depressing I stay in bed late
thinking of you takes me back to last year
sharing a cot under pea-flower eaves
still chanting poems after losing the moon to the pines

A hut in the shade of ten thousand pines
a monk at the foot of Dead Tree Cliff
living like this ten or twelve years
choosing plain virtue over empty fame

56. Ancient Woodcutter

A shadowless tree from before the last kalpa
the only thing holding up Heaven and Earth
a firewood seller from Hsinchou
gathers enough for a load

57. *No Shore*

A wall of white haze obscures the horizon
all directions are indistinct
don't bother trying to pole yourself over
change your ways and it's time to sail

本源

滔滔心地中流出　低下隨宜不自高
坎止流行皆末事　終歸大海作波濤

石崖

千尋拔地青如玉　萬丈凌雲硬似剛
望見嶮巇多退步　有誰撒手肯承當

無敵

眼空湖海氣凌雲　傑出叢林思不群
古往今來誰是我　得饒人處且饒人

白庵

一色虛明含法界　四簷皎潔若冰霜
小窗幾度雪晴夜　不見梅花只覺香

別澗

湛然不入眾流數　瞪目觀來果必殊
但得煮茶增味好　誰能泛濫落江湖

58. The metaphor of water and waves is used in the *Avatamsaka Sutra* to represent the distinction between phenomenon and noumenon, the false and the real.

60. The last line is from Yao K'uan's *Hsihsi Tsungyu:* "There once was a Taoist chess master from Tsaichou who always let his opponent move first. People made up a poem about him: 'Here is a man without enemies / he goes easy on others when he has the chance.'"

61. The *world* here refers to the *dharma-dhatu,* the realm of reality.

62. *Rivers and lakes* refers to the lower reaches of the Yangtze as well as to a life of seclusion or aimless drifting.

58. *The Source*

An endless stream flows out of the mind
whichever way is down never up
where it rests and moves doesn't matter
reaching the sea it all become waves

59. *Rock Cliff*

Ten thousand feet of the greenest jade
piercing the clouds it's harder than diamond
people turn back at the sight of the heights
who can let go and take up the challenge

60. *No Enemies*

Your eyes drain oceans your spirit rides clouds
a monk among monks your thoughts are unique
but who were you once and who are you now
go easy on others when you have the chance

61. *White Hut*

The world is surrounded by a one-color sky
my eaves are white as ice
at night through my windows when the snow stops
no sign of plum blossoms only their scent

62. *Another Stream*

Too clear to be part of the common flow
look and you'll see that it's different
use it for tea and taste the improvement
how does it end up in rivers and lakes

別峰

峭峻萬山齊不得　孤危眾嶽勢難同
善財參見德雲處　又在那邊蒼翠中

出山佛二首
頭髮鬖鬆下翠微　凍雲殘雪綴伽梨
不須更問山中事　觀著容顏便得知
肘破衣穿骨裡皮　下山回首步遲遲
父王休遣人來問　顏貌不如宮裡時

觀音大士二首
長天萬里無雲夜　月在波心說向誰
童子南詢尚未回　白花巖下望多時
水即是波　巖即是石　坐證圓通　斯為第一

羅漢二首
這漢何為　長年打坐　執法修行　如牛拽磨
寂滅見超空劫前　待出定來重勘過

63. Sudhana was one of Shakyamuni's disciples. In the final chapter of the *Avatamsaka Sutra*, Sudhana visits more than fifty different masters in an effort to learn all the practices of a bodhisattva. In the *Wuteng Huiyuan*, Manjushri sends Sudhana into the mountains to find a plant that has no medicinal uses. When he can't find such a plant, Manjushri tells him to bring back any plant. When he does so, Manjushri holds it up before the assembly and says, "This medicine can kill, and it can cure." I'm guessing *Cloud of Virtue* is another name for Manjushri. See also gatha 29. §The *peak* is that of Sumeru.

64.1 Prior to his Enlightenment under the Bodhi Tree, Shakyamuni practiced austerities in a cave known as Praghbodhi on a mountain across the river from Bodhgaya.

64.2 Suddhodana was Shakyamuni's father. The remains of his palace have been found about fifty kilometers west of the Nepalese border post of Belhiya on the road from Bihar State to Katmandu.

65. Avalokiteshvara, the Goddess of Compassion, has kept watch over sailors from her lookout on Putuo Island ever since the ninth century, when a Japanese monk was repeatedly shipwrecked there while trying to carry a statue of Avalokiteshvara back to Japan and concluded it must be her home. The island is located northeast of the port of Ningpo and southeast of Shanghai. §The *white flowers* are those of the heavenly *mandarava* tree, whose blooms also appear in connection with the island in verse 21. The cliff named after these flowers is on the southeast corner of the island, where waves crash against the rocks and their white spray hangs like flowers in the air.

66.1 The arhat is the fourth and final goal of Hinayana Buddhists and is defined as being "free of passion." But unlike the bodhisattva of Mahayana Buddhists, the arhat is incapable of compassion.

63. *Another Peak*

The myriad mountains of the realm are no match
even the great peaks lie below its lone spire
Sudhana visits Cloud of Virtue
up there on its slopes again

64. *The Buddha Leaving the Mountains — two poems*

He comes down the mountain long shaggy hair
patches of clouds and snow on his robe
no need to ask what he does up there
one look at his face and you'll know

Sack full of bones worn at the elbows
looking back at the peak he falters
his father doesn't bother asking for news
his face has changed since the palace

65. *Avalokiteshvara — two poems*

A young man is still on his southern mission
on White Flower Cliff how long do you wait
when the night sky is clear for a thousand miles
who do you tell about the moon on the waves

The water is waves
the cliff is rocks
to know perfect union
this is the goal

66. *Arhat — two poems*

What are you doing
meditating all year
cultivating the Dharma
like an ox at a mill
free now of passion you can see the last world
but what about your faults when your zazen is done

一箇渾身　一瓶秋水　物外生涯　只這便是

白眼看他世上人　手捺雙跌笑而已

達磨二首

面黑齒缺　心粗膽大　梁王殿上　撒沙拋土

少室峰前　開花結果　椻葉嚴臺　蒙頭宴坐

夫是謂之　菩提達磨

無限家私狼藉盡　何爭一隻破皮鞋

一言不契渡江淮　熊耳峰前去活埋

及菴和尚并師同慎

二老比丘　有何因由　先覺後覺　東州西州

建陽山中相見時　好於骨肉　西峰寺裡再參後

惡似冤讎　從此父南子北　不如雲散水流

在你也　報盡已歸兜率　在我也　業煩尚寄閻浮

是非恩怨難分處　一片松陰蓋石頭

67.1 Bodhidharma was from southern India and is usually depicted as dark-skinned, blue-eyed, and buck-toothed. His biography in the *Chuantenglu,* published in 1004, records a meeting with Emperor Wu at the Liang dynasty capital in Nanking. During their meeting, Bodhidharma dismissed the emperor's attempts to gain merit by building temples and supporting monks and explained to him the doctrine of emptiness. Failing to find a receptive audience, Bodhidharma crossed the Yangtze (artists depict him doing so on a single reed) and eventually settled southeast of Loyang in a cave near the summit of Sungshan's Shaoshih Peak. After transmitting the Dharma to Hui-k'o, Bodhidharma composed this gatha: "The reason I came to this land / was to transmit the Dharma and save sentient beings / once the flower unfolds five petals / the fruit will form by itself." The five petals refer to the five Chinese patriarchs, and the fruit to the Zen tradition. After Bodhidharma's death in 528, he was buried on Hsiungershan, or Bear Ear Mountain, about two hundred kilometers southwest of Shaoshih Peak near the small town of Lushih.

67.2 When officials dug up Bodhidharma's grave, all they found was a single sandal. I am unfamiliar with Huyeh Cliff but suspect it must be a local name for the site of Bodhidharma's stupa on Bear Ear Mountain.

68. Stonehouse first met Chi-an at West Peak Temple on Chienyangshan, also known as Langyashan, three kilometers south of Chienyang. §Tushita Heaven is where bodhisattvas are reborn before their final rebirth. §Jambudvipa is the continent of Asia.

An amorphous body
a jar of still water
the transcendental life
nothing else is true
meanwhile notice worldly people
slapping their thighs in laughter

67. *Bodhidharma – two poems*

Dark-skinned and gap-toothed
impulsive and brave
in the emperor's palace
he scattered dust and dirt
below Shaoshih Peak
his blossom bore fruit
before Huyeh Cliff
he sits covered up
he's the one we call Bodhidharma

No one understood so he crossed the river
on Bear Ear Peak he was buried alive
his limitless wealth is a pile of rubble
why fight over a worn-out shoe

68. *Master Chi-an's Warning*

Two old monks
what was our link
waking in turn
in the east and the west
meeting on Chienyang Mountain
we were closer than kin
staying at West Peak Temple
we were like enemies
then we went our separate ways
clouds and rivers flowed on unaware
as for you
you paid your debt and left for Tushita
as for me
karma still troubles me here in Jambu
where good is hard to tell from bad
where pine shade covers the rocks

珣上人求讚

板齒生毛　面孔無肉　受靈山記　欠人天福
瘦稜稜　卻如碧海波心　湧起一座玉巖
硬剝剝　好侶白雲堆裡　突出千尋石屋
道是天湖菴主　不是我同流　謂是福源住持
亦非吾眷屬　眼裡無筋底
未免向影子上胡猜亂猜　皮下有血底
終不向丹青上東卜西卜　珣禪善記吾囑
切須莫展與人看　挂向閒房伴松竹

禪人求讚

髮白面皺　皮黃骨瘦　用盡自己心　笑破他人口
情知衰世道難行　卻來靜處閒叉手
看天湖鵝湖　二水同流　對霞峰胥峰　兩山並秀
何緣得此優遊　端的自能跳透
不是禪翁自點胸　古今盡道蘇州有

69. The Buddha lived on Vulture Peak for thirty-five years and delivered most of his sermons there. It was located just outside the ancient capital of Rajgir and named for a rock formation near the summit. §Often during his sermons, the Buddha foretold the future buddhahood of his disciples.

70. Wild Goose Pond is in Kiangsi province near the modern town of Shangjao and was the site of a famous Neo-Confucian academy as well as several important Zen monasteries. Hsu Peak (also called Mount Wu) is near the southeast corner of Hangchou's West Lake and was home to several dozen Buddhist temples. Apparently, the monk to whom this poem was addressed had spent time in these places and was expecting Stonehouse to point him elsewhere. §Suchou, situated between the Yangtze and Lake Taihu, was a center of silk commerce, high society and, it would seem, braggart monks.

69. *For Monk Hsun Seeking Advice*

There's hair on my teeth
no flesh on my face
since Vulture Peak predestined
my debt to the world remains unpaid
on a thin and ragged edge
on a wave in an emerald sea
on a surging cliff of jade
on a rocky barren peak
on a mountain range of clouds
my stone house rises ten thousand feet
who calls me the Hermit of Sky Lake
isn't any friend of mine
who calls me the Abbot of Fuyuan
isn't one of my disciples
an eye without a muscle
still searches in the shadows
blood beneath the skin
doesn't choose if it's red or blue
Zen Monk Hsun
Zen Monk Hsun
remember well my advice
and don't show anyone else
hang it inside your hut in the woods

70. *Advice for a Zen Monk*

Your hair is white your face is brown
your skin is leather your body is bones
you've exhausted your mind
while others have died from laughter
I know the world is hard to accept
but why disturb me with your bows
consider Sky Lake and Wild Goose Pond
both waters flow the same
look at Hsiamu and Hsu Peak
both mountains rise as one
how did I find such freedom
I simply learned to transcend
I'm not a Zen monk who brags
Suchou I hear has plenty of those

師。於元統辛未四月十三日入寺。指山門云。

豁開戶牖。當軒者誰。喝一喝

佛殿。因我得禮你。自倒還自起。鵓鳩樹上

啼。意在麻畬裡

據室。拈拄杖云。從上諸佛祖師。天下老和

尚。總是揚塵於水底。摘楊華於火中。新福

源。又作麼生。卓拄杖。喝一喝

拈廣教府疏云。老瞿曇。二千年前未了底公

案。琪上座。今日就廣教府官手裡。與他了

卻。呈疏云。所供詣實

The following record was compiled by Stonehouse's disciple Chih-jou while Stonehouse was abbot of Fuyuan Temple. The temple was located near the South Gate of the town of Pinghu, about one hundred kilometers southwest of what is now Shanghai. Stonehouse was asked to take over the temple following its reconstruction in 1330, and he served as its abbot from 1331 until 1339. In the course of addressing the monks, Stonehouse often spoke in rhymed verse. I have indicated these sections with slashes.

1.1 Fuyuan Temple was first built in 1312 and named for a well (*fu-yuan:blessed spring*) that supplied it with water, even during droughts. It was originally located about five hundred meters outside the South Gate of Pinghu at the edge of East Lake. But during the Ming and Ch'ing dynasties, the town expanded at the lake's expense, and the temple eventually found itself just inside the town's South Gate. 1.2 Assuming that Chih-jou was correct concerning the year cycle, he must have been mistaken about the reign period. The Yuan-t'ung period did not begin until 1333, or two years after Stonehouse arrived. 1.3 *Ho:hey* is my rendering of the shout used by Zen masters to awaken their dozing disciples or to supply a shortcut to the more roundabout route taken by language in expressing the truth.

2.1 The shrine hall is where most ceremonies are conducted and includes at least one central altar with a statue of a buddha or bodhisattva. 2.2 As its name suggests, the sound of the rain-pigeon heralds rain. 2.3 Hemp fields were usually located at the periphery of villages on marginal, if not hilly, land, and their irrigation often required carrying water considerable distances.

3.1 Along with the whisk, the staff is the abbot's symbol of authority. 3.2 While Buddhists recognize countless buddhas, their use of the term "patriarch" is restricted to the founders of the various Zen lineages.

4.1 The office of general preceptor was established in the second month of 1331 in each of the sixteen provinces of China and was given responsiblity for monastic discipline and administration. It eliminated three years later in 1334. 4.2 The term *koan* (Chinese: *kung-an*), originally used with reference to a court case, was later applied to the statements of Zen masters that expressed the truth while rising above the limitations of language. 4.3 Gautama was Shakyamuni's personal name. 4.4 Stonehouse refers to himself here by the second part of his monastic name, Ch'ing-hung. 4.5 Stonehouse's point is that the Buddha did not speak the Truth but simply presented expedient teachings, for the Truth cannot be expressed.

BOOK THREE
ZEN TALKS

1. The Master entered the temple[1] on the thirteenth day of the fourth month of the Hsin-wei year of the Yuan-t'ung period.[2] Pointing to the front gate he said, "Open your doors. Who is it at the threshold? Hey!"[3]

2. In the shrine hall,[1] the Master said, "To pay my respects to you / I bow down and stand back up / the rain-pigeon[2] cries from a tree / all thoughts are in the hemp fields."[3]

3. Accepting control of the temple, the Master grabbed his staff[1] and said, "All the buddhas and patriarchs[2] of the past and all the old monks in the world do nothing but stir the mud at the bottom of the pond and pick willow fuzz out of the fire. What about this new abbot?" Lifting up his staff, he shouted, "Hey!"

4. Accepting the decree appointing him general preceptor,[1] the Master said, "The koan[2] that Old Gautama[3] didn't understand two thousand years ago, Abbot Hung,[4] in accepting the office of general preceptor, now completes for him. It reads: 'To supply instruction in the Truth.'"[5]

拈山門疏云。鑊子大小。杓柄短長。自家裡
事。何必論量

指法座云。人天寶座。曲彔木床。我今要坐即
便坐。更不作禮須彌王。便陞座。拈香祝　聖
畢。次拈香云。此一瓣香。爇向爐中。奉為前
住湖州路道場禪寺及菴大和尚。用酬法乳之
恩。乃云。把住也鋒芒不露。放行也十字縱
橫。水雲深處相逢。卻在千峰頂上。千峰頂上
相逢。卻在水雲深處。今朝福源寺裡。開堂演
法。昨日天湖菴畔。墾土耕煙。所以道。法無
定相。遇緣即宗。可傳真寂之風。仰助無為之
化。正與麼時如何。拈拄杖卓一下云。九萬里
鵬纔展翼。一千年鶴便翱翔

6.1 The *fa-tso:dharma seat* is not usually located in the main shrine hall but in a secondary or adjacent hall reserved for lectures on the Dharma, or Buddhist Doctrine. This, though, is a special occasion, hence its presence in the main shrine hall. 6.2 Mount Sumeru is the axis of the universe, and its king is Shakyamuni. 6.3 It was customary to begin all public ceremonies by wishing the emperor long life. Unfortunately, Emperor Wen-tsung, under whose patronage the temple was reconstructed, died the year after Stonehouse arrived. 6.4 Chi-an was Stonehouse's teacher. Though the two first met at Chienyangshan's West Peak Temple, Chi-an ended his years on Taochangshan outside Huchou. 6.5 These lines contrast the lakeside mist of Fuyuan Temple with the expansive view from Stonehouse's hut on Hsiamushan. 6.6 The P'eng appears at the beginning of the first chapter of *Chuangtzu* as a symbol of transcendence and is so large it must rise ninety thousand miles above the sea before it has room to spread its wings. 6.7 The Chinese consider the crane the embodiment of a Taoist adept preparing for his final flight to the Islands of the Blessed.

5. Accepting the decree appointing him abbot, the Master said, "The capacity of your wok or the length of your spatula is your own affair. There's no need to discuss sizes."

6. Pointing to the dharma seat,[1] the Master said, "This treasured seat among gods and men, this high-backed wooden chair, if I want to sit on it, I'll sit. I don't need to bow to the King of Sumeru."[2] He then sat down. After honoring the emperor[3] with incense, he picked up another stick and said, "I place this incense in the censer in honor of Master Chi-an,[4] formerly of Huchou's Taochang Temple, and in gratitude for his kind instruction in the Dharma."

Afterward he said, "When you hold on to something, don't let the smallest hair show. When you let go of something, let it go in all directions. Meeting in heavy mist, we turn out to be at the top of a thousand peaks.[5] Meeting at the top of a thousand peaks, we turn out to be in heavy mist. Today I am at Fuyuan Temple inaugurating this hall and preaching the Dharma. Yesterday I was outside my hut at Sky Lake ploughing in the clouds. Thus it is said that the Dharma has no fixed shape but adapts to conditions. It stirs the wind of perfect stillness and makes effortless transformation possible. But at this moment, what is it like?"

Taking hold of his staff and lifting it up, he said, "Only after ninety thousand miles does the P'eng[6] unfold its wings. Only after a thousand years does the crane[7] take flight."

復舉三聖道。我逢人則出。出則不為人。興化
道。我逢人則不出。出則便為人。師云。只如
今日山僧。是為人也。不為人也。若道為人。
則屈著三聖。若道不為人。則屈著興化。且作
麼生得恰好去。擊拂子云。戎夷蠻貊分諸國。
總在吾皇化育中

當晚小參。現前一眾。久在叢林。謂之參禪。
謂之辦道。殊不知。一念未生已前。更無別
物。纔擬心時錯了也。雪峰和尚。三登投子。
九到洞山。如渴鹿趁陽焰。不知費了多少腳
頭。如今要得現成。直下自家看取。復有何
事。無事切莫妄求。妄求而得。終非得也

7.1 San-sheng and Hsing-hua were the two most prominent disciples of the ninth-century Zen master Lin-chi (Japanese: Rinzai). In fact, it was San-sheng who recorded Lin-chi's sermons and talks. 7.2 Along with the briarwood staff, the fly-whisk is an abbot's symbol of authority, and he often uses it to punctuate his remarks.

8.1 Hsueh-feng was one of the most famous Zen masters of the late ninth century, and his disciples numbered in the hundreds. As a young monk, he traveled from his hometown in central Fukien to western Anhui to visit Master Ta-t'ung on Toutzushan. He then proceeded to northern Kiangsi to see Master Liang-chieh on Tungshan. He traveled back and forth between these two masters but was finally enlightened during his stay in western Hunan with Master Te-shan when the latter told him, "What enters the gate isn't your own treasure" (*Chuantenglu*: 16).

7. The Master recalled the time San-sheng[1] said, "When I meet someone, I leave. But by leaving, I don't help anyone." And Hsing-hua said, "When I meet someone, I don't leave. If I left, I would help someone."

The Master said, "Now, is this mountain monk here to help you or not? If you say I'm here to help you, you wrong San-sheng. If you say I'm not here to help you, you wrong Hsing-hua. How can you get through this?"

Snapping his whisk,[2] he said, "The tribes beyond the borders have their own kingdoms, but all of them benefit from our emperor's instruction."

8. At an informal talk later that evening, the Master said, "All of you present have lived in monasteries for a long time and think you've been practicing Zen and cultivating the Tao. But how many of you realize that before a single thought stirs nothing exists and that the moment you think you become confused?

"Master Hsueh-feng[1] climbed Toutzushan three times and traveled to Tungshan nine times. Like a thirsty deer racing toward a mirage, he wasted so much energy. If you want to find out what is already here, look at yourselves right now. What else is there? Since there's nothing else, don't chase delusions. No one has ever caught a delusion."

復舉南泉和尚道。自小牧一頭水牯牛。擬向溪
東牧。未免食他國王水草。擬向溪西牧。亦未
免食他國王水草。不如隨分納些些。總不見
得。頌云。南泉放牧沒東西。兩岸春風綠草
齊。總是國王家水土。不如隨分納些些

結制上堂。四月十五日已前。夜短睡不足。四
月十五日已後。日長饑有餘。正當四月十五
日。福源寺裡禪和子。粥亦足。飯亦足。睡亦
足。游戲圓覺伽藍。安居平等性智。敢問諸
人。因甚得到這般田地。熏風入戶自生凉。湖
水到門非有意

謝專使並三塔和尚首座都市。上堂。睦州噇臨
濟喫棒。不是好心。楊岐逼慈明晚參。不是好

9.1 Nan-ch'uan was an eminent Zen master of the early ninth century and one of the foremost disciples of Ma-tsu. 9.2 The water buffalo and the herdboy became such a common motif in Zen they were used in both pictures and verses to depict the course whereby the student of Zen trains his unruly mind.

10.1 Chinese Zen monasteries followed the Indian model and held a three-month summer retreat during which the emphasis was on meditation and sleep was limited to only a few hours a night. 10.2 The middle and lower reaches of the Yangtze are the hottest and most humid areas in all of China, and any breeze at all is welcome during summer retreat. 10.3 Fuyuan Temple was just outside Pinghu's South Gate at the edge of the city's famous East Lake.

11.1 The *shou-tso:rector* was in charge of lecturing and usually served as a temple's abbot as well. Rector San-t'a was from the temple of the same name just outside the West Gate of the nearby prefectural seat of Chiahsing and was apparently there to convey the decree appointing Stonehouse abbot of Fuyuan. The emissary was from the capital and was there to present the decree appointing Stonehouse general preceptor of the region. 11.2 During the Yuan dynasty, the capital was called Tatu and was located in what is now Peking. 11.3 Mu-chou and Lin-chi were both disciples of the ninth-century Zen master Huang-po, at whose hands Lin-chi was eventually enlightened, thanks to Mu-chou's encouragement. Here, and in his following remarks, Stonehouse implies that compassion alone is of no use unless it is paired with wisdom and that wisdom should be the goal of those taking part in the three-month meditation retreat. 11.4 Yang-ch'i was a disciple of the eleventh-century Zen master Tz'u-ming, who was kept up late at night trying to enlighten his thick-headed student. 11.5 Chaochou and Tao-wu were disciples of the early ninth-century Zen master Nan-ch'uan, and often discussed their understanding of their master's teaching with each other. 11.6 *Coral pillows* are a euphemism for the hard wooden pillows normally used by monks. Coral is one of the seven gems from which everything in Amida's paradise is constructed.

9. The Master recalled the time Nan-ch'uan[1] said, "Ever since I was a boy, I've herded a water buffalo.[2] Whenever I let it graze east of the river, it can't help eating the grass of the eastern king. Whenever I let it graze west of the river, it can't help eating the grass of the western king. Neither compares to accepting one's lot and making do with less. Nothing else works."

The Master said, "Nan-ch'uan didn't herd east or west / though both shores had fresh spring grass / the land belonged to other kings / thus he made do with less and less."

10. At the beginning of retreat,[1] the Master said, "Before the fifteenth day of the fourth month, the nights are short, and you don't get enough sleep. After the fifteenth, the days are long, and you're always hungry. Today it's the fifteenth, and all you Zen monks here at Fuyuan get enough porridge and rice and enough sleep.

"As you wander through this monastery of perfect enlightenment and take refuge in undifferentiated wisdom, may I ask how you ended up in such a place? A welcome breeze[2] enters the door, and you feel cool. Lake water[3] reaches the gate but without any purpose."

11. After thanking Rector San-t'a[1] and the emissary from the capital,[2] the Master said, "When Mu-chou[3] caused Lin-chi to get hit, it wasn't out of compassion. When Yang-ch'i[4] made Tz'u-ming stay up late, it wasn't out of compassion. When Chao-chou[5] visited Tao-wu, it wasn't out of compassion. Today the emissary is making us stay at Fuyuan. Tell me, is it out of compassion or not? From our coral pillows[6] come two streams of tears: one because we love our lord, the other because we hate him."

趙州訪道吾。不是好心。福源專使。逼人
住院。且道。是好心。不是好心。珊瑚枕上兩
行淚。半是思君半恨君

上堂。若論此事。如農夫耕田相似。耕之以
深。種之以時。所收必豐。輸官奉己之外。綽
綽有餘裕者。無他。力乎精勤而已。耕之不
深。種之非時。所收必寡。輸官奉己不足者。
亦無他。困於怠墮而已。然而不責自己怠墮所
需之。匱而反妒他人精勤而得之多。斯等人。
名為可憐憫者。福源說話。意在於何。不圖打
草。且要驚蛇

謝殿主淨頭。上堂。一身清淨。則多身清淨。
一世界清淨。則多世界清淨。東司頭臭氣。佛

12.1 During the Yuan dynasty, taxes were collected in South China in summer and also in autumn by
merchant corporations that bought "tax-farming" rights from the government. The summer tax was
payable in currency or cloth, while the autumn tax was payable in grain. The coastal province that in-
cluded Chekiang and Fukien (and hence, Fuyuan Temple) provided the Yuan government with more
than one-third of its total revenue.

13.1 The *tien-chu:senior verger* was in charge of the main shrine hall, and the *ching-t'ou:sanitation steward*
was in charge of the latrine.

12. The Master said, "If I had to describe what we're doing here, I would say it's like farming. If you till the soil deeply and plant in season, your harvest will be great, and there will be more than enough left over after paying the authorities their taxes.[1] It's all due to making an effort. If you don't till deeply or you plant out of season, your harvest will be poor, and there won't even be enough to pay the taxes. It's all due to being lazy. And yet how many people ignore the defect of their own laziness and criticize the diligence of others? Such people are pathetic. When I speak, what am I trying to do? I'm not trying to beat the grass. I'm trying to chase the snakes."

13. After thanking the senior verger and the sanitation steward,[1] the Master said, "If one person is pure, other persons are pure. If one world is pure, other worlds are pure. Where does the smell in the latrine or the dust in the shrine hall come from?" Holding his nose, he said, "There it is again."

殿裡蓬塵。從什麼處得來。以手掩鼻云。又有

一點也

上堂。三月安居一月過。園林是處綠陰多。蛙
聲只在池塘裡。試問禪流會也麼。此方真教
體。清淨在音聞。觀音菩薩。將錢買胡餅。放
下卻是饅頭。擊拂子云。打麵還他州土麥。唱
歌須是帝鄉人

散青苗會上堂。天得一以清。地得一以寧。聖
人得一天下和平。衲僧得一。事事現成。拄拄
杖云。拄杖子得一。任運騰騰。晚來縱步東湖
上。笑指禾苗一色青

14.1 The three-month summer retreat began on the fifteenth day of the fourth month, or two days after Stonehouse arrived at Fuyuan. 14.2 Kuan-yin, whose name means "Seer of Sounds," was enlightened when she saw sound, that is, when all of her senses merged into one. Thus, for her, fried bread became steamed buns.

15.1 The Sprout Law, formally introduced by Wang An-shih in the Sung dynasty, was a controversial measure designed to provide farmers with sufficient capital to farm — but at 20 percent interest payable after the harvest. Apparently the temple was distributing its own verson of the government's "largesse," probably with donated sprouts and intended for farmers too poor to pay the government interest. 15.2 The first two lines are from the *Taoteching*: 39. 15.3 Here the *sage* refers to the emperor. 15.4 East Lake was just beyond Fuyuan Temple and the wall that surrounded the town of Pinghu.

14. The Master said, "A month of our three-month retreat[1] is gone / the gardens and groves are dark with shade / the sound of frogs is in the pond / I wonder if you monks understand.

"The true teaching of this place is the perfect clarity we hear in sound. Kuan-yin[2] bought fried bread, but it turned out to be steamed buns instead."

The Master then snapped his whisk and said, "To make dough you can use wheat from other places. But to sing a song you need someone from your own hometown."

15. At the Rice Sprout Assembly,[1] the Master said, "When Heaven becomes one, it's clear. When Earth becomes one, it's still.[2] When the sage[3] becomes one, peace prevails throughout the land. When poor monks become one, they have everything they need."

Grabbing his staff, the Master said, "When this staff becomes one, I don't care what happens. At dusk I stroll along the shore of East Lake[4] and laugh at the rice sprouts all the same green."

復舉溈山開田次。仰山云。這頭得恁麼低。那
頭得恁麼高。溈云。水能平物。但以水平。仰
云。水也無憑。但高處高平。低處低平。溈山
然之。頌云。片段高低總是田。溈山父子見何
偏。福源手不沾泥水。坐看禾收勝去年

解制小參。不觸事而知。金井欄邊絡緯啼。不
對緣而照。明月堂前秋已早。統無邊剎境。為
一微塵。無一塵不是大圓覺海。融十世古今。
作箇念頭。無一念不是自恣時節。便與麼去。
不涉程途。況乃橫擔。拄杖。緊峭草鞋。足跡
四方。鄉關萬里。謂之游江海涉山川。尋師訪
道為參禪。盡是瘋狂外邊走。更饒你跳上三十
三天。一剎那間。遊遍百億須彌盧。百億香水
海。拈拄杖卓一下云。也離不得這裡

16.1 Kuei-shan and his disciple Yang-shan both lived in the ninth century and are the patriarchs of the Yang-Kuei Zen sect. This exchange appears in *Chuantenglu*: 11.

17.1 Because its life is limited to summer, the cricket is said to know nothing of winter. 17.2 *Release*, or *pravarana* in Sanskrit, refers to the last day of retreat. 17.3 The Thirty-third Heaven of Indra is at the top of Mount Sumeru, and Mount Sumeru is surrounded by a perfumed sea.

16. The Master recalled the time Kuei-shan[1] was clearing a field, and Yang-shan said, "How come this part is low and that part is high?" Kuei-shan said, "Water can level anything. Let's let water take care of it." Yang-shan said, "Water is unreliable. All it does is level the high places and level the low places." Kuei-shan nodded in agreement.

The Master said, "High places low places all of them are fields / Kuei-shan and Yang-shan both of them were partial / here at Fuyuan we don't touch the mud / we wait to see if this harvest beats last year's."

17. At an informal talk at the end of retreat, the Master said, "Without knowing what's coming, the cricket[1] sings beside the golden well. Shining for no reason, the moon before the shrine hall announces early autumn. If you can unite limitless worlds into a single speck of dust and let every speck of dust be a great sea of enlightenment, if you can combine ten lifetimes into a single thought and let every thought be the day of release,[2] then leave here like this, without taking roads, much less a staff or bindle or tightly woven shoes, and without leaving your footprints throughout the four quarters a thousand miles from home.

"If you think practicing Zen means traveling across rivers and mountains in search of a teacher or the Tao, you're just running around like lost fools. Even if you jump as high as the Thirty-third Heaven[3] in the blink of an eye or circle Mount Sumeru and its perfumed sea a million times ..."

Grabbing his staff and raising it, the Master said, "You still can't leave here."

解制上堂。今朝七月十五。涼風開我竹戶。嶺上一片兩片白雲。被他吹得七橫八豎。輕飄飄浮遍遍。欲散不散。欲聚不聚。老僧招手向白雲。白雲白雲何不住。到頭終是覓山歸。流落天涯與途路。喝一喝

中秋謝藏主。上堂。天上月正圓。人間月方半。諸人恐未知。打鼓普請看。道是如來藏裡摩尼珠。又似賓頭盧尊者手中琉璃碗。比也不可比。辨也不可辨。天風吹露濕桂華。香浸雲邊廣寒殿

上堂。達磨居少林。九年面壁。牆塹不牢。疏山賣布單。千里見人。路頭繁雜。福源這裡牆塹堅牢。路頭平直。諸人。每日行在正路上

18.1 This woven bamboo screen was hung across the doorway of the meditation hall during summer retreat to ensure privacy while allowing at least some air to enter. 18.2 *Clouds* refers to wandering monks, who traditionally visit other temples in search of instruction following their three-month summer retreat.

19.1 Mid-Autumn Festival is celebrated on the eighth full moon and is second only to New Year in terms of family gatherings. 19.2 The *ts'ang-chu:librarian* was in charge of the sacred texts that were usually kept on the second floor of the shrine hall. 19.3 The second line of the poem refers to the world's more mundane view of the fifteenth day of the month as another month half gone rather than the occasion of another full moon. 19.4 The *magic pearl* is the mind. 19.5 The *Tathagata Treasury* refers to the collection of sutras under the care of the librarian and also to the storehouse of the mind that contains the seeds of all things. 19.6 Beryl, or aquamarine, is chief among the gemstones of paradise. 19.7 Master Pindola is the first of the sixteen (sometimes eighteen) arhats whose statues often line the shrine halls or galleries of Buddhist temples. He is also known as the Old Man of the Mountains. 19.8 The *cassia flowers* are on the moon, where their fragrance confers immortality. 19.9 The monks have ended summer retreat and have gone off on pilgrimage. Hence, Stonehouse finds himself relatively alone during a festival normally marked by family gatherings.

20.1 Bodhidharma spent nine years meditating in a cave on Shaoshih Peak near Shaolin Temple before he finally broke his silence and transmitted his understanding of Zen to Hui-k'o. 20.2 Shu-shan was a ninth-century Zen master and disciple of Tung-shan who spent many years visiting different masters. When someone asked what kind of Zen he taught, Shu-shan said, "One and a half feet of cloth." Asked to explain what this meant, he said, "You can't find it inside a circle" (*Chuantenglu*: 17). 20.3 While Theravada monks refrain from farming out of fear they'll kill insects or worms, Zen monks live by the rule: no work, no food.

18. At the end of retreat, the Master said, "On the fifteenth day of the seventh month / a breeze blows open the bamboo screen[1] / on distant peaks are scattered clouds[2] / moving one way then the other / lightly drifting slowly floating / they try to part but can't / they try to merge but can't / this old monk waves to the clouds / white clouds white clouds why not stop / your search for a mountain home never ends / wandering across Heaven and down every road. Hey!"

19. On Mid-Autumn Festival,[1] after thanking the librarian[2] the Master said, "The moon in the sky is perfectly round / the moon in the world is exactly half[3] / afraid you don't understand / I strike the drum and convene the assembly.

"We call it the magic pearl[4] in the Tathagata Treasury,[5] the beryl bowl[6] in the hands of Master Pindola.[7] Incomparable and indescribable. A heavenly wind scatters dew and drenches the cassia flowers.[8] Their perfume permeates the clouds and fills the desolate shrine hall."[9]

20. The Master said, "When Bodhidharma[1] lived at Shaolin, he faced the rocks for nine years. But the walls and moats were not impregnable. When Shu-shan[2] sold cloth, he traveled thousands of miles to pay someone a visit. But the roads were confusing.

"Here at Fuyuan, the walls and moats are impregnable, and the roads are straight and smooth. Whenever you walk, walk in the middle of the road. Whenever you stop, stop where it's safe. And if you encounter a piece of farm land in between, why shouldn't you set foot on it?"[3]

行。住在穩密處住。中間一片田地。因甚踏不
著

復舉僧問古德。如何是清淨法身。古德云。家
無小使。不成君子。師云。諸禪德。古人與麼
答話。大似認奴作郎。今日忽有人間福源如何
是清淨法身。只對他道。家無二主

臘八上堂。只在山中多少好。無端走入鬧籃
來。眾生福薄難調制。一點明星是禍胎

上堂。我有一句子。欲與諸人說破。又恐諸人
罵我。不與諸人說破。又恐諸人疑我。且如今
説即是。不説即是。撫膝云。知我罪我。我無
辭焉

21.1 The *dharmakaya* (*kaya:body*) is the ultimate undifferentiated body of a buddha. While the *sambhogakaya* is the body a buddha experiences by himself, and the *nirmanakaya* is the body a buddha manifests to others, the *dharmakaya* is beyond the dualistic labels of self and other.

22.1 *Lapa* is a winter festival held on the eighth day of the last lunar month to commemorate Shakyamuni Buddha's Enlightenment. It is marked in Chinese Buddhist temples by the eating of rice porridge containing a variety of dried fruits and nuts. 22.2 According to the account of Shakyamuni's life in the *Lalitavistara Sutra,* his Enlightenment occurred when he beheld Venus on the western horizon.

23.1 This was a favorite expression of the ninth-century monk Yueh-shan, who often used it to elicit a response from his listeners. However, he met his match one day when he said, "I have something to say that I have never told anyone," and Tao-wu stepped forward and said, "Here it comes" (*Chuantenglu:* 14).

21. The Master recalled the time a monk asked an eminent priest, "What is the pure dharma body[1] like." And the priest said, "A home without servants isn't fit for a lord."

The Master said, "My fellow Zen monks, this is the same as saying a slave is a free man. If somebody suddenly asked me what the pure dharma body was like, I would tell him, 'A home doesn't have two owners.'"

22. On Lapa Festival,[1] the Master said, "When I was in the mountains everything was fine / somehow I entered this noisy cage / where virtue and self-control are rare / and a tiny star[2] becomes a seed of trouble."

23. The Master said, "I have something to say.[1] But if I tell you, I'm afraid you will curse me. And if I don't tell you, I'm afraid you won't believe me. Now, should I tell you or not?" The Master brushed off his knees and said, "Who knows me wrongs me. To him I have nothing to say."

解制上堂。九旬同禁足。自恣是今朝。暮雨青
燈寺。西風白石橋。孤身三事衲。萬里一輕
包。若到溈山處。須防笑裡刀

除夜小參。年亦窮月亦窮。三十六旬窮伎倆。
破除全在五更鐘。窮則變破變則通。尋常一樣
窗前月。纔有梅華便不同。三條椽下禪和子。
囊亦空缽亦空。拾得斷麻穿破衲。不知身在寂
寥中。惟有福源拄杖子。不屬陰陽造化功。了
無春夏秋冬。自古自今。撐天拄地。同行同
坐。嘯月吟風。又誰管你。江湖滾滾。日月
匆匆。等閒靠在禪床角。一片雲中掛黑龍

歲朝上堂。鏡清道。新年頭佛法有。明教道。
新年頭佛法無。道是有也未必有。道是無也未

24.1 It was customary at the end of the summer retreat to undertake pilgrimages to sacred sites and to visit other Zen masters. 24.2 Kuei-shan was a disciple of Pai-chang and lived on a mountain of the same name near the western border of Hunan province. The sect that he and his disciple Yang-shan founded in the ninth century was second only to that of Lin-chi in the history of Zen. The verbal and nonverbal exchanges that he and Yang-shan used to demonstrate their understanding of Zen were characterized by their biographers as "swordplay."

25.1 The traditional Chinese week had ten days. 25.2 Three rafters was the equivalent of three feet and was the width of the space allotted to each monk inside the meditation hall for meditation and sleep. 25.3 The *straw* is from worn-out meditation cushions. 25.4 The abbot's staff stands for the Dharma. 25.5 The *black dragon* refers to the rain as well as the new moon, which the Chinese New Year celebrates. The black dragon also repressnts our karma, which keeps us from finding the pearl of wisdom.

26.1 Ching-ch'ing lived in the tenth century, and Ming-chiao was an eminent eleventh-century monk. Once Hsuan-sha asked Ching-ch'ing, "I have heard it said that the bodhisattvas and mahasattvas were wrong not to see a single thing. What was the thing they didn't see?" Ching-ch'ing pointed to the pillar and said, "Is this not the thing they didn't see?" (*Chuantenglu:* 18) 26.2 Chao-chou was a ninth-century monk and a disciple of Nan-ch'uan. Although I am not familiar with Chao-chou's connection with the calabash, to hang a calabash on the eastern wall means to leave with nothing. The phrase comes from Li Pai's poem *To the Former King of Wu* and recalls the story of the impoverished hermit Hsu Yu who was once given a calabash to use for drinking water. He took one drink with it and left it behind, preferring not to be burdened by such a possession.

24. At the conclusion of retreat,[1] the Master said, "For ninety days you have been deprived / your freedom returns this morning / the evening rain in a wayside temple / the west wind at an old stone bridge / a solitary patched-robe monk / a thousand miles with a light armbag / if you reach Kuei-shan's[2] abode / beware of the knife inside his smile."

25. At an informal talk on New Year's Eve, the Master said, "The year is ending / the month is ending / thirty-six weeks[1] are about to end / they're over when the dawn bell rings / but ending means changing and changing means beginning / the moon lights the window the same as before / only the plum blossoms are different / my fellow three-rafter[2] students of Zen / your bags are empty / your bowls are empty / beneath your straw-covered[3] worn-out robes / your unaware bodies reside in solitude / here at Fuyuan only this staff[4] / is free of the workings of yin and yang / of spring and summer and autumn and winter / today as in the past / it holds up the sky and supports the earth / it joins you when you walk or sit / it sings to the moon and wind / but who cares / the Yangtze rolls on / the sun and moon don't slow their pace / and all you do is sit on your beds / while a black dragon[5] lurks in the clouds."

26. On New Year's Day, the Master said, "Ching-ch'ing[1] said, 'At the beginning of the year the Dharma exists.' And Ming-chiao said, 'At the beginning of the year the Dharma doesn't exist.' What we say exists doesn't really exist / what we say doesn't exist doesn't really not exist / when Mister Chang drinks wine Mister Lee gets drunk / Chao-chou[2] hung his calabash on the eastern wall."

必無。張公喫酒李公醉。趙州東壁掛胡蘆

上堂。春風開竹戶。夜雨滴華心。一一與諸
人。發向上機。演第一義。因甚不知。良久云
莫怪山僧太多事。光陰似箭暗相催

元宵謝東班殿主並無念西堂。上堂。進以禮退
以禮。天地與我同根。萬物與我一體。爛生薑
陳皂角。舊笊籬破木杓。東頭賣賤。西頭賣
貴。有利無利。不離行市。夜來無位真人。提
金剛圈。點飛龍馬。走遍四天下。卻與寰中和
尚。在蟭螟眼裡。共賞元宵。天曉起來。依然
即在赤肉團上。卓拄杖一下云。我見燈明佛本
光瑞如此

27.1 The bamboo screen is hung over the doorway to the meditation hall. 27.2 In the Western Paradise of Amida, the flowers preach: "All is suffering, all is empty, all is impermanent, all is selfless."

28.1 Lantern Festival is celebrated on the first full moon, or fifteen days after New Year's Eve. 28.2 The residents of a monastery were divided into two groups, each with its own set of duties and ranks. In general, the eastern ranks were in charge of administration and took care of the shrine halls, while the western ranks were in charge of instruction and took care of the meditation and guest halls. 28.3 The honey locust, or *Gleditsia sinensis,* is a large tree grown for its shade and large brown pods, which are used in Chinese medicine as an expectorant. 28.4 The *true man of no rank* is one's original face, and the *cushion of red flesh* is the body. Lin-chi says, "On your meditation cushion of red flesh is the true man of no rank who goes in and out of your faces" (*The Recorded Words of Lin-chi:* 3). 28.5 The *diamond fist* refers to the full moon.

27. The Master said, "Spring wind lifts the bamboo screen.[1] Night rain moistens the hearts of flowers. One by one they work their peerless magic and reveal to all the supreme truth.[2] Why are you still blind?"

After a long silence, he said, "Don't blame this mountain monk if you have too much to do or if time is like an arrow or if darkness is pressing in."

28. On Lantern Festival,[1] the Master thanked the chief monks of the eastern and western ranks[2] and said, "We proceed according to rules and retire according to rules. We share the same root as Heaven and Earth and the same essence as all other creatures. Overripe ginger, old locust pods,[3] worn-out sieves, and broken ladles: in the east they're priced low, in the west they're priced high. Whether or not there's a profit depends on the market.

"Tonight, the true man of no rank[4] will raise his diamond fist[5] and summon his dragon steed. Racing through the four quarters, he will enjoy the Lantern Festival together with all the monks of the realm inside the eye of a mite. And when the dawn breaks, he will be back on his meditation cushion of red flesh the same as before." Raising his staff, the Master said, "When I see the lantern light, it reminds me of the Buddha's radiance."

佛涅槃上堂。四十九年。賣弄脫空。二月十
五。一場合殺。直饒藏得渾身。未免露出雙
腳。百萬人天。雲散水流。丈六金身。煙消火
滅。迦葉自歸雞足山。魔王嫉妒心方歇。諸仁
者。要見釋迦老子麼。卓拄杖一下云。遍地春
風桃李華。紅者自紅白者白

上堂。知見立知。即無明本。知見無見。斯即
涅槃。春山疊亂青。春水漾虛碧。寥寥天地
間。獨立望何極。拈拄杖云。放過釋迦老子。
卓拄杖云。穿卻雪竇鼻孔。良久云。劍為不平
離寶匣。藥因救病出金瓶

浴佛上堂。舉世尊初生下。一手指天。一手指
地。周行七步。目顧四方。乃言。天上天下。

29.1 Following his Enlightenment at the age of thirty-five, Shakyamuni preached for forty-nine years, until his Nirvana at the age of eighty-five. I have amended the text, which has seventy-nine years instead of forty-nine. 29.2 The Buddha's funeral pyre refused to ignite until Kashyapa, the first patriarch of the Zen lineage in India, arrived from the capital of Rajghir. Following the division of relics and the recording of the Buddha's sermons, Kashyapa then traveled to southwest China, where he disappeared into a rock cliff near the summit of Chitzushan, or Chickenfoot Mountain. 29.3 Mara, king of the realm of desire, tried in vain to distract Shakyamuni from his quest for Enlightenment.

30.1 These remarks were apparently made soon after the preceding talk on the anniversary of the Buddha's Nirvana. 30.2 Hsueh-tou was an eleventh-century monk and the author of the one hundred verses that form the basis of the koan collection known as the *Blue Cliff Record*. Zen masters often liken the mind to an ox, whose nose the student must pierce in order to control the unruly beast with the rope of discipline.

31.1 Small statues of the infant Shakyamuni pointing to the sky and earth are bathed in Buddhist temples on his birthday, which falls on the eighth day of the fourth lunar month. 31.2 The fragrant blooms of the loquat, *Eriobotrya japonica,* appear on the hillsides of South China in November and its fruit in June. Here, however, we have flower and fruit appearing simultaneously, mimicking the infant Shakyamuni's behavior.

29. Celebrating the Buddha's Nirvana, the Master said, "For forty-nine years,[1] he sold everyone on liberation and emptiness. Then, on the fifteenth day of the second month, the monks gathered around. Even though they managed to cover up his body, they couldn't keep his feet from sticking out. Before a million gods and men, before billowing clouds and flowing streams, his six-foot golden body was consumed by smoke and flames. But only after Kashyapa[2] retired to Chickenfoot Mountain was Mara's[3] jealous heart finally quenched.

"Good monks, if you want to see Old Shakyamuni . . ." Lifting up his staff, the Master said, "The spring wind covers the land with the petals of peach and plum flowers. The pink ones are pink. The white ones are white."

30. The Master said, "Knowledge that contains knowledge is the root of delusion. Knowledge that contains no knowledge is nirvana.[1] Spring mountains are mounds of green / spring lakes are ripples of blue / how vast are Heaven and Earth / standing alone which way do you face?"

Grabbing his staff, the Master said, "Let old Shakyamuni go." Lifting up his staff, he said, "Pierce the nose of Master Hsueh-tou."[2]

Finally, after a long silence he said, "The sword is removed from its jeweled scabbard because of injustice. The pill is taken out of its golden bottle to cure illness."

31. While bathing[1] the Buddha, the Master recalled when the World-Honored One was born, he pointed to the ground with one hand and to the sky with the other, walked in a circle for seven steps, looked in the four directions and said, "In Heaven above and on Earth below, I alone deserve praise."

The Master said, "Pointing to the earth and sky he babbled / if no one was there such boasts were vain / adding bravado on top of bravado / a grove of perfumed dew-drenched loquats."[2]

唯我獨尊。頌云。指天指地日吧吧。傍若無人
自説誇。有意氣時添意氣。滿園香霧濕枇杷

結制小參。明朝結制。今夜小參。福源不是琅
琊。點出五般病。西院商量兩箇錯。一夏九十
日。諸人不得妄動一步。一日十二時。諸人不
得妄起一念。不起一念。而即證無生。不動一
步。而遍遊沙界。如斯履踐。無一日不是安
居。自能笑傲林泉。誰管坐消歲月。纔與麼便
不與麼。不見雲門和尚道。直得盡乾坤大地。
無纖毫過患。始是轉句。不見一法。猶是半提
更須知有向上全提時節。卓拄杖一下云。我愛
夏日長。人皆苦炎熱

32.1 *Langya* was the name of the mountain south of Chienyang where Stonehouse studied with Chi-
an. It was also the name of the temple on Langyashan's West Peak. 32.2 Yun-men was a disciple of
Hsueh-feng and one of the great Zen masters of the tenth century. His biography and recorded talks
appear in the *Chuantenglu:* 19, and a number of his koans are recorded in the *Blue Cliff Record*.

32. The Master said, "Tomorrow we begin summer retreat, and tonight we are holding an informal talk. Fuyuan isn't Langya.[1] Pointing out the faults of others or talking in the meditation hall are both infractions. During the ninety days of summer none of you will be allowed to make a single false move. And during the twelve periods of the day, none of you will be allowed to think a single false thought. But by not thinking a single thought, you will become aware of the uncreated. And by not making a single move, you will travel through countless worlds. If you continue to practice like this, every day will be a retreat. And if you are able to enjoy yourselves among forests and streams, why should anyone care if you sit away your months and years? What difference does it make?

"Do you recall when Yun-men[2] said, 'Can you travel through the whole world and all of creation and not find the slightest thing wrong?' If you don't see anything in his words, you're only halfway there. You still need to know what it's like when you're all the way there."

Lifting up his staff, the Master said, "I love summer days because they're long. Everyone else complains about the heat."

結制上堂。諸人未結制已前。天台南嶽。峨眉五臺。要去便去。要來便來。因甚結制已後。頂笠腰包。草鞋拄杖。總用不著。咄。莫道布袋頭不在山僧手裡好

上堂。十五日已前。夜短睡不足。十五日已後。日長饑有餘。正當十五日。飯白如雪。扇團似月。打扇喫飯。猶嫌道熱。釋迦老子道。知足之人。雖臥地上。猶為安樂。不知足者。雖處天堂。亦不稱意。又道。假使百千劫。所作業不忘。因緣會遇時。果報還自受。灼然灼然。善惡若無報。乾坤必有私

復舉東印土國王。請般若多羅齋次。乃謂祖日。諸僧皆轉經。惟師為甚不轉經。祖日。出

33.1 All of these mountains are centers of religious pilgrimage.

34.1 The fifteenth day of the fourth month, or the beginning of summer retreat, is meant.

33. At the beginning of summer retreat, the Master said, "Before we begin retreat, if any of you want to go to Tientai or Nanyueh or Omei or Wutai,[I] then go. If you want to stay, then stay. Once retreat begins, you won't need your hat or your bag or your sandals or your staff. In fact, everything you own will be in the hands of this mountain monk!"

34. The Master said, "Before the fifteenth day of the month,[I] the nights are short, and you don't get enough sleep. After the fifteenth, the days are long, and you don't get enough to eat. But today is exactly the fifteenth, and the rice is as white as snow, and the fans are as round as the moon. Wave your fans and eat your rice and avoid talking about the heat.

"Old Shakyamuni said that people who know contentment can live in the dirt and still be happy, while people who don't know contentment can live in paradise and still complain. He also said that even after a hundred thousand kalpas the karma we create doesn't disappear. When conditions come together, we suffer the fires of retribution. If good and evil had no reward, yin and yang would pursue their own interests."

息不涉眾緣。入息不居陰界。常轉如是經。百
千萬億卷。豈止一卷兩卷。師云。諸禪德。般
若多羅。與麼答話。醫得眼前瘡。剜卻心頭
肉。若有人問福源。諸僧皆轉經。長老因甚不
轉經。只對他道。白日窗前。青宵月下。要轉
便轉。要罷便罷。且道。與般若多羅。還有優
劣也無。若檢點得出。許你具一隻眼

及菴和尚忌日拈香。有來由沒巴鼻。建陽山西
峰寺。蒲團頭拾得底。無眼無耳。無頭無尾。
道是一塊兜樓。嗅著又無香氣。家醜不可外
揚。明人不作暗事

上堂。黃梅俾老盧踏碓。石頭譏藥山不為。有
一丈蓬。可以使八面風。無三尺鞭。難以控千

35.1 During the fifth century, the Pallavas controlled southeast India from their capital at Kanchipurum. 35.2 Prajnatara was Bodhidharma's teacher. 35.3 Stonehouse is referring to the middle, or dharma, eye, which perceives the true nature of things.

36.1 *Chienyangshan* is the name of the mountain where Stonehouse first studied Zen with Chi-an. 36.2 Frankincense, sandalwood, and aloe were among the major trade goods imported to China from India via the Silk Road. 36.3 *Family matters* refers to the transmission of understanding that takes place in a Zen lineage.

37.1 *Huang-mei* was the name of the Fifth Zen Patriarch. 37.2 *Lu* was the family name of the Sixth Patriarch, who hulled rice at the monastery where Huang-mei served as abbot. For more on their relationship, see *The Sutra of the Sixth Patriarch: 1*. 37.3 Shih-t'ou was the First Patriarch of the Shihtou (Japanese: Soto) Zen sect. 37.4 Yueh-shan was the sect's Second Patriarch, who revealed his understanding of Zen by "doing nothing at all," for which see *Chuantenglu: 14*. 37.5 The six-foot briarwood staff is one of an abbot's symbols of authority, the other being his whisk. 37.6 Eravana trees are known for their noxious blooms. 37.7 The philodendron is also known as the cork tree.

35. The Master recalled the time the Pallava[1] king of Eastern India invited Prajnatara[2] to a feast and asked, "All the other monks read sutras. Why doesn't the Master read them?" Prajnatara replied, "When I exhale, I don't become involved in the external world. When I inhale, I don't dwell in the inner realm. This is the kind of sutra I read. It's millions of volumes long. Why should I settle for a few books?"

The Master said, "My Zen brethren, Prajnatara's answer can cure ailments of the eyes and eliminate wounds of the heart. If someone asked me why all the other monks read sutras and this abbot doesn't, I would tell him: 'When sunlight streams in through the window or the moon shines high in the sky, if I feel like reading, I read. If I feel like resting, I rest.' Tell me, is this better than Prajnatara's answer or not? To find out, you'll need at least one eye."[3]

36. Commemorating the death of Chi-an, the Master held up a stick of incense and said, "It has a beginning but nothing to grab / at West Peak Temple on Mount Chienyang[1] / I found it on my zazen mat / it has no eyes or ears / it has no head or tail / I call it a stick of frankincense[2] / smell it but it has no smell / family matters[3] shouldn't be broadcast / those who know shouldn't act dumb."

37. The Master said, "Huang-mei[1] chided Old Lu[2] for hulling rice. Shih-t'ou[3] laughed at Yueh-shan[4] because he didn't. A six-foot briarwood staff[5] can direct the winds of the eight directions. Without a three-foot whip, you can't control a thousand-mile horse. Sandalwood doesn't grow in an eravana grove.[6] What sort of fruit do you find on a philodendron tree?"[7]

里馬。伊蘭園裡。不生栴檀。黃蘗樹頭。有甚
蜜果

上堂。動若行雲。止猶谷神。水中鹹味。色裡
膠青。細雨濕衣看不見。閒華落地聽無聲

上堂。神光不昧。萬古徽猷。但從已覓。莫向
外求。養雞意在五更頭

上堂。所聞不可聞。所見不可見。昨夜五更
風。吹落桃華片。蒼苔面上生紅霞。百鳥不來
春爛熳

上堂。我本山林拙比丘。等閒來此伴禪流。縱
饒相聚人情好。那箇人情得到頭。休休休。綠

39.1 The monastic day begins an hour or so before dawn.

40.1 Birds are embarrassed by the glory of spring.

41.1 Apparently the end of summer retreat is at hand, and the temple's monks are preparing to go off on their separate pilgrimages.

38. The Master said, "It's as fleeting as a cloud / it's as still as a valley / it's the salt in water / it's the dye in color / it's the mist that soaks your clothes unseen / it's the flower that falls to earth unheard."

39. The Master said, "The spiritual light that never fades / noble deeds that shine forever / seek them in yourself / don't search for them outside / the reason for raising chickens has to do with the dawn." [1]

40. The Master said, "What I hear can't be heard / what I see can't be seen / last night the wind before dawn / scattered petals everywhere / turning green moss into a peach pink sky / birds don't come when spring is in its glory." [1]

41. The Master said, "I'm just a stupid mountain priest / merely here to be with you monks / despite our desire to be together / what desire was ever satisfied / enough is enough is enough / green mist and red clouds a tapestry of peaks / west wind and yellow leaves a sky full of autumn." [1]

霧紅霞千嶂錦。西風黃葉一天秋

上堂。月出海門東。金波浩渺渺。圓又圓不
虧。明又明得好。寄語白兔翁。說與嫦娥道。
收彩不宜遲。潛光須及早。莫待黑雲四面來。
一天光彩都無了。世間惟有道人心。歷劫至今
常皎皎

謝藏主上堂。今朝八月十五。樹凋葉落金風
露。野狐窟宅梵王宮。狗子尾巴書卍字。大藏
小藏從何來。拈拄杖云。盡從這裡流將去。等
閒道箇鉢囉娘。截斷古今聞露布

上堂。一日一日復一日。二三四五八九十。數
到紅殘綠暗時。人間又是四月一。朝悠悠暮悠

42.1 One day Ch'ang-o drank an elixir given to her husband by the Queen Mother of the West. Unprepared for its effects, she floated up to the moon. And she has been there ever since, kept alive by the white hare that also lives on the moon and that provides her with more elixir.

43.1 The full moon of the eighth month is celebrated as the harvest festival in China. 43.2 There once was a wild fox that memorized the sutras it heard a monk chanting and convinced all the animals in the forest to proclaim it their king. The fox then proceeded to the palace of Brahma to find a suitable wife but was stopped in its tracks when it heard a lion roar. 43.3 Brahma is the lord of creation. 43.4 *Dogs* refers to those who memorize the sutras without having any idea what they mean. 43.5 The *sauvastika* 卍 is an ancient Indian symbol for the infinite as it appears to us from This Shore, while its reverse, the *svastika* 卐, represents the vision of the infinite from the Other Shore. 43.6 The Buddhist Canon, or Tripitika, included 1440 titles in Stonehouse's day. 43.7 Prajapati was Shakyamuni's nurse and the first nun admitted into the Buddhist Order. After agreeing to her admission, Shakyamuni said the flourishing of the Dharma would henceforth be reduced by five hundred years. Thus, Stonehouse attributes to her the shorter form of the Canon, which he, however, welcomes.

44.1 The middle of the fourth month is when the three-month summer retreat begins. 44.2 Vairochana is the Sun Buddha and represents the *dharmakaya,* or essential body of the Buddha. 44.3 The *bubble* refers to our transient, corporeal selves.

42. The Master said, "The moon rises east through the ocean's door / gold waves light the horizon / rounder than round it's perfectly full / brighter than bright it's lovely / here's a message to the old white hare / tell Ch'ang-o[1] for me / don't delay hiding your splendor / conceal your light while there's time / don't wait until dark clouds gather / and the whole sky loses its glory / only a monk's mind here in this world / since time began still shines."

43. Thanking the chief librarian, the Master said, "Today is the eighth month the fifteenth day[1] / barren trees falling leaves autumn wind and dew / foxes[2] are living inside Brahma's[3] palace / dogs[4] are writing sauvastikas[5] with their tails / where are the Great and Small Canons[6] from?"

Grabbing his staff, the Master continued, "They all come flowing out of here / it's simply that old Prajapati[7] / cut out the useless pronouncements of the past."

44. The Master said, "One day another day and still one more / two three four five eight nine ten / count until red fades and green grows dark / the first day of the fourth month[1] is back again / we think all day and think all night / and filling our eyes is Vairochana's[2] Sea / which we exchange for a bubble[3] / enough is enough / to cultivate the mind without the ground of no-mind / is to follow a hundred thousand streams."

悠。滿目毗盧藏海。棄之認一浮漚。休休。修
心未到無心地。萬種千般逐水流

上堂。喫飯要止饑。飲水要止渴。著衣要免
寒。歸鄉要到家。學道要到三世諸佛開口不得
處。參禪要到天下祖師插腳不入處。若不如
此。倚他門戶。傍他牆壁。聽人指揮。喫人啼
唾。總不丈夫。福源與麼說話。良藥苦口。忠
言逆耳

空巖印首座至。上堂。陸州唆臨濟。問黃蘗佛
法大意。三度六十拄杖。口乃招禍之門。還有
免得此過者麼。良久云。空生巖下坐。天雨四
華來

46.1 *Mudras* are hand gestures that summarize the oral teachings of various Hindu and Buddhist sects. 46.2 Mu-chou was the head monk at Huang-po's congregation and encouraged Lin-chi to ask Huang-po for instruction in the Dharma. Three times Lin-chi asked Huang-po, and three times Huang-po struck him with his staff. Lin-chi eventually founded his own congregation and a Zen lineage that still exists in both China and Japan. This story is reported in *Chuantenglu*: 11. 46.3 The text reads *sixty*, which I have read as an error for "six-foot." 46.4 Lin-chi used gestures as words and words as gestures and didn't let himself be bound by either in instructing others in Zen. 46.5 Celestial flowers are bestowed on bodhisattvas by various heavenly beings. But, as Vimilakirti makes clear, their recipient must be careful not to let them cling to his body lest another round of attachment result.

45. The Master said, "You eat to satisfy your hunger and drink to quench your thirst. You wear clothes to keep warm and go home to be with your families. You cultivate the Tao to reach the place even the buddhas can't describe. And you practice Zen to find the place even the patriarchs can't enter. But if you rely on the doors and walls of others and you listen to their instruction and accept their drivel, you'll never stand on your own. I put it like this: Good medicine tastes bitter. True words sound harsh."

46. On the arrival of Mudra[1] Master K'ung-yen, the Master said, "Mu-chou[2] provoked Lin-chi into asking Huang-po the meaning of the Dharma. And Huang-po struck Lin-chi three times with his six-foot[3] staff. The mouth[4] is a door that invites trouble. Is there anyone who can avoid this mistake?" After a long silence, the Master said, "On the venerable K'ung-yen, Heaven rains down celestial flowers."[5]

上堂。六月七月天不雨。農夫曉夜忙車水。背
皮焦裂腳底疼。眼華無力欲悶死。公人又遍
夏稅。稅絲納了要盤費。大麥小麥盡量還。一
日三餐不周備。思量我輩出家兒。現成受用都
不知。進道身心無一點。東邊浪蕩西邊嬉。三
箇五箇聚頭坐。開口便說他人過。及乎歸到暗
室中。背理虧心無不做。莫言墮在異類中。來
生定作栽田翁。前來所說苦如此。那時難與今
時同。古德訓徒有一語。對人天眾拈來舉。緇
田無一簣之功。鐵圍陷百刑之苦

上堂。佛法無人說。雖慧莫能了。開口便不
是。我宗無語句。亦無一法與人。不開口也不
是。五馬不嘶。一牛飲水。開口不開口總不
是。仁者見之謂之仁。智者見之謂之智

47.1 During the Yuan dynasty, taxes were collected in the summer as well as in the fall. Summer taxes were usually paid in money or cloth, while fall taxes were almost always paid in grain.

48.1 The *five horses* refers to the five senses and the ox to the sixth sense, namely the mind.

47. The Master said, "Two months now the sky hasn't rained / farmers haul water from dawn to dusk / their backs are burned their feet are sore / they're dizzy and exhausted and depressed / now officials come demanding summer taxes[1] / they want silk and travel money too / barley and wheat they take it all / there isn't enough left for daily meals / then there are those like you without a home / strangers to what lies before you / making no progress on the Way / indulging yourselves in the east and the west / sitting in groups of four or five / opening your mouths to criticize / then retiring to unlit rooms / unfaithful ungrateful there's nothing you won't do / don't think you're destined for a better state / next life you'll all be planting fields / suffering the suffering I've described / then is never better than today / the ancient worthies and teachers had a saying / they quoted before men and gods / who does no work in a monastery field / suffers endless tortures in an iron hell."

48. The Master said, "The Dharma isn't spoken. Nor can wisdom comprehend it. Speaking isn't it. This sect of ours doesn't have any words, nor does it have a teaching to give to others. Not speaking isn't it either. When the five horses[1] don't neigh, the ox drinks water. Neither speaking nor not speaking are it. The kind who see it call it kindness. The wise who see it call it wisdom."

上堂。百丈教人開田。通身泥水。佛眼俾僧修
造。滿地木楂。楊岐遍慈明晚參。成人不自
在。趙州教嚴陽放下。自在不成人。福源與麼
道。也是為他閒事長無明

上堂。是聖是凡。入門便見波斯鼻孔。開眼便
見蚌蛤心肝。開口便見諸人兩莖眉毛橫在面
上。因甚看他不見。明眼人前三尺暗

病起上堂。舉苕溪和尚示眾云。吾有大病。非
世所醫。後有僧問曹山。未審。是甚麼病。山
云。攢簇不得底病。又問。一切眾生。還有此
病也無。山云。老僧正覺起處不得。師云。這
僧是病過的人。極是搜尋。得到頭髮尖裡。也
不放過。若非曹山。知他落處。其他難為啟

49.1 Pai-chang established the basic rules for Zen monasteries, which he summarized as "no work, no food." 49.2 The buddha-eye is the eye of enlightenment, and *moksha* is Sanskrit for "liberation." 49.3 Tz'u-ming had to meet with Yang-ch'i repeatedly late at night to help him understand Zen. Thus Tz'u-ming was not free. 49.4 And Chao-chou had to make an effort to teach Yen-yang to let go. Thus Chao-chou did not succeed in letting go.

50.1 The nostrils, the clam, and the eyebrows all obstruct the light, and hence represent the delusion of duality.

51.1 Although I have not found any information on him, I assume T'iao-hsi was an eighth or ninth-century monk. 51.2 Ts'ao-shan Pen-chi was a ninth-century Zen master and disciple of Tung-shan Liang-chieh. 51.3 The Chinese prepare herbal decoctions inside an earthenware pot they use exclusively for the purpose and that they heat on the same small portable stove they use to boil water for tea. Stonehouse's point is that medicine can't cure the disease he's talking about, which is also the subject of the *Vimilakirti Sutra*.

49. The Master said, "Pai-chang[1] told people to weed fields and get dirty. Thus the buddha-eye[2] enables monks to work and still cover the ground with *moksha*. Yang-ch'i[3] made Tz'u-ming stay up late. Thus a perfect person isn't free. Chao-chou[4] told Yen-yang to let go. Thus a free person isn't perfect. I put it like this: If you didn't meddle in other people's affairs, you wouldn't still be in the dark."

50. The Master said, "Are you sages or fools? Entering the door, I see a Persian's nostrils. Opening my eyes, I see a clam's insides. Opening my mouth, I see everyone's eyebrows hanging across their faces. Why don't you see them? In front of clear-eyed people is three feet of darkness."[1]

51. When he was ill, the Master recalled the time T'iao-hsi[1] told the assembly, "I have a terrible sickness which no one in the world can cure." Later, a monk asked Ts'ao-shan,[2] "What kind of sickness did T'iao-hsi have?" Ts'ao-shan said, "The sickness of dissolution." The monk asked, "Do all beings suffer this sickness?" Ts'ao-shan said, "This old monk hasn't been able to find out where it begins."

The Master said, "I'm sick, too. And no matter where I look, I see that it doesn't spare even the tip of a hair. If Ts'ao-shan didn't know where it begins, how can others? I've composed another gatha to explain this to the assembly: Our bones suffer then they dissolve / first they're hot then they're cold / we look in vain for where it begins / knock over the stove and the medicine pot."[3]

口。復成一偈。舉似大眾。百骨酸疼攢簇難。
一番熱了一番寒。覓他起處竟不得。藥銚風爐
盡打翻

冬節小參。洞山掇退果卓。取捨未忘。玉泉不
洗布襌。固執難斷。福源寺是箇般時節。就中
卻不同。梅放孤標。依舊暗香浮動。線添寒
影。又逢佳景迎春。燈籠裡帽。水底吹笙。露
柱著衫。雲中作舞。是汝諸人還委悉麼。一百
五日是清明。清明更在寒食後

復舉僧問古德。如何是冬來意。德云。京師出
大黃。頌云。有問冬來意。京師出大黃。地爐
深夜火。茶熟透瓶香

52.1 Stonehouse is apparently referring not to the ninth-century Zen master Tung-shan Liang-chieh,
but to Tung-shan Shou-ch'u, a tenth-century Zen master famous for his spontaneous responses to all
manner of questions. 52.2 The *line* refers to the addition of an unbroken yang line to the five broken
yin lines that represent the end of winter. This is what appears in the hexagram *Fu: Return*. 51.3 I am
unfamiliar with the references in this and the next three lines and can see why Stonehouse asked his
audience if they understood or not. 51.4 Cold Food Day occurs at the beginning of the third lunar
month, one hundred and five days after the winter solstice. The day after Cold Food Day is the day
when people clear the weeds from their family tombs and pay their respects to their ancestors.

53.1 *Rheum officinale,* or medicinal rhubarb, puts forth new leaves during the first week of the new
year. 53.2 Drinking tea at night suggests late night meditation.

52. At an informal talk on winter solstice, the Master said, "Tung-shan[1] succeeded in withdrawing, but he never stopped responding. Even a jade spring can't wash pants clean. Stubborn habits are hard to break. Today at Fuyuan Temple everything is different. When the plum unveils its lone flag, a familiar fragrance drifts unseen. And winter shadows finally add a line.[2] Once again we have fine weather for spring. The lanterns are covered.[3] There's a flute below the water. The pillars wear robes. And the clouds dance. Are you monks clear about all this? In another one hundred and five days comes Grave Sweeping Day. Grave Sweeping Day follows Cold Food Day."[4]

53. The Master recalled the time someone asked an old monk, "Why does winter come?" And the old monk said, "So rheum[1] can appear in the capital."

The Master said, "Someone asked why winter comes / so rheum can appear at court / late at night a stove is lit / when the tea[2] is done the pot smells sweet."

謝都寺冬齋並維那。上堂。一遍一切。一切
遍一一。香積世界。以香飯為佛事。南閻浮
提。以音聲為佛事。東勝神州打槌。西瞿耶尼
普請。懷州牛喫禾。益州馬腹脹。粗餐易飽。
細嚼難饑。只恐不是玉。是玉也大奇。

及菴和尚忌日拈香云。沒興相逢處。西峰與建
陽。不平多少事。盡在一爐香

歲旦上堂。鐘樓上念讚。床腳下種菜。勝首座
道。猛虎當路坐。福源這裡。山門頭賀正歌
唱。佛殿裡祝聖諱經一種是聲無限意。有堪聽
有不堪聽。諸人還曾檢點得出麼。喝一喝。下
座

54.1 The *tu-chien:provost* was in charge of overseeing a temple's business affairs. 54.2 Ghandharva is a legendary land north of India where the inhabitants communicate by means of smell, while Jambudvipa is the continent south of Mount Sumeru inhabited by mankind. Purvavideha is the continent east of Mount Sumeru, and Aparagodaniya is the continent to the west. 54.3 During the Yuan dynasty, *Yichou* was the name for Chengtu, the capital of Szechuan province, and Huaichou was the adjacent prefecture to the northeast. If there's a story here, and I assume there is, I don't know what it might be. 54.4 *Jade* is a euphemism for fine food, although Taoists actually included it in their elixirs.

55.1 Stonehouse was enlightened while staying with Chi-an at Chienyangshan's West Peak Temple.

56.1 The bell tower is usually to the right of a temple's main gate, while the drum tower is to the left. 56.2 The *shang-tso:rector* is in charge of a temple's daily affairs. 56.3 The Chinese add another year to their ages on New Year's Day rather than on their birthdays. Hence the wishes for the emperor's continued longevity.

54. After thanking the provost[1] and the meditation master at the winter solstice banquet, the Master said, "Each and every thing includes all things. All things include each and every thing. In Gandharva,[2] they use fragrant rice to transmit the Dharma. In Jambudvipa, we use our voices. In Purvavideha, they beat hammers. And in Aparagodaniya, it's communal work. When a water buffalo eats rice sprouts in Huaichou,[3] a horse's stomach swells in Yichou. Simple food fills you up faster. Chewing longer keeps away hunger. Perhaps this isn't made of jade.[4] But if it was, it would be a great surprise."

55. On the day commemorating the death of Chi-an,[1] the Master held up some incense and said, "The incomparable place we met / West Peak and Mount Chien-yang / all the unsettled events / are in this incense burner."

56. On New Year's Day, the Master said, "Sing praises from the bell tower.[1] Plant vegetable seeds under your bed. Rector[2] Sheng says there's a ferocious tiger sitting in the road. Here at Fuyuan, the gatekeeper greets the year with song. And inside the shrine hall, the sounds of 'Long live the Emperor'[3] and the chanting of sutras never seems to stop. Some hear. Some don't. Can you tell them apart? Hey!"

佛涅槃上堂。身口意清淨。是名佛出世。身口
意不淨。是名佛涅槃。人情不能恰好。世界難
得團欒。晝長夜短。秋熱冬寒。一把柳絲收不
得。和煙搭在玉蘭干

聖節上堂。蟠桃三千年華開。聖人五百歲出
現。拈拄杖云。蟠桃華開也。卓拄杖云。聖人

元宵上堂。南閻浮提。以音聲為佛事。十方俱
擊鼓。十處一時聞。福源寺裡上堂。西林寺裡
一一聽得。西林寺裡念佛。福源寺裡一一聽
得。讚嘆也獲一分功德。毀謗也獲一分功德。
一即一切。一切即一。鸚湖市上做元宵。因
甚東家點燈。西家暗坐。你也理會不得。我也
理會不得。冷水浸冬瓜。大家相瀉漓

57.1 Lantern Festival is celebrated on the first full moon of the year. 57.2 In Buddhist geography, Jambudvipa is equivalent to Asia. 57.3 Fuyuan Temple was just outside Pinghu's South Gate, and Hsilin Temple was just outside its West Gate. 57.4 No doubt the name of Amida Buddha, the buddha of the Western Paradise, is meant. 57.5 *Parrot Lake* is another name for East Lake, whose shore wraps around the east and south gates of Pinghu. 57.6 "One is all, and all is one" is from Seng-ts'an's *Believing in Mind*. 57.7 Winter melons, or *Benincasa cerifera,* grow as large as three or four watermelons combined and are kept fresh by immersion in cold water.

58.1 The Buddha's Nirvana is normally celebrated on the fifteenth, or full moon, of the second month. 58.2 The body, the mouth, and the mind are the three sources of karma. 58.3 The *perfect circle* refers to the full moon. 58.4 In the last line, Stonehouse pokes fun at excessive and impossible desires.

59.1 Toghon Timur ascended the throne in 1333 at the age of thirteen as Emperor Shun-ti and was the last emperor of the Yuan dynasty. He died in 1370 in the Steppes after being driven from the dynasty's capital in 1368 by the founders of the succeeding Ming dynasty. 59.2 The peach tree of immortality grows in the garden of the Queen Mother of the West and blooms every three thousand years. 59.3 The expectation of the birth of a sage every five hundred years goes back to Mencius, who noted that the lapse of time between China's earliest sages, namely Yao, Shun, T'ang, Wen, and Confucius, was more or less five hundred years (*Mencius: 7B.38*).

57. On Lantern Festival,[1] the Master said, "In Jambudvipa,[2] we use the voice to transmit the Dharma. When drums sound throughout the ten directions, everyone in the ten realms hears the sound at the same time. When we conduct services here at Fuyuan, everyone at Hsilin Temple[3] hears us. When they chant the name of the Buddha[4] at Hsilin, all of us here at Fuyuan hear them. Those who praise others receive a certain amount of merit. Those who slander others receive the same amount of merit. One is all, and all is one.[5]

"When we celebrate the Lantern Festival here in the city of Parrot Lake,[6] why do those to the east light their lanterns, while those to the west sit in darkness? You don't understand, and I don't understand. When you drop a winter melon in a tub of cold water,[7] everyone gets soaked."

58. On the Buddha's Nirvana,[1] the Master said, "When a person's body, mouth, and mind[2] become pure, we say a buddha appears in the world. When his body, mouth, and mind become impure, we say a buddha enters nirvana. Human desires can't be satisfied. It's hard to find a perfect circle[3] in the world. The days are long, and the nights are short. The falls are hot, and the winters are cold. And I can't reach the willow catkins hanging in the mist at my jade balcony."[4]

59. On the emperor's[1] birthday, the Master said, "The peach tree of immortality blooms every three thousand years.[2] A sage appears every five hundred years."[3] Grabbing his staff, he said, "The peach tree of immortality is in bloom." Lifting his staff, he said, "The sage has appeared." Leaning on his staff, he said, "Peace prevails throughout the realm."

出現也。靠拄杖云。天下太平

結制上堂。福源今日結制。不得不為諸人議定。第一。從朝至暮。舉足下足。不得踏著常住地。若踏著常住地。定犯著波羅夷罪。第二。十二時中。不得向鼻孔裡出氣。若向鼻孔裡出氣。定犯著波羅夷罪。第三。件事且莫說且莫說。留在七月十五日也未遲。甕裡何曾走卻鱉

上堂。日日日東出。日日日西沒。出沒知幾廻。又是五月一。咄哉門外人。把手牽不入。拽杖獨歸來。門開空嘆息

60.1 The *Parajika* comprises the first section of the *Vinaya,* or rules of the Buddhist Order, and lists the offenses that demand expulsion. 60.2 The three-month summer retreat ends on the seventh full moon.

170

60. At the beginning of retreat, the Master said, "Today at Fuyuan we begin retreat, and I have to go over the rules with you. First, from dawn to dusk, whenever you lift your feet or put your feet down, you may not step on permanent ground. Anyone who steps on permanent ground is guilty of a Parajika[1] offense. Second, during the twelve periods of the day, you may not exhale through your nose. Anyone who exhales through his nose is guilty of a Parajika offense. Third, you may not talk about anything, anything at all. It won't be long before the fifteenth day of the seventh month[2] arrives. Have you ever seen turtles crawling inside a pot?"

61. The Master said, "Every day in the east the sun rises / every day in the west the sun sets / how many times does it rise and set / the fifth month is here again/ alas for those outside the gate / they can't be pulled inside / I come back alone dragging my staff / the gate is open and my sighs are in vain."

示眾。古德道。結夏半月日了也。水牯牛作麼
生。有者道。結夏半月日了也。寒山子作麼
生。福源道。結夏半月日了也。已躬下事作麼
生。莫是早晨起來洗面。洗面了喫粥。喫粥了
喫飯。喫飯了放參。放參了打眠。是已躬下事
麼。莫是東廊上西廊下。寮舍裡山門頭。鼓扇
是非。是已躬下事麼。莫是看諸子百家。長篇
短章。高談闊論。傍若無人。是已躬下事麼。
莫是經卷上博量。語錄上卜度。未得謂得。未
證謂證。是已躬下事麼。莫是禮幾拜佛。看幾
卷經。燒幾箇指頭。燃幾炷頂香。誑惑世人。
希求利養。是已躬下事麼。莫是長連床上。閉
眉合眼。昏昏沉沉。懵懵懂懂。空過時節。是
已躬下事麼。如此反不及三家村裡拖鋤頭漢。
栽田種地。養口資身。卻無罪過。我輩沙門釋

62.1 Han-shan, or Cold Mountain, was a Buddhist poet-recluse of the late eighth century. 62.2 As a sign of devotion some Buddhists tie strings around one or more fingers to cut off the circulation. Eventually, the finger dries up and is burnt as an offering to the Buddha. One of the most famous Buddhist poets of the Ch'ing dynasty was a monk who used the pen name *Eight Fingers*. 62.3 During Buddhist ceremonies of initiation, monks and nuns often burn cones of incense – one for the Dharma, one for the Buddha, and one for the Order – on top of their shaved heads. Lay members do the same on their forearms. 62.4 A communal sleeping platform is used in the meditation hall and also in the visiting monks' hall.

62. Before the assembly, the Master said, "An ancient worthy once asked, 'At the beginning of summer retreat, when the moon is full, and the sun goes down, what does the water buffalo do?' And someone else asked, 'At the beginning of summer retreat, when the moon is full, and the sun goes down, what does Han-shan[1] do? Well, I ask, 'At the beginning of summer retreat, when the moon is full, and the sun goes down, what do you do?'

"Do you get up in the morning and wash your face; and after you wash your face, you eat porridge; and after you eat porridge, you eat rice; and after you eat rice, you meditate; and after you meditate, you sleep? Is this what you do?

"Do you stir up talk about right and wrong in the east and west wings, in your rooms, and at the front gate? Is this what you do?

"Do you read all the works of the ancient sages and philosophers and rant and rave about them as if no one else existed? Is this what you do?

"Do you analyze sutras and Zen talks and say you understand when you don't and say you see when you don't? Is this what you do?

"Do you worship a few buddhas and read a few sutras, burn off a few fingers[2] and light a few cones of incense on your head,[3] and deceive the common people to gain their favor and support? Is this what you do?

"Do you sit on the communal bed[4] with your eyes closed and waste your time in slumber and obliviousness? Is this what you do?

子。仗如來慈蔭。不耕而食。不蠶而衣。高堂
大廈。廣殿修廊。十指不沾水。百事不干懷。
種種現成。般般便當。只為現成。只為便當。
卻乃縱情放逸。非法貪求。不修僧業。不清戒
律。不明因果。不畏罪福。寬裡做債。造地獄
因。閻家老子。沒人情無面目。一善一惡。主
籍分明。一發與你打筭。莖虀粒米。滴水寸
絲。盡要酬還。福源與麼告報。也是為他閒事
長無明

上堂。一塵起大地收。四月十五日。結卻布袋
頭。一葉落天下秋。七月十五日。解卻布袋
頭。正當自恣。何證何修。草鞋底北鬱單越。
拄杖頭南贍部洲。朝悠悠暮悠悠。無拘無束自
在自由。老豐干忽然出來道。我與汝同往五臺

62.5 *Tathagata* is another name for the Buddha and means "he who truly comes." 62.6 Yama is the Judge of the Dead.

63.1 Uttarakuru is the continent north of Mount Sumeru, while Jambudvipa is the continent to the south. Here, they represent the world. 63.2 Feng-kan was a monk and a friend of the eighth-century recluse Han-shan, or Cold Mountain. One day Feng-kan said to Han-shan, "If you'll go to Wutaishan with me, you'll be my equal. If you don't go with me, you won't be my equal." Han-shan replied, "I won't go." Feng-kan said, "Then you aren't my equal." Han-shan asked, "What are you going to do on Wutaishan?" Feng-kan said, "Pay my respects to Manjushri." Han-shan said, "Then you're not my equal." 63.3 Wutaishan is the residence of Manjushri, the Bodhisattva of Wisdom, and is located in North China. It is customary at the end of summer retreat to make pilgrimages to such sacred sites.

"If so, then you aren't the equal of even the commonest farmer in the poorest village. Hoeing and planting, at least he supports himself and doesn't do anything wrong. But you monks and sons of Shakyamuni take advantage of the Tathagata's[5] shelter. You eat food without ploughing and wear clothes without raising silkworms. You live in great halls and immense temples, your fingers never touch the mud, and you aren't bothered with everyday concerns. Everything is taken care of, and everything is placed before you. But because it's all taken care of and placed before you, you indulge in laziness and greed. You don't act like monks, and you don't observe the precepts. You don't understand cause and effect, and you don't fear retribution. You pile up countless debts and sow the seeds of Hell.

"Old Yama[6] has no sympathy and no constraint. He registers every good deed and every bad deed. And when you leave this life, he adds them up. Every leek and grain of rice, every drop of water and inch of silk must be repaid. This is my advice to you: The reason you're still in the dark is because you meddle in other people's affairs."

63. The Master said, "A speck of dust rises and the earth receives it / in the middle of the fourth month / you put your bags away / a leaf falls and the world enters autumn / in the middle of the seventh month / you take out your bags again.

"But the moment you end retreat, how will you act and how will you practice? Will Uttarakuru[1] be beneath your shoes and Jambudvipa be below your staffs? Will you spend endless days and nights detached and free? And if Old Feng-kan[2] suddenly appears and says, 'Let's go to Wutaishan[3] and pay our respects to Manjushri,' what will you do?" Waving his hand, he said, "You're not my equals."

禮文殊。又且如何。搖手云。你不是我同流

中秋上堂。黑月難見。白月易見。黑白未分已

前。眼見何如心見。所以道。見見之時。見非

是見。見猶離見。見不能及。卓拄杖云。昨夜

蟾宮桂子開。好風吹下天香來。昭王白骨埋青

草。無人為掃黃金臺

上堂。澄一念虛明。未脱三乘羈鎖。認八處出

現。正迷自己靈光。直饒平白地上轉身。荊棘

林中移步。腳跟下好與三十棒。何故。不因樵

子徑。爭到葛洪家

天壽聖節上堂。箕翼長明。地天長泰。風不鳴

條。雨不破塊。君乃堯舜之君。俗乃成康之

64.1 *Toad palace* refers to the moon, which is inhabited by a three-legged toad. 64.2 A huge cassia tree also grows on the moon and confers immortality on those who breathe the fragrance of its blossoms. 64.3 In the fourth century BC, King Chao of the state of Yen built a golden terrace to welcome men of talent from all over China to his government. The remains of his capital have recently been unearthed outside the town of Yihsien southwest of Peking.

65.1 The Three Vehicles are those of the *sravaka,* whose goal is freedom from passion, the *pratyeka-buddha,* whose goal is enlightenment for himself, and the *bodhisattva,* whose goal is liberation for all beings. The three cases cited by Stonehouse are examples of the limitations of each of these vehicles. 65.2 Ko Hung was a fourth-century recluse and the author of several seminal Taoist works, including the first detailed account of the quest for immortality through alchemical and dietic means. His former hermitage and the site of his cauldron can still be visited on Lofushan, one hundred kilometers east of Kuangchou.

66.1 Yao and Shun were two rulers of China's pre-historic period famous for their sagacity and humility. 66.2 Ch'eng and K'ang were two kings of the Chou dynasty known for their leniency and virtue. 66.3 The Queen Mother of the West dwells in the mountains of Central Asia and bestows her peaches of immortality on virtuous rulers. Here, however, the allusion is to the mother of the emperor. 66.4 *Seas and Mountains* (Hai-shan) was the name of Emperor Wu-tsung, the father of Emperor Wen-ti, whose birthday is being celebrated here, as it was he who rebuilt Fuyuan Temple. He died in 1332, the year after Stonehouse took over as abbot. The birthday of the reigning emperor, Shun-ti, was celebrated after the Buddha's Nirvana and before the start of the summer retreat. Here, however, the time must be in the ninth month.

64. On Mid-Autumn Festival, the Master said, "It's hard to see the dark of the moon. It's easy to see the light. But before you distinguish the light and the dark, what your eyes see doesn't compare with what your mind sees. Thus we say when you see seeing, seeing is not seeing. Seeing exists apart from seeing and can't be reached by seeing."

Lifting his staff, the Master said, "Last night in toad palace[1] the cassias[2] bloomed / a favorable wind blew down their perfume / King Chao's[3] bones still lie below weeds / nobody sweeps his golden terrace."

65. The Master said, "Why do those who completely still their minds remain imprisoned by the Three Vehicles?[1] Why do those who recognize what appears around them remain blind to their own divine light? And why do those who find themselves on open ground walk into a forest of thorns where the bottoms of their feet feel as if they had been given thirty lashes? How can you reach Ko Hung's abode[2] if you don't follow woodcutter trails?"

66. On the emperor's birthday, "The Master said, "The undying light spreads forth / peace prevails on Earth and in Heaven / the wind doesn't howl / and the rain doesn't flood / his rule is the rule of Yao and Shun[1] / his ways are the ways of Ch'eng and K'ang[2] / the Queen Mother[3] waves her banner of clouds / in the fourth month the Seas and Mountains produce peaches.[4]

俗。王母畫夜雲旗翻。海山四月蟠桃熟

上堂。十月初一日開爐。諸方説寒道熱。福源
一味尋常。不會安排施設。深深埋兩箇炭團。
滿滿堆一爐黃葉。莫嫌火種無多。只要煖氣相
接。放下重簾。密糊窗縫。又誰管你屋上濃
霜。庭前深雪。但得自家屋裡一團和氣。外邊
冷言冷語不須聽。由他自歇。諸禪德。本色住
山人。且無刀斧痕

上堂。一心不生。萬法無咎。無咎無法。不生
不心。所以道。山僧居菴時。只見居菴時境界
門對千峰。心閒一境。朝看白雲冉冉。暮聽流
水潺潺。煮藜藿于折腳鐺中。穿破衲于尖頭屋
下。自由自在。無束無拘。娑羅樹影落天湖。

67.1 It was once a common practice at Zen temples to light the stoves inside the monastery on the first day of the tenth month. The stoves were kept burning until the first day of the second lunar month. 67.2 Until modern times, most windows were covered with waterproof paper, which required periodic repair, especially after storms. 67.3 The axe scars would be from chopping wood.

68.1 Pigweed, or *Chenopodium scoparia,* is a member of the goosefoot family and similar to spinach. 68.2 The sal tree, or *Shorea robusta,* is a variety of teak found in India. It was between a pair of such trees that the Buddha entered Nirvana at Kushinagar. 68.3 *Sky Lake* is Stonehouse's name for the spring next to his hut on Hsiamushan. 68.4 The flat-topped boulders at the summit of Hsiamushan were Stonehouse's favorite place to enjoy the sun and the view.

67. The Master said, "On the first day of the tenth month[1] we light the stoves. While people elsewhere talk about the cold or the heat, here at Fuyuan everything is normal. We don't need to make special preparations. We put in a few coals and fill our stoves with dry leaves. We don't worry about having so few provisions as long as the heat lasts. We lower our layered curtains and paste over the rips in our windows.[2] We don't care if there's heavy frost on the roof or deep snow in the courtyard, as long as our rooms are comfortable. We don't need to listen to talk about how cold it is outside. Why should we pay it any heed? You Zen monks, you true-natured mountain dwellers, at least you don't have any axe scars."[3]

68. The Master said, "When thoughts don't appear, nothing is wrong. No wrongs, no things. No appearances, no thoughts. When I was living in my mountain hut, all I saw were the scenes around my hut. My door faced a thousand peaks, and my mind was focused on one scene. During the day I watched the clouds drift, and at night I listened to the spring flow. I cooked pigweed[1] soup in my broken-legged pot and wore a ragged robe in my peaked-roof hut. I was free and unattached. The reflection of a sal tree[2] filled Sky Lake,[3] and the scent of peach blossoms in my yard floated up to the boulders.[4] There was no right or wrong, no fortune or fame.

簷蔔華香浮臺石。是非不到。名利杳忘。住院
時。即見住院時境界。門連湖市。地接海州。
早起晏眠。迎來送去。整規模于顛危之際。聚
衲子于寂寞之中。漁歌牧笛長聞。山色溪光罕
見。紅塵滾滾。白日匆匆。且道。住湖寺。居
山菴。是同是別。良久云。無山不帶雲。有水
皆含月

祈雨上堂。記得去年時五月。火雲燒田天不
雨。家家插種望今年。不料今年又如此。偉哉
公侯將相心。憂民切切如憂己。叩之龍神便感
靈。來此閣浮澍甘雨。霈然不止三日霖。天人
群生悉歡喜。敢問諸人。且道承誰恩力。以拂
子擊禪床云。蘇嚕蘇嚕。嗡哩嗡哩

68.5 The *lake town* refers to Pinghu, which was situated on the west shore of East Lake. 68.6 The natural harbor of Tsapu was fifteen kilometers southeast of Pinghu. 68.7 The entire region south of the Yangtze saw a great increase in banditry and the power of local warlords in the 1330s, when Stonehouse was abbot of Fuyuan. Eventually, major rebellions broke out in neighboring Anhui province in the 1340s, and the Yuan dynasty came to an end in the 1360s. 68.8 *Red dust* refers to the world of sensation.

69.1 The residents of Buddhist and Taoist temples continue to serve some of the functions that were once the preserve of shamans and shamanikas. 69.2 Jambudvipa is the Buddhist equivalent of Asia. 69.3 The sounds here are those of loquacious people.

"Now that I live in a monastery, all I see are the scenes around the monastery. The gate faces a lake town,[5] and the land meets the sea.[6] I get up early and go to bed late. I welcome those who come, and I say good-bye to those who go. The whole world is in crisis,[7] but the assembly of monks is at peace. I often hear the songs of fishermen or oxherds and seldom see mountain shadows or stream light. The red dust[8] rises, and the days hurry by. Is living in a lake temple or a mountain hut the same or different?"

After a long pause, he said, "Every mountain has its clouds. Wherever there's water, there's the moon."

69. Giving thanks for rain,[1] the Master said, "The fifth month last year I recall / sun scorched the fields and the sky didn't rain / everyone planted in hopes of this year / but this year alas was the same / our noble lords expressed concern / caring for the people as they do themselves / the dragon spirit answered their prayers / showering Jambudvipa[2] with sweet welcome rain / for three days it poured without stop / the gods and people gave thanks.

"But tell me, by whose grace did this occur?" Snapping his whisk against his meditation seat, he said, "Cackle, cackle. Chirp, chirp."[3]

復舉僧問乾峰。十方薄伽梵。一路涅槃門。未
審。路頭在甚處。峰以拄杖劃一劃云。在這
裡。僧舉似雲門。門拈起扇云。扇子䟓跳。上
三十三天。築著帝釋鼻孔。東海鯉魚打一棒。
雨似盆傾。頌云。萬仞籠門一捺開。傾盆驟雨
假風雷。袈裟打濕歸來看。半是紅雲半海苔

上堂。鴆毛毒。未是毒。箭來不似人心毒。三
伏熱。未是熱。思量無出人心熱。阿修羅王。
當好罵天。善星比丘。偏要謗佛。道高一尺。
魔高一丈。汝之伎倆有盡。我之不採無窮

七月旦上堂。人間秋十日。湖寺便生涼。竹色
溪邊綠。荷花鏡裡香。即心猶未是。作境謾摶
量。空劫已前事。今朝為舉揚

70.1 Ch'ien-feng was a disciple of the ninth-century Zen master Tung-shan. 70.2 *Bhagavan* is Sanskrit for "World-Honored One" and is one of the ten titles of a buddha. 70.3 Yun-men was another eminent ninth-century Zen master. 70.4 The Thirty-third Heaven is at the top of Mount Sumeru and is the abode of Indra, ruler of the gods. 70.5 *Dragon Gate* is the name of a gorge in the middle reaches of the Yellow River. Carp pass through it every year on their way to spawn further upstream. It is also where the dragon spirit that controls the rain resides. 70.6 The *red clouds* are from Indra's palace, and the *seaweed* is from the Dragon King's realm.

71.1 The *chen* is a legendary bird that kills its prey with the touch of its venomous feathers. 71.2 *Asuras* are gods that make war on other gods. 71.3 According to legend, Sutara ("Good Star") was one of Shakyamuni's three sons. Although he attained the highest state of meditation and memorized all the Buddha's sermons, his understanding was not founded on wisdom. Eventually, he followed the heterodox path of a misguided friend and fell into a bottomless hell when he slandered the Buddha.

72.1 The summer heat and humidity of the Yangtze Valley is oppressive, and the first sign of autumn is welcomed by all. Here the first cool breeze arrives just before the conclusion of summer retreat, which ends on the fifteenth day of the seventh month. 72.2 The *mirror* refers to the lake as well as to the mind. 72.3 An empty kalpa is the period of time between the destruction of one universe and the creation of another. *What happened before the last empty kalpa* refers to our original face.

70. The Master recalled the time a monk asked Ch'ien-feng,[1] "The bhagavans[2] of the ten directions all take the same road to the Gate of Nirvana. Could you please tell me where this road begins?" Ch'ien-feng picked up his staff and drew a line on the ground and said, "Right here."

Another monk asked Yun-men[3] to explain this. Yun-men picked up his fan and said, "This fan sails up to the Thirty-third Heaven[4] and hits Indra in the nose. A carp in the East Sea slaps its tail, and the rain comes down in buckets."

The Master said, "Once the towering Dragon Gate[5] opens / torrents of rain ride thunder and wind / my robe gets soaked and I return home / half of me red clouds the other half seaweed."[6]

71. The Master said, "Chen[1] feathers might be deadly / and they might not / but they're not as deadly as the mind / summer months might be hot / and they might not / but they're not as hot as the mind / asuras[2] love to criticize the gods / Sutara[3] couldn't help defaming the Buddha / however great the realm of truth / the realm of lies is ten times greater / your cleverness has its limits / my stupidity knows no end."

72. At the beginning of the seventh month, the Master said, "Ten days into autumn[1] / the lake temple turns cool / streams are green with bamboo / lotuses perfume the mirror[2] / this mind still isn't it / drawing lines sets false limits / what happened before the last empty kalpa[3] / today I bring up again."

解制上堂。有佛處不得住。樓臺月色雲收去。

無佛處急走過。池塘荷葉風吹破。三千里外。

逢人不得錯舉。郎州澧州水。四海五湖皇化

裡。腰包頂笠萬千千。問著盡言山與水。忽有

不甘底。出來道。山但言山。水但言水。有甚

麼過。良久云。未可全拋一片心。逢人且説三

分話

上堂。行腳高人。説箇參禪。説箇辦道。恰如

坐在飯籮裡叫肚饑相似。通身是飯。你自不肯

喫。又干他別人甚麼事。十二時中。動轉施

為。全是一條潑天大路。且無荊棘瓦礫。礙汝

腳跟下。你自不肯進步。又于他別人甚麼事。

諸佛有甚麼勝如凡夫。凡夫有甚麼不如諸佛。

彼既丈夫我亦爾。何得自輕而退屈。驀拈拄杖

73.1 In the first and third lines of this gatha, Stonehouse quotes the koan given to him by his own master, Chi-an. 73.2 *Langchou* and *Fengchou* were the names of two prefectures on the west shore of Tungting Lake in the middle reaches of the Yangtze. The area was the location of a number of well-known Zen temples and the destination of many monks at the end of summer retreat. The *Four Seas* refers to the seacoast and the *Five Lakes* to Lake Taihu, which was said to be made up of five bodies of water. Such place names were shorthand for the major centers of Buddhist practice. 73.3 The shoulder bags and bamboo hats are those of monks preparing to go on pilgrimage. 73.4 The *three explanations* refers to seeing mountains as mountains, mountains as not mountains, and mountains as simply mountains again.

74.1 *Composite things* include anything made of more than one component: the world, the body, the mind.

73. At the end of summer retreat, the Master said, "Where buddhas dwell don't stop[1] / the moon lights the terrace when the clouds withdraw / where buddhas don't dwell hurry past / lotus leaves in the pond are ripped by the wind.

"When you meet someone a thousand miles from home, don't make any judgments. On the mountains of Langchou,[2] on the rivers of Fengchou, on the Four Seas and Five Lakes, in the emperor's realm, amid thousands upon thousands of shoulder bags and hats,[3] everyone you talk to talks about mountains and rivers. Suddenly some unhappy person comes up and says, 'Let's call mountains mountains and rivers rivers.'

"What's wrong with this?" After a long pause, he said, "Until you completely get rid of the mind, you'll have three different explanations[4] for everyone you meet."

74. The Master said, "You wandering monks say you're practicing Zen. You say you're cultivating the Tao. But it's as if you were sitting inside a rice bucket complaining that you're hungry. There's rice all around you. Why don't you eat? What are you doing bothering other people? Everything you do during the twelve periods of the day, every movement, every action, it all takes place on a sun-drenched, rain-washed highway. There aren't any brambles or rocks to obstruct your feet. Why don't you walk straight ahead? What are you doing bothering other people?

"Do buddhas have something that makes them better than ordinary people? Do ordinary people have something that makes them inferior to buddhas? They're men, and so are you. Why do you slight yourselves and act like servants?"

He suddenly grabbed his staff and said, "The Tathagata said, 'All composite things are not composite things.'[1] Where do you find flowering rushes on a moonlit night? I imagine, as usual, along rivers in fall."

云。如來說一合相。即非一合相。明月蘆華何
處尋。想伊只在秋江上

中秋上堂。初三月十五月。缺時無圓。圓時無
缺。圓缺不相干。清光常皎潔。昨夜蟾宮雨露
多。天風吹落黃金屑

復舉嚴陽尊者問趙州。一物不將來時如何。州
云。放下著。嚴云。一物不將來。放下箇甚
麼。州云。放不下擔取去。頌云。香飄桂子十
分月。雨滴芙蓉一半秋。門外任他時節換。穩
將衲被自蒙頭

上堂。學道參禪。心地未明。已眼未開。情塵
未脱。命根未斷。恰如甚麼相似。恰如有眼人

75.1 Mid-Autumn Festival is celebrated on the fifteenth day, or full moon, of the eighth month.
75.2 Normally, the moon doesn't become visible until the third day of the month. 75.3 *Toad palace*
refers to the moon.

76.1 Chao-chou was an eminent Zen master of the ninth century, and Yen-yang was his disciple.
Later, when Yen-yang was the abbot of his own temple, he kept a pet snake and a pet tiger, both of
which followed him everywhere and ate out of his hand. See *Chuantenglu:* 11. 76.2 As noted else-
where, the cassias that bloom on the moon confer immortality on those fortunate enough to breathe
their perfume.

75. On Mid-Autumn Festival,[1] the Master said, "The third[2] and fifteenth of the month / when it's empty it's not full / when it's full it's not empty / neither interferes with the other / the pure light shines without cease / last night toad palace[3] rained down dew / a heavenly wind showered us with stardust."

76. The Master recalled the time Yen-yang[1] asked Chao-chou, "What is it like when nothing appears?" Chao-chou answered, "Put it down." Yen-yang then asked, "But when nothing appears, what is there to put down?" Chao-chou said, "If you can't put it down, take it out of here."

The Master said, "The perfume of cassias[2] a perfect moon / rain drops on lotuses midway through autumn / outside the gate let the seasons change / wrap your ragged quilts over your heads."

步入千年暗室中相似。目前雖有一切物色相
傾。竟不知其是青是黃。是赤是白。是長是
短。是方是圓。懵然無知。黑漫漫地。若如
此。在裰裟下。如何消得人天供養。學道參
禪。心地已明。已眼已開。情塵已脫。命根已
斷。千年暗室。一照照破。目前所有一切種
種物色。青黃赤白。長短方圓。一一明了。一
一分曉。那時正好向三條椽下。七尺單前。長
養聖胎。閒閒度日。若如此。在裰裟下。方始
消得他人天供養。然雖如是。更須知道。福源
門下。一條生鐵門檻。高而無上。廣寞可測。
在外者。要入不能得入。在內者。要出不能得
出。也須是著些精彩。用些氣力。跳過始得。
若也擬議。不是撞頭磕腦。便是墮坑落塹。莫

77.1 The K'un is a legendary leviathan who lives in the ocean and who appears at the very beginning of *Chuangtzu*. 77.2 In a Zen monastery, the space allotted to each monk's bed in the meditation hall was limited to the width between three rafters, or about three feet. The length was seven feet, with the last foot containing the monk's name board. Below the bed and in front of the name board was a lower step on which the monk sat in meditation.

77. The Master said, "What is it like to cultivate the Tao and practice Zen if you haven't yet fathomed your mind, or opened your eyes, or freed yourselves of passion, or severed your attachment to life? It's as if someone who could see entered a room that had been dark for a thousand years. Even though all manner of things might appear before him, he would have no idea which was blue or yellow, which was red or white, which was long or short, and which was square or round. He would be completely unaware and oblivious. If someone like this wears a monk's robe, he doesn't deserve the support of gods and men.

And what is it like to cultivate the Tao and practice Zen once you fathom your mind, and open your eyes, and free yourselves of passion, and sever your attachment to life? It's as if the K'un[1] sent the red sun shooting out of the ocean. The room that was dark for a thousand years is suddenly full of light. And everything before your eyes, the blue and the yellow, the red and the white, the long and the short, the square and the round, is clear and visible. And there you are sitting below your three rafters in front of your seven-foot bed,[2] nourishing the sacred womb, and idly passing your days. If someone like this wears a monk's robe, he alone deserves the support of gods and men.

Even so, you need to be aware that below the gate at Fuyuan there's a cast iron threshold too high to scale and too wide to measure. People outside who want to get in can't get in. And people inside who want to get out can't get out. If you want to jump across it, you'll need to summon all of your energy and all of your strength. If you stop to think about it, you'll either crack your skull or fall into an abyss. Don't say I didn't warn you."

言不道

臘八上堂。雪山高且深。忍凍吞麻麥。如此過
六年。酌然是快活。無端睹明星。剛言成正
覺。拂袖下山來。早是低一著。更云度眾生。
重重露拴索。看他世上榮。何似山中樂。錯
錯。年年有箇臘月八

入新僧堂上堂。直為柱。曲為梁。矩中圓。規
中方。匠氏取材之良也。歸其圓。泯其方。捨
其短。取其長。主人立法之妙也。所以福源僧
堂。建柱石于丙子孟春。畢斧斤于戊寅之重
九。六窗炯炯。洞一色之虛明。萬瓦鱗鱗。絕
三種滲漏。低頭不見地。還他擔板禪和。仰面
不見天。卻許蒙頭衲子。老竹溪。豈止一生行

78.1 *Lapa* falls on the eighth day of the last lunar month. 78.2 The poem more or less recapitulates Shakyamuni's career, which took place in the Gangetic Plains south of the Himalayas. According to the *Lalitavistara Sutra,* Shakyamuni was enlightened after seeing Venus on the horizon. 78.3 It was customary for hermits to come down to their "mother temple" on *Lapa,* if only for provisions.

79.1 The *six windows* are the senses. 79.2 And the three sources of karma are the body, the mouth, and the mind. 79.3 Someone who carries a board on his back must stoop over to do so and is only able to see the ground in front of him. Hence the expression has become a cliché for people of limited vision. Here, though, the board is being carried by hand and thus blocks the view of the ground. Stonehouse's point is that those who work are liable to lose sight of the true ground while those who meditate are liable to lose sight of the true heaven. 79.4 The *bamboo stream* refers to a place of the same name near the foot of Taishan where the poet Li Pai and the Taoist Wu Yun built huts with four other friends around 740, resolving to spend the rest of their lives in seclusion. Their seclusion, however, did not last long. In 742, both Wu and Li accepted an opportunity to appear at court and took up posts in the prestigious Hanlin Academy.

78. On Lapa Festival,[1] the Master said, "The Himalayas are high and remote / if you can stand the snow and coarse fare / and do this for six long years / and be content with poverty / one day you will see a bright star[2] / and all at once you'll be enlightened / and shaking your sleeves you'll come down the mountain[3] / and as soon as you're down / you'll say you're here to liberate all beings / to expose their countless attachments / but when you behold the glories of the world / how will they compare with the joys of the mountain? Forget it. Every year there's a Lapa Festival."

79. Entering the new meditation hall, the Master said, "The straight become pillars, the crooked become beams. The carpenter's trick to selecting wood is to look for the circle inside the square and the angle inside the compass. The ruler's secret to enacting laws is to trust the round and get rid of the square, to chose the long and abandon the short. Thus the pillar bases of Fuyuan's meditation hall were laid in the first month of 1336, and the axe work was finished on the ninth day of the ninth month of 1338.

"The six shining windows[1] all let in the same colorless light, and the ten thousand glistening roof tiles keep out the three leaks.[2] Monks who carry boards[3] look down without seeing the ground. Monks who cover their heads look up without seeing the sky. How could an old bamboo stream[4] divert a lifetime of resolution? As usual, through pride.

願。憍陳如。頓增萬倍威光。遵行百丈叢林。壯觀千年常住。直得十方諸佛。異口同音。宣說偈言。佛子住此地。則是佛受用。常在於其中。經行及坐臥。又有龐居士。說箇頌子讚嘆云。十方同聚會。箇箇學無為。此是選佛場。心空及第歸。然雖如是。其奈張無盡。忍俊不禁。出來道。汝等諸人。即解樹頭喫果子。不知樹曲錄。殊不知。作此堂者。有損有益。居此堂者。有利有害。這般說話。也怪伊不得。何故。人無遠慮。必有近憂。此事且拈放一邊。祇如衲僧自己分上得力句子。作麼生道。良久云。饑餐渴飲渾無事。聽雨聞風閑打眠

開爐上堂。法昌和尚道。法昌今日開爐。行腳僧無一箇。惟有十六高人。緘口圍爐打坐。福

79.5 Pai-chang was an eighth-century monk who laid down the basic rules for Zen temples.
79.6 Layman P'ang was a disciple of Ma-tsu.

"The light has suddenly increased ten thousand fold in this monastery where the rules of Pai-chang[5] prevail. May his stern gaze last a thousand years. Even though the buddhas of the ten directions have different mouths, they preach the same message. They all preach: 'The place where a buddha dwells / that place becomes his own / there he is in the middle / walking sitting lying down.'

"Layman P'ang[6] presented his own version of this: 'They assemble from the ten directions / students of inactivity / this is where buddhas are tested / where graduates with empty minds return.' This may be so, but why couldn't he stay quiet and thus avoid our laughter?"

Coming out of the hall, the Master said, "All of you know how to eat the fruit of trees, but you don't understand trees, much less chairs. Those who built this hall have lost and gained. Those who live in this hall have been helped and harmed. Don't blame me for saying this. And why not? People who don't think far ahead have too many worries nearby. Choose one side over the other. Be like those monks who find their own solutions.

"And what do they say?" After a pause, he said, "When you're hungry, eat. When you're thirsty, drink. What else is there? Listen to the rain. Listen to the wind. When you have nothing else to do, sleep."

源不與塵道。福源今日開爐。炭墼也無一箇。

五湖四海禪和。衲被蒙頭打坐。不是冷眼傍

觀。免見挑灰弄火。寬心寧耐到春來。屋外梅

花香朵朵

冬節小參。諸禪德。如今是甚麼時節。群陰欲

去未去。一陽欲來未來。陰不得為陰。陽不得

為陽。山不得為山。水不得為水。日月星辰。

六十甲子。一齊打亂。沒商量處。水泄不通。

無奈何時。放開一線。便見地中雷復。律管灰

飛。餒發冰河。筍抽寒谷。依舊山即是山。水

即是水。日月星辰。六十甲子。各歸舊位。是

法住法位。世間相常住。卓拄杖下座

80.1 According to custom, stoves were lit at Zen monasteries on the first day of the tenth month, and they were kept burning until the first day of the second month. See also 67 above. 80.2 Fa-ch'ang was a Vinaya master of the ninth century. Note that he took his name from the monastery of which he was the abbot. 80.3 Most Zen monasteries include the statues of sixteen (in some cases, eighteen) arhats, or worthies from India and Central Asia. 80.4 The *Five Lakes* refers to Lake Taihu, which was viewed as being made up of five bodies of water. And the *Four Seas* refers to the ocean along the central coast.

81.1 The Chinese associate the changing seasons with the hexagrams of the *Yiching*. The hexagram *K'un: Earth,* with six broken yin lines, represents the end of winter, while the hexagram *Fu:Return,* with five broken yin lines on top and a single solid yang line on the bottom, represents the beginning of spring. 81.2 Stonehouse's point is that yin can only become yang. 81.3 The Chinese use a cycle of sixty successive time periods to plot the movements of the heavens. 81.4 The *thread* refers to a peculiarity of the old Chinese solar calendar, to which stitches of red thread were added as the sun began to lengthen its arc. 81.5 *Thunder, pitch pipes, flames,* and *bamboo shoots* are all metaphors for the reappearance of yang. 81.6 These two lines are from the *Lotus Sutra*: 2.

80. On lighting the stoves,[1] the Master said, "Fa-ch'ang[2] once said, 'Today at Fa-chang we light the stoves, and I don't see a single homeless monk. All I see are sixteen[3] masters sitting around the stove in meditation with their lips sealed.'

"I put it differently: Today at Fuyuan we light the stoves, and I don't see a single coal. All I see are Zen monks from the Five Lakes[4] and Four Seas sitting in meditation wrapped in their blankets.

"You're either disinterested by-standers trying to avoid starting the fire, or you're patient ascetics waiting for spring to come and the plum blossoms outside to send forth their fragrance."

81. At an informal talk on winter solstice, the Master said, "You Zen monks, what day is it today? The assembled forces of yin[1] are about to leave but haven't quite left. The first sign of yang is about to arrive but hasn't yet appeared. Yin can't become yin,[2] and yang can't become yang. Mountains can't become mountains, and rivers can't become rivers. The sun and moon and stars and the sixty divisions[3] of the sky are all confused. There's no way in and no way out. There's no alternative but to take out a thread[4] and watch thunder return to the earth, pitch pipes blow ashes into the air, flames rise from glaciers, and bamboo shoots appear in cold ravines.[5]

"Once again mountains are mountains, and rivers are rivers, and the sun and moon and stars and sixty divisions of the sky all return to their former places. Thus 'the Dharma dwells in the Dharma's place. It dwells forever in the forms of the world.'"[6]

The Master then lifted up his staff and left the hall.

冬節上堂。昨夜陰回陽復爻。曉來湖岸冰消。
皇宮日影喜添線。胡地筍長梅破梢。春漏依痕
舒柳眼。雲拖五色束天腰。明明空劫已前事。
不是虛言誑爾曹

上堂。臘月一。水生骨。虛明自照。不勞心
力。白鷗寒雁蘆花。無處尋他綜跡。待得日煖
冰融水面寬。依舊飛來照破碧光碧

復舉麻谷至章敬。遶禪床一匝。振錫一下。卓
然而立。敬云。是是。又至南泉。遶禪床一
匝。振錫一下。卓然而立。泉云。不是不是。
谷云。章敬道是。和尚因甚麼道不是。泉云。
章敬是是。汝不是。此是風力所轉。終歸敗
壞。輒成一頌。普告人天。尺可量弓秤可平。

82.1 See the notes to 81.

83.1 The lake is frozen over.

84.1 Ma-ku, Chang-ching, and Nan-ch'uan were all disciples of the eighth-century Zen master Ma-
tsu. This account appears in the *Blue Cliff Records:* 31.

82. On winter solstice, the Master said, "Last night yin left and yang returned[1] / ice began to melt on the lake this morning / the sun's shadow adds a thread in the palace / shoots appear in foreign lands and plum blossoms fall / spring leaves a scar on budding willow eyes / clouds drag their colors across Heaven's waist / clearly the events of the last empty kalpa / aren't empty talk meant to make us crazy."

83. On the first day of the last month, the Master said, "The water grows bones.[1] The empty light shines on its own. It doesn't require any effort of the mind. Neither seagulls, nor winter geese, nor rush flowers leave tracks. Waiting for the sun to grow warmer and the ice to melt and the water to expand, they come flying as always and drive away the dark-blue of the dark-blue light."

84. The Master recalled the time Ma-ku visited Chang-ching,[1] Ma-ku walked around Chang-ching's meditation seat, shook his staff in the air, and stood still. And Chang-ching said, "Right." Then Ma-ku visited Nan-ch'uan and walked around Nan-ch'uan's meditation seat and shook his staff in the air and stood still, and Nan-ch'uan said, "Wrong." Ma-ku said, "Chang-ching said, 'Right.' Why do you say, 'Wrong?'" Nan-ch'uan said, "Chang-ching was right. You are wrong. Whatever is exposed to the wind doesn't last long."

The Master then composed this gatha: "This is for men and gods everywhere / a ruler can measure and a scale can weigh / length and weight are thus distinguished / if all you have is two hands / how can you cover the eyes of the world."

短長輕重要分明。都盧祇是一雙手。難掩世間

人眼睛

九皋學士至。上堂。諸佛廣大門風。祖師向上

巴鼻。初非明悟見知。而可擬議。又非世智辯

聰。而能㕙佛。直使盡天下衲僧。捫摸他不

著。亦不令住在無捫摸處。有此大丈夫氣慨。

方能成辦大丈夫事。此非一生兩生行願得成。

乃是多劫多生淨業增熏。方能如此。無一法從

懶墮懈怠中生。豈不見。二祖立雪。五祖栽

松。六祖踏碓。仰山牧牛。雪峰在德山做飯

頭。疏山賣了布單。三千里外行腳。長慶坐破

七箇蒲團。香林侍雲門十八年。張無盡一宿

龍安。黃太史十遊幕阜。裴丞相悟心於黃蘗言

下。龐居士得旨於馬祖室中。先輩大儒。古來

85.1 The Second Patriarch was the sixth-century monk Hui-k'o, who had to stand in the snow for days on end before Bodhidharma would agree to instruct him. 85.2 The Fifth Patriarch was the seventh-century monk Huang-mei. 85.3 The Sixth Patriarch was the seventh-century monk Hui-neng. 85.4 Yang-shan was a ninth-century Zen master who studied with Kuei-shan. 85.5 Hsueh-feng was a ninth-century Zen master who studied with Te-shan on the mountain of the same name. 85.6 Shu-shan was a ninth-century Zen master who studied with Hsiang-yen. 85.7 Ch'ang-ch'ing was a tenth-century Zen master who studied with Hsueh-feng. 85.8 Hsiang-lin was a tenth-century Zen master and disciple of Yun-men, whose Zen talks Hsiang-lin wrote down on a paper robe. 85.9 Chang Wu-chin (Chang Shang-ying) was a famous lay Buddhist and statesman of the twelfth century. Lungan Temple is in Hunan. 85.10 I'm not sure who Historian Huang was or where Mufu was located. 85.11 Prime Minister P'ei (P'ei Hsiu) visited many eminent ninth-century Zen masters, including Huang-po, whose sermons he recorded during several official postings in the Chiangnan region. 85.12 Layman P'ang Yun was enlightened while living with Ma-tsu.

85. Upon the arrival of Scholar Chiu-kao, the Master said, "The great teachings of the buddhas and the incomparable techniques of the patriarchs can't be understood by intellect or knowledge. Nor can they be comprehended by common sense or logic. There isn't a monk in the realm who can grasp them. And yet no one can find a place where they can't be grasped.

"Only someone with the determination of a truly great man can perform the deeds of a truly great man. This isn't something that the resolve of one or two life-times can achieve. It's only possible as a result of the accumulated effects of the pure karma of many kalpas and many lifetimes. No teaching has ever come out of lazi-ness or negligence.

"Do you not recall how the Second Patriarch[1] stood in the snow, how the Fifth Patriarch[2] planted pines, how the Sixth Patriarch[3] hulled rice, how Yang-shan[4] tended water-buffalo, how Hsueh-feng[5] worked as a rice steward on Teshan, how Shu-shan[6] traveled by foot for a thousand miles to sell cloth, how Ch'ang-ch'ing[7] wore out seven meditation cushions, how Hsiang-lin[8] served Yun-men for eighteen years, how Chang Wu-chin[9] spent one night at Lungan, how Historian Huang[10] visited Mufu ten times, how Prime Minister P'ei[11] was enlightened by the words of Huang-po, or how Layman P'ang[12] received instruction in Ma-tsu's chamber?

老衲。是皆苦志勞形。究明此道。豈似如今。
禪和家。華居豐食。致身於叢林中。視叢林如
驛舍。口裡說道。參禪辦道。聞說禪道。如風
過樹。此等名為可憐憫者。我此現前一眾。宿
因深正。得在此處。清淨伽藍。同居共處。當
生希有難遭之想。豈可也學他。今時流輩荒
逸。終日無所用心。逐隊隨群。說黃道黑。略
無少念回光返照。我今此身。四大和合。所謂
毛髮爪齒。皮肉觔骨。髓腦垢色。皆歸於地。
唾涕膿血。津液涎沫。痰淚精氣。大小便利。
皆歸於水。煖氣歸火。動轉歸風。四大各離。
今者妄身。當在何處。若向這裡。回光返照。
著得一隻眼。便見應菴和尚道。若作地水火風
商量。釋迦老子。盡塵沙劫。無出頭分。不作
地水火風商量。如將魚目擬比明珠。二途不

85.13 *Sangharama* is Sanskrit for a "monastery," the place where the sangha dwells. 85.14 *Yellow* and *black* refer to yin and yang. 85.15 The *four elements* comprise the constituents of all matter: earth, water, fire, and air. 85.16 The dharma eye, which perceives reality, is meant. 85.17 Ying-an was a twelfth-century Zen master and member of Stonehouse's own Tiger Hill lineage. 85.18 I have read *er-t'u:two paths* as a mistake for *tz'u-t'u:this path*.

"The great Confucian scholars and virtuous monks of the past all wore themselves out trying to understand the Way. How unlike the Zen monks of today who retire to monasteries for their elegant lodgings and fine food and who treat monasteries as inns. All they do is talk about practicing Zen and cultivating the Tao. But when they finally hear someone speak about Zen, it's like the wind blowing through the trees. Such people are pathetic.

"The members of the present assembly have planted deep roots in past lives to reach this place. Here, where we live and dwell together in this pure sangharama,[13] you should think rare and daring thoughts. How can you study anything else? Nowadays most people are so lazy, they don't think about anything all day. They just follow the crowd and call yellow black[14] and never stop to reflect.

"This body of ours is made up of the four elements.[15] Its hair and nails and teeth, its skin and flesh, its tendons and bones, its marrow and brains are earth. Its saliva and mucus, its pus and blood, its tears and semen, its urine and feces are water. Its warmth is fire, and its movements are wind. When the four elements separate from each other, where then is this illusory body of ours? If you reflect on this and focus on it with one eye,[16] you will see what Ying-an[17] was talking about. If you meditate on the four elements, Old Shakyamuni won't have an opening for countless kalpas. Those who don't meditate on the four elements, think a fish eye is a pearl. And those who don't take this path[18] are no different from someone who draws a loaf of bread to satisfy his hunger.

"This mountain monk thus proclaims: those whose wisdom is equal to their knowledge are able to believe and understand, while those whose wisdom is overwhelmed by doubts and regrets are lost forever."

涉。何異畫餅充饑。山僧與麼舉揚。有智若
聞。則能信解。無智疑悔。則為永失

復舉東坡。夜宿東林。與照覺道話有省。呈頌
云。溪聲便是廣長舌。山色豈非清淨身。夜來
八萬四千偈。他日如何舉似人。師云。諸仁
者。我觀王公大臣。好此道極多。至於談道之
際。箇箇喜人順已。怕人針箚。所以東坡居
士。被照覺活埋。在聲色堆裡。至今無出身
路。翰林九峯學士。來我山中。清話連日。述
偈數篇。等是一種語言三昧。中未曾道著元字
腳。祇這便是出他古人一頭地了也。乃撫膝
云。鶴有九峯難餘翥翼。馬無千里謾追風

86.1 Su Tung-p'o lived in the eleventh century and was one of China's greatest poets and calligraphers. He was also friends with many monks, and on one occasion he stopped overnight at Lushan's Tunglin Temple in the middle reaches of the Yangtze, where he had an illuminating conversation with its abbot, Ch'ang-ts'ung Chao-chueh. 86.2 The Hanlin Academy was charged with drafting most of the documents used at court, with writing the history of the previous dynasty, and with any other projects the court deemed worthy of the highest scholarship. 86.3 The expression *mountains* is euphemistic and is often used in reference to a monastery, where solitude rivals that of more remote places. 86.4 *Samadhi* is Sanskrit for "the state attained when one's mind is focused on one thing."

86. The Master recalled the time Su Tung-p'o[1] stayed overnight at Tunglin Temple, was enlightened while talking with Chao-chueh and composed this gatha: "The sound of the stream is a buddha's long, wide tongue / and how could the mountains not be his perfect body / the night inspires a million songs of praise / how will I explain this tomorrow to others."

The Master said, "My fellow monks, I have heard that many kings and nobles and ministers love the Way. But when it comes to discussing the limits of the Way, each prefers to acquiesce to others and avoid criticism. Thus Layman Tung-p'o was buried alive by Chao-chueh in a pile of sights and sounds that he still hasn't found his way out of. Scholar Chiu-kao of the Hanlin Academy[2] has been visiting us here in the mountains,[3] and for several days now he has been talking spontaneously and writing gathas, a kind of language samadhi[4] within which not a word touches the ground and wherein he has found a place for the ancients to appear."

Brushing off his knees, he concluded, "But a crane can't carry Chiu-kao on its wings, and an ordinary horse can't chase the wind."

除夜小參。北禪分歲。三代禮樂全。該王老燒
錢。一種盃盤狼籍。珙上座。固守清貧。兼逢
歡歲。難與諸方鬥富。從年頭直至年尾。共諸
人同家共活。豐儉隨宜。終不陪面去。借地栽
花。虛妝好漢。且就自家屋裡。量水打碓。免
見求人。但每日二時。牽補得過。便可塞住持
之責。古人有言。時挑野菜和根煮。旋斫青柴
帶葉燒。不是爺貧連子苦。免教家富小兒嬌

歲旦上堂。新年頭說話。舊年裡不同。舊年裡
說話。新年頭不同。秦山雪解。湖岸冰融。髮
從今日白。華是去年紅

元宵上堂。山堂兀坐思悠悠。節令推遷莫暫
留。新歲始聞歌鼓吹。元宵又見挂燈毬。心田

87.1 I presume the Yuan dynasty capital of Tatu (Peking) in North China is meant. 87.2 The Chinese burn paper money drawn on the Bank of Hell to afford their departed ancestors a modicum of happiness in the afterlife. 87.3 Stonehouse uses his Buddhist name here: Ch'ing-hung.

88.1 Taishan, in Shantung province, is China's most sacred mountain and where all departed spirits rest before passing on to the afterlife. During the previous dynasty, Taishan was actually given a rank equal to that of the emperor. 88.2 Pinghu's East Lake is meant, just outside the temple's gate.

89.1 Lantern Festival is celebrated on the first full moon of the new year. 89.2 Fuyuan Temple is located beside a laketown in the plains, hence *mountain temple* is euphemistically meant.

87. On New Year's Eve, the Master said, "The sacrifice in the north[1] marks the year's end, complete with the ritual and music of the ages. The elders burn money,[2] and bowls and plates are laid out in profusion. Meanwhile, Abbot Hung[3] remains poor.

"Encountering a year of want, I have found it hard to compete with others for wealth. From the beginning to the end of the year, we have lived and worked together regardless of whether or not we had enough. We've never chased after reputation or used our land for flowers.

"My fellow unadorned men, in your own rooms you have measured your capacities and worked hard at your practice and have not sought anything from others. Every day from morning until night, you have managed to pull yourselves through and to avoid the abbot's reproach.

"The ancients had a saying: 'Gather wild plants and roots for dinner / chop green wood and burn leaves for heat / fathers might want and sons might suffer / but at least the children aren't spoiled.'"

88. On New Year's Day, the Master said, "What I say at the start of this year / isn't the same as what I said last year / what I said last year / wasn't the same as this year / snow disappears from Taishan[1] / ice melts on the lakeshore[2] / my hair turns white beginning today / the red of the flowers is from last year."

89. On Lantern Festival,[1] the Master said, "Inside our mountain temple[2] we sit while thoughts drift off / the seasons change and never rest / at New Year we had music and song / on Lantern Night the hanging light shines / the brambles of the mind reach up to the sky / the waves of karma keep rolling on / unless you make a plan before you die / weeds will shackle your dried up bones."

荊棘參天長。業海波濤滾底流。不向死前先畫
策。草根從自鎖枯髏

上堂。報緣虛幻。豈可強為浮世。幾何隨家豐
儉。淡靜生涯水一湖。寂寞相從雲數片。思量
誰是箇般人。獨自舉頭天外看。擊拂子下座

二月旦上堂。道遠乎哉。觸事而真。自攜瓶去
沽村酒。卻著衫來作主人。聖遠乎哉。體之則
神。但見落花隨水去。不知流出洞中春。要識
肇法師麼。豎起拂子云。枇杷葉是馬家親。眼
裡無筋一世貧

上堂。春眠不覺曉。處處聞啼鳥。夜來風雨
聲。花落知多少。世尊三昧。迦葉不知。迦葉

91.1 Stonehouse is referring to T'ao Yuan-ming's story about the fisherman who saw peach petals floating in a stream and followed them upstream to a cleft in the rocks beyond which he found a group of refugees leading an idyllic life. 91.2 Seng Chao was a disciple of Kumarajiva and the author of several brilliant, if complex, treatises on Madhyamika philosophy. 91.3 The leaves of the loquat, *Eriobotrya japonica,* are used as a cough suppressant and an expectorant, and apparently to feed horses.

90. The Master said, "The conditions of retribution are empty illusions. How can you cling to transient existence? How long will you be rich or poor?

"The tranquil life of a placid lake / the company of occasional clouds / consider who this person is / lift your eyes beyond the sky."

Snapping his whisk, the Master left the hall.

91. On the first day of the second month, the Master said, "The Way may be distant, but everything we touch is real. If you go around selling homemade wine, wear a gown and act like a merchant. The sages may be distant, but we embody their spirit. Just because you see flower petals drifting down the stream doesn't mean you know what springtime is like on the other side of the cave. [1]

"If you want to understand Master Chao ..." [2] holding up his whisk, the Master said, "Loquat leaves [3] are a horseman's friends / to an eye without muscles the whole world is poor."

三昧。阿難不知。山僧三昧。諸人不知。所以
道。諸法無作用。亦無有體性。是故。彼一切
各各不相知。雖各不相知。諸法元無二。便與
麼去苦樂逆順。道在其中。若不然者。柳絮隨
風自西自東。卓拄杖下座

天壽聖節

聖節上堂。盡大地是國王水土。無一物不受王
恩。盡十方是古佛道場。無一日不為佛事。莫
有知恩報恩者麼。下座。同詣大雄寶殿。啟建

上堂。收足上蒲團。坐一參禪則易。伸手展鉢
盂。喫三廚粥則難。夜短眠不足。日長饑有
餘。置而勿論。你道。賓頭盧走入僧堂裡。與
憍陳如商量箇甚麼事。良久云。縱然為客好。

92.1 Kashyapa became the First Patriarch of Zen when he smiled. 92.2 *The World-Honored One* refers to the Buddha. 92.3 *Samadhi* is Sanskrit for "mental or spiritual concentration." 92.4 Ananda became the Second Patriarch when he knocked down the flagpole.

94.1 Pindola is the first of the sixteen (sometimes eighteen) arhats whose statues often line the shrine halls of Buddhist temples. He is also known as the Old Man of the Mountains and here takes Shakyamuni's place. 94.2 Kaundinya was Shakyamuni's uncle and his first disciple, whom he met at Sarnath following his Enlightenment at Bodhgaya. For him and his four fellow ascetics, the Buddha first turned the Wheel of Dharma, teaching them the Four Noble Truths and the Eightfold Path.

92. The Master said, "Dawn finds us dreaming in spring / everywhere we hear singing birds / at night the sounds of wind and rain / and countless flowers falling.

"Kashyapa[1] didn't understand the World-Honored One's[2] samadhi.[3] Ananda[4] didn't understand Kashyapa's samadhi. And none of you understand this mountain monk's samadhi. Thus we say that nothing moves or exists and no one understands anyone else. But even though we don't understand each other, nothing is separate from anything else. Thus we turn away from happiness and sorrow, agreement and disagreement and take the Middle Way instead. Those who don't are like willow catkins blown back and forth by the wind."

Then he raised his staff and left the hall.

93. On the emperor's birthday, the Master said, "The whole earth is the property of the emperor, and there isn't a creature that doesn't enjoy his kindness. The ten directions are the sacred realm of the ancient buddhas, and not a day passes that they don't preach the Dharma. Is there anyone who doesn't know enough to repay kindness?"

Stepping down, he said, "Let us proceed to the buddha hall and begin the celebration of the emperor's birthday."

94. The Master said, "Tucking in your legs on straw cushions and practicing meditation is easy. But holding out your begging bowl and eating three meals of porridge a day is hard. The nights are short, and you don't get enough sleep. The days are long, and you don't get enough to eat. But let's not talk about this.

"Tell me, when Pindola[1] walks into the meditation hall, what does he say to Kaundinya?"[2] After a pause, he said, "Being a guest is all right. But it doesn't compare to being poor and at home."

爭似在家貧

結制上堂。今朝四月十五日。行腳師僧念頭
息。草鞋乾晒待秋風。金錫罷遊留靠壁。鷗鷺
偏愛守空池。鳳凰豈肯棲荊棘。平生肝膽向人
傾。相識猶如不相識

聖節滿散上堂。天下無二道。混四海而為一
家。聖人無二心。視百姓猶如一子。所以道。
心同虛空界。示等虛空法。證得虛空時。無是
無非。法如天普蓋。似地普擎。元元自化。蕩
蕩難名。好。諸禪德。但見皇風成一片。不知
何處是封疆

95.1 The phoenix alights only on the paulownia tree.

96.1 Here, *sage* ostensibly refers to the emperor.

95. At the beginning of retreat, the Master said, "Today is the fourth month the fifteenth day / put your wandering-monk thoughts away / let your sandals dry until fall / lean your staffs against the wall / cormorants prefer a secluded pool / a phoenix[1] can't nest among brambles / those of you partial to lifelong ties / know each other yet don't."

96. At the conclusion of the emperor's birthday, the Master said, "There aren't two Ways in the world. Everyone within the Four Seas belongs to one family. The sage[1] doesn't have a divided heart. He regards the people as his only child.

"Thus it is said, when your mind is an empty universe, what appears is the empty Truth. Once you realize such emptiness, there is no right or wrong. The Truth is like the sky that covers everything and like the earth that supports everything. Its transformations are numberless, and it's too vast to itemize. Virtuous Zen monks, behold how the imperial wind blows without paying attention to borders."

平山和尚至。上堂。即心即佛也不是。非心非
佛也不是。不是心不是佛不是物也不是。恁麼
也不是。不恁麼也不是。恁麼不恁麼總不是。
子細看來。直教你無用心處。正好用心。卓拄
杖云。藕穿平地為荷葉。筍過東家作竹林

復舉芙蓉訪實性大師。以右手拈拄杖安左邊。
良久云。若不是芙蓉師兄。也大難委悉。師
云。諸仁者。實性大師。聞名富貴。見面貧
窮。自家骨肉相看。也只作路岐相待。今日平
山法兄。久出歸來福源。雖則囊空橐虛。未免
將無作有。卓拄杖云。人情淡處道情濃。燙斗
煎茶銚不同

97.1 P'ing-shan was a fellow disciple of Chi-an and was the abbot of Ching-tzu Temple in Hangchou.
97.2 *This mind is the buddha* and *what isn't the mind isn't the buddha* were both teachings used by Ma-tsu, to whom both Stonehouse and P'ing-shan traced their dharma lineage.

98.1 Fu-jung Tao-k'ai was a Sung-dynasty Zen master and a disciple of Yi-ch'ing. I'm truly mystified by this exchange. 98.2 Again, P'ing-shan and Stonehouse shared the same teacher.

97. On the arrival of Master P'ing-shan,[I] the Master said, "It isn't 'this mind is the buddha.'[2] And it isn't 'that which isn't the mind isn't the buddha.' And it isn't 'it isn't the mind, it isn't the buddha, and it isn't anything else' either. 'It's like this' isn't it. 'It's not like this' isn't it. And 'it's like this and not like this' isn't it. Looking at it carefully, I can only tell you that where you don't use your mind is where you should use your mind."

Lifting up his staff, he said, "A lotus root breaks through the mud and becomes a lotus leaf. A bamboo shoot enters a neighbor's yard and becomes a bamboo grove."

98. The Master recalled when Fu-jung[I] visited Master Shih-hsing he grabbed Shih-hsing's staff with his right hand and placed it on his left side. After a moment, Shih-hsing said, "If it isn't my brother Fu-jung, then I'm truly mystified."

The Master said, "Good monks, Master Shih-hsing's reputation was lofty, yet his appearance was quite humble. Even in the case of our own kin, we don't treat each other the same. Today our Dharma Brother P'ing-shan[2] has returned to Fuyuan after a long absence. Although his purse and bag are empty, he couldn't help bringing us something useless."

Raising his staff, he said, "Where human sentiment is superficial, spiritual sentiment is deep. Using a clothes iron to heat water for tea isn't the same."

迴院上堂。老牯偷閑去半年。祖翁田地草芊
芊。歸來懶更重還債。犁杷春風又上肩。是即
是祖禰不了。逃難逃宿業拘牽。四蹄耕白水。
兩角指青天。拍膝一下云。可惜無人知此意。
風前令我憶南泉

退院上堂。卸卻頂上鐵枷。颺下手中木杓。合
眼跳過黃河。騰身衝開碧落。獅子趯倒玉闌
干。象王擺壞黃金素。白雲兮處處相逢。青山
兮步步踏著。喝一喝云。舉頭天外看。誰是箇
般人

示眾云。吾佛世尊。有四種清淨明誨。所謂攝
心為戒。因戒生定。因定發慧。云何攝心。何
名為戒。若諸世界六道眾生。其心不婬。則不

99.1 Stonehouse relinquished control of Fuyuan Temple in 1339, after serving as its abbot for eight years. 99.2 There isn't much for a water buffalo to do after harvest until the following spring. The harvest also marks the end of the summer-long meditation retreat. 99.3 Stonehouse's teacher was Chi-an, whose remains were interred in a stupa near his hut on Hsiamushan. 99.4 Nan-ch'uan was one of the greatest Zen masters of the T'ang dynasty and often likened himself to a water buffalo. In fact, just before he died, he said he would be one in his next life. Here, the wind of spring reminds Stonehouse it's time to plough the fields around his hut.

100.1 The cangue was similar to the pillory and worn by criminals as part of their punishment. 100.2 This particular kind of spoon was used in the preparation of tea and thus refers here to meditation. 100.3 The capital of Tatu was north of the Yellow River.

101.1 The Buddha's first sermon, delivered at Sarnath, concerned the Four Noble Truths: all existence entails suffering, suffering is the result of desire, the extinction of desire results in an end of suffering, and the way to extinguish desire is by following the Eightfold Path that begins with mindfulness and blameless action and ends with concentration and wisdom.

99. Announcing his departure from the temple,[1] the Master said, "This old buffalo has been idle since fall[2] / my master's fields[3] are covered with weeds / once I leave I'll be too tired to return / the plough on my shoulders in spring once more / this is something my master didn't teach / how to escape hardship and the bondage of the past / four hooves ploughing in the water / two horns pointing to the sky."

Slapping his knee, he said, "It's too bad nobody understands what this means. It's the wind that makes me think of Nan-ch'uan."[4]

100. Turning over control of the temple, the Master said, "I remove the iron cangue[1] from around my neck / I put down the wooden spoon[2] in my hand / I close my eyes and leap over the Yellow River[3] / I jump up and fly through the heavenly vault / the lion knocks down the jade bars / the elephant breaks the gold chain / I meet white clouds wherever I go / I walk into green mountains with every step.

"Hey! Lift up your heads and look beyond the sky. Who is this person anyway?"

101. The Master addressed the assembly, "Concerning the World-Honored Buddha's Four Perfect Truths,[1] what he calls mindfulness becomes morality, and morality becomes the basis of meditation, and meditation becomes the basis of wisdom. But how does one become mindful? And what is morality?

隨其生死相續。又道。若不斷婬修禪定者。如蒸砂石欲其成飯。經百千劫。祇名熱砂。何以故。此非飯本砂石成故。汝以婬身求佛妙果。縱得妙悟。皆是婬根。根本成婬。輪轉三途。必不能出。又道。若不斷殺修禪定者。譬如有人自塞其耳。高聲太叫。求人不聞。此等名為欲隱彌露。清淨比丘。於岐路行。不踏生草。況以手拔。云何大悲。取諸眾生血肉充食。名為釋子。又道。若不斷偷修禪定者。譬如有人水灌漏巵。欲求其滿。縱經塵劫。終無平復。若諸比丘。衣鉢之餘。分寸不畜。乞食餘分。施餓眾生。又道。若諸世界六道眾生。雖則身心無殺盜婬。三行已圓。若大妄語。則三摩地不得清淨。如刻人糞。為旃檀形。欲求香氣。無有是處。婬殺盜妄。既已消亡。戒定慧學。

101.2 The six states of existence include gods, asuras, humans, beasts, hungry ghosts, and the demons of hell. 101.3 The three lower realms among the six states of existence include beasts, ghosts, and the demons of hell.

216

"Beings in the six states[2] of existence who aren't driven by sex are able to free themselves from birth and death. It's said that if you don't quit having sex, practicing meditation is like steaming gravel to make rice. Even after a hundred thousand kalpas, all you get is hot gravel. You can't make rice from gravel. And if you seek the divine fruit of enlightenment in order to have sex with someone, you may gain wonderful insights, but the root of sex only results in sex. Meanwhile, you remain in the three lower realms[3] of rebirth without hope of escape.

"It's also said that if you don't quit killing, practicing meditation is like covering your ears and screaming that you can't hear or like trying to hide Mount Sumeru. When a blameless monk walks down a road, he doesn't step on the grass much less pull up plants, such is his compassion. And yet those who use the flesh and blood of other creatures to satisfy their hunger call themselves the followers of Shakyamuni.

"It's also said that if you don't quit stealing, practicing meditation is like trying to fill a leaky cup. Even after countless kalpas, it still won't be full. If you monks have spare clothes or bowls, don't store them away. And if you collect more food than you need, give it those who are hungry.

"It's also said that even if the beings of the myriad worlds in the six states of existence don't use their bodies or minds to engage in murder, theft, or sex, and even if they manage to avoid the karma of good deeds, bad deeds, and inactivity, if they deceive others with words, their meditation won't be true. It's like carving a turd to look like sandalwood. You can carve all you want, but you can't make it smell like incense.

自然清淨。若太虛之雲散。如大海之波澄。得
到這般田地了。方可以參禪。方可以學道。你
且道。禪又作麼生參。道又作麼生學。從上以
來。多有樣子。福源不惜口嘴。略舉數段。二
祖初到少林。參禮達磨。斷臂立雪。悲泣求
法。達磨曰。諸佛最初求道。為法忘形。汝今
斷臂。求亦可在。二祖曰。諸佛法印。可得聞
乎。達磨曰。諸佛法印。匪從人得。二祖曰。
我心未安。乞施安心。達磨曰。將心來。為汝
安。二祖曰。覓心了不可得。達磨曰。我為汝
安心竟。二祖於此悟入。這箇。便是為法忘
軀。參禪學道第一樣子。大梅常禪師。參問馬
祖。如何是佛。祖曰。即心是佛。常領旨。直
入大梅山卓菴。後馬祖聞之。令僧去問曰。和
尚見箇甚麼道理。便住此山。常曰。馬祖向我

101.4 The Second Patriarch of the Zen sect was Hui-k'o, who studied with several masters in the Loyang area in the early sixth century before finally visiting Bodhidharma at his cave on Sungshan's Lesser Peak, just above Shaolin Temple. 101.5 Fa-ch'ang, who is usually called Ta-mei after the mountain on which he lived, was an eighth-century Zen master. Ta-mei means "great plum." Ma-tsu, or Patriarch Ma, was the only Zen master after Hui-neng to receive the title of Patriarch.

"Once you free yourselves of sex, murder, theft, and deceit, your practice of morality, meditation, and wisdom will naturally be true. It will be as if the clouds vanished from the sky or the ocean's waves suddenly stilled. Once you reach this state, you are finally ready to practice Zen. You are finally ready to cultivate the Way.

"If you want to know how to practice Zen and cultivate the Tao, there have been many ways since time began. Here at Fuyuan we aren't miserly with our words. Let me give you a few examples.

"When the Second Patriarch[4] first arrived at Shaolin and paid his respects to Bodhidharma, he cut off his arm and stood in the snow and begged for the Dharma in tears. Bodhidharma said, 'When the ancient buddhas went in search of the Truth, they gave up their bodies for the sake of the Dharma. Anyone who cuts off his arm will find what he seeks.'

"The Second Patriarch said, 'Please tell me about the Truth that buddhas teach.' Bodhidharma said, 'The Truth that buddhas teach isn't learned by anyone.' The Second Patriarch said, 'My mind is still confused. Will the Master please clear up my mind?' Bodhidharma said, 'Give it to me, and I'll clear it up.' The Second Patriarch said, 'I've looked everywhere, but I can't find it.' Bodhidharma said, 'Then I've cleared up your mind for you.' The Second Patriarch was suddenly enlightened. This is an example of forsaking the body for the Dharma. This is the first way to practice Zen.

"When Master Fa-ch'ang[5] visited Ma-tsu, he asked, 'What is a buddha like?' And the Patriarch said, 'This mind is the buddha.' Fa-ch'ang understood and left immediately for Tamei Mountain, where he built a hut. Later, when Ma-tsu heard of his whereabouts, he sent a monk to inquire after him. The monk asked Fa-ch'ang, 'What truth did you discover that made you move to this mountain?'

道。即心是佛。我向這裡住。僧曰。馬祖佛法。如今又別了也。常曰。作麼生別。僧曰。如今又道。非心非佛。常曰。這老漢。惑亂人未有了日在。任他非心非佛。我只管即心即佛。其僧回舉似祖。祖曰。梅子熟也。這箇。便是有決定信。無疑惑心。參禪學道第二箇樣子。臨濟。初在黃檗會下。行業純一。首座問曰。上座在此多少時也。濟曰。三年。首座曰。曾參問也無。濟曰。不曾參問。不知問箇甚麼。首座曰。汝何不去問堂頭和尚。如何是佛法的的大意。濟便去問。聲未絕。藥便打。如是三度發問。三度被打。濟白座云。幸蒙慈悲。令某問話。三度發問。三度被打。自恨障緣不領深旨。今且辭去。座云。汝若去時。須辭方丈去。座先到方丈云。問話底後生。甚是

101.6 Lin-chi was the ninth-century founder of one of the most important Zen sects, known to the West by his Japanese name: Rinzai. His records and those of his teacher, Huang-po, have been translated into English.

"Fa-ch'ang said, 'Patriarch Ma told me "this mind is the buddha," so I moved here.' The monk said, 'The Patriarch's teaching is different now.' Fa-ch'ang asked, 'How is it different?' The monk said, 'Now he teaches "that which isn't the mind isn't the buddha."' Fa-ch'ang said, 'That old geezer still isn't done confusing people. He can have 'that which isn't the mind isn't the buddha.' I'll stick with 'this mind is the buddha.' When the monk returned and reported this conversation, Ma-tsu told his disciples, 'The plum is ripe.' This is an example of resolute belief and a mind impervious to doubt. This is the second way to practice Zen.

"When Lin-chi[6] studied with Huang-po, he was simple and sincere in his actions. One day the rector asked him, 'How long have you been here?' And Lin-chi said, 'Three years.' The rector said, 'Have you asked any questions yet?' Lin-chi said, 'No, I haven't. I wouldn't know what to ask.' The rector said, 'Why don't you ask the abbot about the essential meaning of Buddhism.' So Lin-chi went to ask. But before the words were out of his mouth, Huang-po struck him. Three times Lin-chi asked, and three times he was struck.

"Lin-chi went back and told the rector, 'I appreciate your kindness encouraging me to question the abbot. But I asked three times and was struck three times. I'm afraid the weight of my karma prevents me from gaining a deeper understanding, so I've decided to leave.'

"The rector said, 'Before you go, you should say good-bye to the abbot.' The rector then went to Huang-po and said, 'This young monk is a good prospect. If he comes to say good-bye, please help him. In the future, he could grow into a great tree and provide many people with shade.'

如法。若來辭時。方便接他。向後成一株大
樹。與天下人作陰涼去在。濟去辭。藥云。不
得往別處。向高安灘上大愚處去。濟到大愚。
愚問。甚麼處來。濟云。黃蘗處來。愚云。黃
藥有何言句。濟云。某甲三度問佛法的的大
意。三度被打。不知某甲有過無過。愚云。黃
藥與麼老婆。為汝得徹困。更來這裡問有過無
過。濟於言下大悟云。元來黃蘗佛法無多子。
愚搊住云。這尿床鬼子。適來道有過無過。如
今卻道黃蘗佛法無多子。你見箇甚麼道理。速
道速道。濟於大愚肋下築三拳。愚托開云。汝
師黃蘗。非干我事。濟辭大愚。卻回黃蘗。藥
見來便問。這漢來來去去。有甚麼了期。濟
云。祇為老婆心切。藥問。什麼處去來。濟
云。昨蒙慈旨。參大愚去來。藥云大愚有何言

101.7 Ta-yu was a disciple of Kuei-tsung.

"The next day, when Lin-chi went to say good-bye, Huang-po said, 'Go see Ta-yu.'7 When Lin-chi reached the place where Ta-yu was living, Ta-yu asked him, 'Where have you come from?' Lin-chi said, 'From Huang-po.' Ta-yu said, 'What did Huang-po teach you?' Lin-chi said, 'I asked him three times to tell me the essential meaning of Buddhism, and each time he beat me. I don't know what I did wrong.' Ta-yu said, 'Huang-po is an old grandmother to give you such an opportunity. What are you doing here asking me if you did something wrong or not?' Suddenly Lin-chi was enlightened and said, 'So, Huang-po's Buddhism doesn't amount to much after all.'

"Ta-yu grabbed him and said, 'You bed-wetting son of a ghost, you come here wondering if you did something wrong or not, and now you're saying Huang-po's Buddhism doesn't amount to much. What do you understand all of a sudden? Tell me right now!' Lin-chi gave Ta-yu three pokes in the ribs. Ta-yu let him go and said, 'Your teacher is Huang-po. This doesn't have anything to do with me.' Lin-chi said good-bye and returned to Huang-po.

"When Huang-po saw Lin-chi return, he said, 'This fellow comes and goes. When is he going to stop?' Lin-chi said, 'It's all due to your grandmotherly kindness.' Huang-po said, 'Where have you come from?' Lin-chi said, 'After I received your kind instruction, I went to visit Ta-yu.' Huang-po said, 'And what did Ta-yu tell you?' When Lin-chi reported what had happened, Huang-po said, 'Who does Ta-yu think he is? Wait until I give him a taste of my stick.'

句。濟遂舉前話。藥云。作麼生得這漢待來痛
與一頓。濟云。說什麼待來。即今便喫。隨後
便掌。藥云。這風顛漢。卻來這裡捋虎鬚。濟
便喝。藥云。侍者引這風顛漢。參堂去。這
箇。便是宿因深正。有大根器。參禪學道第三
箇樣子。長慶稜禪師未悟時。看箇驢事未去馬
事到來。如是在雪峰玄沙。往來三十年。坐破
蒲團七箇。一日捲簾。豁然大悟。便說箇頌
子。道也大差也大差。捲起簾來見天下。有人
問我解何宗。拈起拂來劈口打。這箇便是不肯
造次承當。必欲見大休歇田地。參禪學道第四
箇樣子。仰山。在百丈會下。問一答十。口吧
吧地。百丈曰。汝已後去遇人在。後到溈山
處。溈問曰。承聞。子在百丈。問一答十。是
不。仰云。不敢。溈云。佛法向上一句。作麼

101.8 Ch'ang-ch'ing was a tenth-century Zen master and a disciple of Hsueh-feng. The remark about the donkey and horse suggests Ch'ang-ch'ing was still dependent on the gradual approach to understanding and unwilling to make the intuitive leap required of Zen students.

101.9 Yang-shan was a ninth-century Zen master who, together with his teacher Kuei-shan, founded one of the five most popular sects of Zen, known as the Kuei-Yang sect.

"Lin-chi said, 'Why wait? Have a taste right now.' And he hit Huang-po. Huang-po yelled, 'This mad man is trying to grab the tiger's whiskers!' Lin-chi shouted, 'Hey!' Then Huang-po said, 'Attendants, take this mad man to the meditation hall.' This is an example of deep karma from past lives and the capacity of deep roots. This is the third way to practice Zen and cultivate the Tao.

"Before Ch'ang-ch'ing[8] was enlightened, he couldn't distinguish a donkey from a horse. He visited Master Hsueh-feng for thirty years and wore out seven meditation cushions. Then one day, as he was raising a bamboo blind, he was suddenly enlightened and composed this gatha: 'The Truth is a mistake a big mistake / rolling up a blind I see the whole world / if someone asks me what Zen means / I'll hit him in the mouth with my whisk.' This is an example of being unwilling to undertake anything in a hurry and waiting for the field of great repose to appear by itself. This is the fourth way to practice Zen and cultivate the Tao.

"When Yang-shan[9] was with Pai-chang, every time he was asked a question, he gave ten different answers and couldn't do anything but mutter. Pai-chang said, 'You'll meet your teacher in the future.'

"Later, when Yang-shan arrived at Kuei-shan's place, Kuei-shan said, 'I've heard that when you were with Pai-chang, you gave ten answers to every question. Is that true?' Yang-shan said, 'I'm afraid so.'

生道。仰擬開口。溈便喝。如是三問。仰三擬
答。三被喝。仰低頭垂淚云。先師道。教我更
遇人始得。今日便遇人也。遂發心。看牛三
年。一日。溈山見仰在樹下坐禪。溈以拄杖點
背一下。仰回首。溈云。寂子道得也未。仰
云。雖道不得。且不借別人口。溈云。寂子會
也。這箇。便是去卻知解真實。參禪學道第五
箇樣子。保寧勇禪師。初入天台教。更衣謁雪
寶顯禪師。顯以為堪任大法。乃熟視。呵之
日。央庠座主。勇發憤下山。望雪竇山禮拜
日。我此生。行腳參禪。道不過雪竇。誓不歸
鄉。便往泐潭踰年。疑情未泮。後參楊岐。頓
明心地。岐沒。更從同參白雲端。研極玄奧。
這箇。便是具決定志。無退轉心。參禪學道第
六箇樣子。雲峰悦禪師。在大愚芝座下。一日
芝示眾曰。大家相聚喫莖齏。喚作衣莖齏。入
地獄如箭。悦聞之駭然。便上方丈請開示。芝
曰。法輪未轉。食輪先轉。後生家。趁色力
健。何不為眾乞食。我忍饑不暇。何暇為汝說

101.10 Pao-ning was an eleventh-century Zen Master. 101.11 The Tientai sect rivaled that of Zen in popularity during the T'ang and Sung dynasties. Named for the Tientai Mountains, where its first patriarchs had their center, it divided the various teachings of the Buddha into progressive stages culminating with those contained in the *Lotus* and *Nirvana* sutras. 101.12 Hsueh-tou was an eleventh-century Zen master and the author of the poems in the *Blue Cliff Records*. 101.13 Yun-feng was a ninth-century Zen master and disciple of Ta-yu. 101.14 Buddhist monks and nuns in China do not normally eat leeks, onions, or garlic, due to their power as aphrodisiacs.

"Kuei-shan said, "Tell me, what's the most important expression in Buddhism?" Just as Yang-shan was about to speak, Kuei-shan yelled, 'Hey!' Three times Kuei-shan asked, and three times Yang-shan tried to answer, and three times he was cut short with a 'Hey!' In tears, Yang-shan lowered his head and said, 'My old master told me I would meet my teacher someday. Today I've met him.' After that Yang-shan vowed to spend the next three years taking care of the temple's water buffalo.

"One day Kuei-shan saw Yang-shan sitting under a tree in meditation and tapped him once on the back with his staff. When Yang-shan turned around, Kuei-shan asked, 'Have you found the Tao yet?' Yang-shan said, 'I haven't found the Tao, but at least I don't steal the words of others.' Kuei-shan said, 'Then you understand.' This is an example of eliminating knowledge and truth. This is the fifth way to practice Zen and cultivate the Tao.

"Pao-ning[10] first studied the Tientai[11] doctrine then changed his attire and visited Hsueh-tou.[12] Thinking he was worthy of the Dharma, Hsueh-tou looked at Pao-ning for a long time then yelled, 'Abbot Pao-ning!' Pao-ning turned and ran down the mountain. Then, looking back, he bowed and said to himself, 'I've wandered on foot and practiced meditation all my life, but my path ends here with Hsueh-tou. I vow never to return.'

"He then traveled to Tungshan to live out his years, but his doubts remained unresolved. Later, he visited Yang-ch'i and suddenly beheld the ground of his mind. After Yang-ch'i died, Pao-ning resumed his study of white clouds and mysteries. This is an example of unwavering resolution. This is the sixth way to practice Zen and cultivate the Tao.

"When Yun-feng[13] was with Ta-yu, one day Ta-yu told the assembly, 'Everyone here eats leeks.[14] But if anyone calls them leeks, they'll go straight to Hell.' When Yun-feng heard this, he was perplexed and asked the abbot to explain.

"Ta-yu said, 'The food wheel turns before the Dharma Wheel. Why don't you youngsters use your sexual energy to collect some food for the monks? We don't have time to be hungry.

禪乎。悦不敢違。未幾。芝遷翠巖。悦納疏罷。復過翠巖求開示。芝曰。佛法不怕爛卻。

今正雪寒。可為眾乞炭。悦亦奉命。化炭歸。

復上方丈請益。芝曰。堂司即目缺人。今已煩汝。悦受之不樂。恨芝不去心。一日。後架桶箍忽散。自架墮落。豁然大悟。頓見芝用處。

急趨方丈。芝見來。笑曰。且喜。維那大事了畢。悦不措一詞。禮拜了退。這箇。便是為眾竭力。不廢寸陰。參禪學道第七箇樣子。更有

第八箇樣子。此是微塵佛一路涅槃門。過去諸如來。斯門已成就。現在諸菩薩。今各入圓

明。未來修學人。當依如是法。卓拄杖一下。下座

結制小參。佛祖門風將委地。說著令人心膽碎。扶持全在我兒孫。不料兒孫先作弊。紛紛走北又奔南。昧卻正因營雜事。滿目風埃滿面

101.15 Tsuiyen is the middle peak of Wutaishan's five peaks and is in North China.

Do you think I have time to explain Zen to you?' Yun-feng didn't dare argue.

"Not long after that, Ta-yu moved to Tsuiyen,[15] and Yun-feng stayed behind. Later, Yun-feng passed by Tsuiyen and stopped to ask for instruction. Ta-yu said, 'Don't be in such a hurry, the Dharma won't spoil. Today the weather is ice cold. Why don't you go collect some charcoal for the monks?' Yun-feng did as he was asked. Afterwards, he asked the abbot for instruction again. Ta-yu said, 'Right now I need someone to act as meditation master. Do you mind?' Although he really wanted to leave, Yun-feng grudgingly agreed.

"One day not long afterward, Yun-feng saw a bucket hoop suddenly break. As the bucket fell apart, Yun-feng was suddenly enlightened. Realizing Ta-yu's intention, he hurried to see the abbot. When Ta-yu saw him coming, he laughed, 'I'm glad to see the meditation master has finished his task.' Without saying a word, Yun-feng bowed and left. This is an example of using your strength for the benefit of other monks and not wasting a moment. This is the seventh way to practice Zen and cultivate the Tao.

"There is also an eighth way. This is the road taken by numberless buddhas to the gate of nirvana. The tathagatas of the past created this gate. And the bodhisattvas of the present all reach perfect enlightenment by entering it. And those who practice in the future should rely on this dharma." Lifting up his staff, the Master stepped down from his seat.

102. At an informal talk at the end of retreat, the Master said, "The teaching of the patriarchs spreads across the land / their very words rend people's hearts / our support depends completely on our children / but our children have turned out bad / they run north and south in confusion /

塵。業識茫茫無本據。縱饒挂搭在僧堂。直待
板鳴歸被位。聚頭寮舍鼓是非。收足蒲團便瞌
睡。癡雲靉靆性天昏。石火交煎心鼎沸。暫時
寂寂滯輕安。一向冥冥墮無記。百丈清規不肯
行。外道經書勤講議。因果分明當等閒。罪福
昭然渾不懼。或遷一榻一間房。放逸總由身口
意。頭上瓦腳下磚。身上衣口中味。一一皆出
信心檀越人家施。未成道業若為消。捫心幾箇
知慚愧。今日三明日四。閒處光陰盡虛棄。一
朝老病來相尋。閻翁催請死符至。從前所作業
不忘。三塗六趣從茲墜。袈裟失卻復再難。鱗
甲羽毛披則易。看他古之學道流。直忘人世輕
名利。煮黃精煨紫芋。飯一搏水一器。為療形
枯聊接氣。石爛松枯竟不知。洗心便作累生
計。物外清閒一味高。世上黃金何足貴。劫空
田地佛華開。香風觸破娘生鼻。選佛場中及第
歸。圓覺伽藍恣遊戲。茲因結制夜小參。不覺
所言成此偈

102.1 Karmic consciousness is that aspect of awareness that results from our previous actions. 102.2 The meditation signal. 102.3 The void is also a bottomless hell. 102.4 The rules followed by all Zen temples were established by Pai-chang in the ninth century. 102.5 A private room or bed was the perogative of senior monks. 102.6 The body, the mouth, and the mind are the three sources of karma. 102.7 There once was a monkey trainer who fed his charges three acorns in the morning and four in the evening. One day they complained that this wasn't enough. When the trainer changed their ration to four in the morning and three in the evening, they stopped complaining (*Chuangtzu:* 2). 102.8 One of the three lower states of existence: as a beast, a hungry ghost, or in one of the hells. 102.9 The *kasaya* is a monk's robe, which protects its wearer from the obstacles of existence. 102.10 Solomonseal, or *Polygonatum cirrhifolium,* ranks among the survival foods upon which all hermits depend.

blind to the root they chase twigs / eyes full of dust they face the wind / karmic consciousness[1] provides them no help / even when they stay in a meditation hall / and they take their seats when the clapper[2] sounds / they stir up discension in the hall / and sit on their cushions and doze / covering their natures with clouds of delusion / striking rocks to warm their minds / then for a moment they're still and at peace / but entering the darkness they fall into the void[3] / unwilling to follow Pai-chang's pure rules[4] / they talk about the ways of other sects / cause and effect they treat the same / reward and punishment don't concern them / and if they get their own bed and room[5] / they indulge their bodies their mouths and their minds[6] / with tiles overhead and bricks underneath / clothes to wear and food to eat / they offer more incense than others / but it doesn't help someone in the dark / how many know to be embarrassed / with three today and four tomorrow[7] / they waste their time and don't do a thing / "until one day old age or illness finds them / and Yama announces their time has arrived / everything they ever did is counted / and forthwith they fall into a lower state[8] / who loses his kasaya[9] won't get another soon / more likely a shell or feathers, fish scales or fur / consider those who practiced in the past / ignoring the world and making light of glory / living on taro and solomon-seal[10] / a bowl of rice a cup of water / keeping frail bodies healthy / rock-hard pine trees might wither / while they sat cleansing their minds / planning their future lives / they achieved peace and detachment / worldly wealth meant nothing to them / when the buddha flower blooms in the empty kalpa / its fragrance is sensed by the nose born of woman / candidates return to your buddha seats / do what you will in this temple of awareness / I have talked tonight to end this retreat / suddenly my words have turned into a gatha."